HINDU SELVES IN A MODERN WORLD

This book explores devotional Hinduism in a modern context of high consumerism and revolutionized communications. It focuses on a fast-growing and high-profile contemporary Hindu guru faith originating in India and attracting a transnational following. The organization is led by an extremely popular female guru, Mata Amritanandamayi, whom devotees worship as an avatar and a healer of the ills of the contemporary world. By drawing upon multi-sited ethnographic fieldwork among the Mata's primarily urban, educated 'middle-class' Indian devotees, the author provides crucial insights into new trends in popular Hinduism in a post-colonial and rapidly modernizing Indian setting.

Maya Warrier teaches Indian Religion and the Anthropology of Religion at the University of Wales, Lampeter. Her research interests centre on popular Hinduism in contemporary India and among Indian immigrants in the West, with particular focus on issues to do with modernity and globalization.

RoutledgeCurzon South Asian Religion Series

HINDU SELVES IN A MODERN WORLD
Guru faith in the Mata Amritanandamayi Mission
Maya Warrier

HINDU SELVES IN A MODERN WORLD

Guru faith in the Mata Amritanandamayi Mission

Maya Warrier

RoutledgeCurzon
Taylor & Francis Group

LONDON AND NEW YORK

First published 2005
by RoutledgeCurzon
2 Park Square, Milton Park, Abingdon, Oxon OX14 4RN

Simultaneously published in the USA and Canada
by RoutledgeCurzon
270 Madison Ave, New York, NY 10016

RoutledgeCurzon is an imprint of the Taylor & Francis Group

© 2005 Maya Warrier

Typeset in Times by Keystroke, Jacaranda Lodge, Wolverhampton
Printed and bound in Great Britain by
TJ International Ltd, Padstow, Cornwall

British Library Cataloguing in Publication Data
A catalogue record for this book is available from the British Library

Library of Congress Cataloging in Publication Data
A catalog record for this book has been requested

ISBN 0–415–33988–X

FOR ATCHAN, CHECHI AND RICHARD

CONTENTS

Acknowledgements   ix

1   Introduction   1

2   Encountering the Mata   25

3   An avatar with a mission   43

4   Choosing to surrender   65

5   Spiritual pathways   83

6   Experiencing divine love   102

7   East meets West?   119

8   Conclusion   138

    Appendix   143
    Glossary   145
    Notes   148
    References   168
    Index   182

ACKNOWLEDGEMENTS

I wish to thank the authorities at the Mata Amritanandamayi Mission in India for their readiness in granting me permission to study their religious organization. The ascetic disciples of the Mata in Kerala, Tamil Nadu and Delhi, as well as several of her lay devotees from India as well as abroad whom I had a chance to meet and interview in Delhi, in Kerala, and later in London, were all extremely forthcoming in extending their help and support towards this study. I am grateful to them all. I also wish to thank my friends and kinsfolk in Delhi and Kerala, who were generous with their hospitality and support throughout my fieldwork.

I am indebted to my teacher at the Delhi School of Economics, Professor André Béteille, whose ideas and work have long been a source of inspiration. At Cambridge, where this research first shaped up as a PhD thesis, my thanks are due to James Laidlaw and Leo Howe at the Department of Social Anthropology for their invaluable comments. Thanks go also to Marcus Banks and Fiona Bowie for their encouragement and insightful observations on my thesis. The influence of the many friends I made while at Cambridge has had a substantial impact on me and my research efforts. Newnham College provided me with a friendly and stimulating environment in which to live and work. I particularly wish to thank Patrick Welche at Newnham for his timely help during the worst of my computer crises!

Colleagues at the Department of Theology and Religious Studies at the University of Wales, Lampeter, provided encouragement and advice towards the completion of this manuscript. My thanks are due to them. Most of all, I wish to thank my supervisor at Cambridge, Susan Bayly, from whom I have learnt much. Susan's constant encouragement, astute inputs into my research, and unfailing support, have all gone a long way in developing my academic skills and making my research a constantly stimulating and pleasurable exercise. I consider myself extraordinarily fortunate to have had, as my supervisor, someone who corresponded so closely with the ideal-typical guru of my imagination.

The finances for this research came mainly from the Cambridge Commonwealth Trust and Charles Wallace Bursary, who were generous in their support before, during and after my fieldwork. I have also benefited from grants from the Henry Ling Roth fund, Worts Fund, Smuts Memorial Fund and Richards Fund.

1

INTRODUCTION

This study explores one of the most dramatic and important developments in present-day Hinduism – the growth of vast and popular transnational devotionalist organizations led by charismatic Indian gurus. While some of these organizations address a primarily Indian following in India and abroad, often narrowly defined in terms of linguistic and caste identities, others attract a more diverse following, cutting across national, cultural, even religious boundaries. In this book I focus on a devotionalist organization that fits the latter description, the Mata Amritanandamayi Mission (henceforth MAM, or simply the 'Mission'), which operates in a visibly 'globalized' and transcultural environment. This organization is led by Mata (mother) Amritanandamayi, a female spiritual leader from the south Indian state of Kerala. The Mata Amritanandamayi Math and Mission Trust was established in 1981 and has its headquarters in the leader's native village of Parayakadavu, now Amritapuri, in Kerala's Kollam district. The Mission has grown, in the twenty-odd years since its inception, from its small, village-based beginnings, into the vast global, urban and largely multicultural organization it is today.

As a transnational spiritual leader, the Mata addresses an extremely diverse following. Her message is at once universalistic and pluralistic. She respects cultural, regional and religious differences among followers and adopts an inclusivistic stance vis-à-vis persons from diverse backgrounds, and of diverse faiths and traditions. She stresses not uniformity of belief and standardization of practice within her fold, but freedom for her followers to engage with her and with her teachings in the manner best suited to their personal tastes and inclinations. Followers celebrate this aspect of their guru, and value the respect she accords to their individuality and personal freedom. The most crucial aspect of faith within the MAM is the individualized, personalized and often highly intimate bond that comes to be established between the guru and each individual devotee who enters her fold. It is this one-to-one bond,

1

rather than any notion of collective identity or group affiliation, that forms the cornerstone of faith in this organization.

The Mata addresses the needs of a specifically modern world, identifying problems with modern world-views and lifestyles and offering solutions to these. It is not surprising that the majority of her devotees outside India, both Indian as well as non-Indian, Hindu as well as non-Hindu, come from the industrialized, affluent and 'modern' nations of the world. These include USA, Canada, UK, France, Italy, Germany, Spain, the Netherlands, Finland, Sweden, Australia, Japan and Singapore.[1] Within India she attracts followers primarily from urban educated middle-class backgrounds. In this study I examine the high-profile spirituality popularized by the Mata from the vantage point of her Indian urban 'middle-class' devotees. The desire to be 'modern' and to keep pace with the rapid transformations in the objective conditions of their existence is a central concern in the lives of these individuals. By their own reckoning, they are situated in a context of 'modernity'.

Modernity is a central theme in this book. The term 'modernity' here refers not to an analytical concept, a historical process, or a particular trajectory of intellectual thought. I use it instead in the sense in which my informants come to understand it through their engagement with the teachings of this guru, and which they then express through their own narratives on their guru-faith. In my treatment of 'modernity' in this book, I engage with three levels of narrative. First, I examine the Mata's own narrative pertaining to the modern world and its problems. Second, I explore devotees' engagement with this narrative and the subsequent narratives they then construct about the Mata as a modern guru, and about themselves as actors in a modern world. These narratives are shaped by, and in their turn shape, devotees' experiences of their lived realities. Third, there is my own narrative, as it unfolds in the pages of this book, about how modernity is constructed and negotiated within the Mata Amritanandamayi Mission. All three levels of narrative are in fact attempts at apprehending the larger course of events in the contemporary world.[2] All three are commentaries on social change, the first and second offering analyses using emic categories, the third (mine) providing an analysis using an etic standpoint. My aim in this book is to explore, by placing my own narrative in creative tension with those of my informants, how modernity and modern selfhood come to be negotiated in this guru's fold.

In the following sections of this chapter, I discuss in turn the key concerns of this study: Mata Amritanandamayi and her Mission; her urban Indian middle-class devotees; and the context of modernity and modern selfhood in which my study is located.

Mata Amritanandamayi and her Mission

The Mata is a relatively recent addition to India's vast spiritual landscape teeming with gurus and guru organizations. According to popular belief, Mata Amritanandamayi[3] is an avatar-guru, a divine incarnation who has descended to the earth in order to fulfil a divinely ordained mission. She was born in 1953 to a 'low-caste' family of fisherfolk in the south Indian state of Kerala.[4] At the age of twenty-one she is believed to have realized her identity first with the Hindu deity Krishna, and subsequently with the goddess Devi. Her claims to spiritual knowledge and enlightenment are based not on systematic striving within any of the established devotionalist and/or renunciatory orders in Hindu religious traditions, but on the strength of spontaneous ecstatic visions and mystical states.[5] Central to her self-representations today are her 'Devi *bhava*', regular public appearances when she dresses up in the regalia of the goddess and thus 'reveals' her goddess aspect (*bhava*) to her devotees.

The Mata's teachings convey in essence the message of universal love. She sees the modern world as depleted of selfless love and consequently as a place of immense suffering. Her mission, as she defines it, is to alleviate humanity's suffering by restoring selflessness, love and compassion to their rightful place in the modern world. Perhaps the most striking aspect of the Mata is the distinctive way in which she relates to her devotees and disciples. She seeks to communicate her message of love by enfolding individuals in her 'divine' embrace. At public *darshans*[6] devotees queue up in order to receive her embrace. The Mata takes each waiting devotee into her arms, and lavishes her love on them individually. She comforts those troubled by pressing personal problems in much the same way as a loving mother comforts a troubled child, and offers solutions. For most devotees the embrace is an intensely emotional experience, and many cry openly in her arms, even as they relish the comforting intimacy of her motherly touch.

Crucial to her reputation as guru and goddess are the countless miracles attributed to her. Devotees cherish every opportunity to narrate their own and others' experiences of miracles worked by the Mata. These include stories of how she heals the sick and dying, how she solves the financial problems of her devotees, rids alcoholics of their addiction, grants childless couples the boon of children, blesses the jobless with employment, resolves family disputes and settles marital discord. All of this the Mata is believed to effect simply by making a divine resolve, a *sankalpa*, willing that her devotees' wishes be granted. The Mata travels widely, moving from city to city within India visiting her Mission branches and offering local devotees a chance to meet her and receive her embrace. She also travels abroad every year, covering most MAM centres outside India. These annual 'world tours' and 'India tours', and the public programmes she conducts in the course of these, are the most visible feature of the Mata's mission to serve humanity and alleviate its suffering.

The Mata is known to be single, celibate and to lead a life of asceticism and austerity. In this respect, she conforms to the renunciatory ideals which govern the lives of ascetics in Hindu renunciatory orders even though, as I noted earlier, she does not belong to any such order herself. Yet, as Fuller (1992: 180) argues, it is crucial to the appeal of 'god-persons' like the Mata, that their divinity does not depend on legitimation through succession from an ancient line of precedent gurus. It is certainly true of Mata Amritanandamayi that because she is not in any way bound by a given tradition, nor in any sense answerable to a prior lineage of gurus, she exercises a great deal of flexibility in creating, choosing, combining and mixing religious symbols. Her independent claims to divinity confer upon her an autonomy from existing religious practices that she uses to full advantage. She draws heavily on established mythical, ritual and doctrinal elements within popular Hinduism, and reinterprets and remixes these in novel and ingenious ways, so as to weave together a unique system of meanings particularly relevant to modern times.

Though no two gurus in India are exactly alike, some often share broad and often striking similarities which invite comparison between them. Mata Amritanandamayi has important parallels with Sathya Sai Baba, arguably the most popular living guru in India today. Among important points of similarity between the two are their respective self-definitions as avatar-gurus (though each leader fosters a distinctive devotionalist style among devotees), their reputation for miracle-working (their miracle working styles, however, are again distinctive), the institutional structure of their respective Missions, their transnational spread, and their popularity among urban middle classes in India. Throughout the discussion in this book, I draw out points of comparision (and indeed of contrast) between the two gurus where appropriate.

Because of the highly eclectic nature of her professed divinity, it is impossible to place the Mata within any known categories of popular religion and/or spirituality. Devotees are divided in their views on whether or not hers is a 'Hindu' organization. She herself prefers to refer to her spiritual precepts and recommendations as *sanatana dharma*, which she describes thus: 'the preceptors of old presented Sanatana Dharma (eternal religion) not as a narrow religion constrained to a particular caste, creed or sect but rather as open to anyone and everyone. All are welcome to this path. This is everyone's'.[7]

Despite the reservations expressed by the Mata and some of her devotees about perceiving this faith as Hindu, in this study I locate this guru organization very much within the 'Hindu' pale, since the Mata's teachings and ritual prescriptions borrow heavily from traditions that are popularly recognized as 'Hindu'. It is impossible to situate the beliefs and practices of the MAM squarely within any one path or stream of Hindu spirituality. It appears to belong mainly to the *bhakti* or devotionalist tradition of Hindu faith, where individuals seek spiritual salvation by means of intense and personalized devotion to particular gods in the Hindu pantheon under the guidance of a spiritual preceptor. Yet, alongside the path of *bhakti* or devotion, the Mata recommends equally the paths of *karma* (selfless service) and *jnana* (knowledge) as legitimate means to attain spiritual salvation. It is also impossible to locate the MAM within any one Hindu devotionalist tradition – Shaiva, Vaishnava or Shakta.[8] The Mata encourages devotees to worship god in the form to which they can best relate. For most devotees, the object of worship is the Mata herself, whom they regard as a goddess.

In seeking to fulfil her mission to alleviate humanity's suffering, the Mata relies on the MAM's vast organizational network. The Mission, according to its promotional literature, was founded 'in order to disseminate the message of spirituality, Universal Love, and selfless service to humanity, which shines through the life and teachings of the Divine Mother, Her Holiness Mata Amritanandamayi Devi'. In the course of the 1980s and 1990s, the Mission shot to prominence as a fast-growing and highly successful enterprise, drawing hundreds of thousands of new devotees into its fold every year both in India and abroad. In India, besides its numerous branches and centres in towns and cities through the length and breadth of the country, the Mission also runs a chain of temples called Brahmasthanams, a network of schools, called Amrita Vidyalayams, a high-cost 'multi-super-speciality' hospital in Kerala, a hospice for the terminally ill in Mumbai (Bombay) as also an array of high profile engineering and management colleges and computer training schools in south India. Its charitable activities in Kerala include the provision of free housing for the poor, a monthly pension scheme for poor widows, a project for tribal welfare, and the running of various charitable institutions including an orphanage, a youth hostel and an old-age home. Abroad, as in India, the more active of the MAM centres consist of an ashram or centre headed by a disciple of the Mata, who engages local devotees in regular spiritual activities. The biggest of these is a 160-acre ashram in San Ramon, California, headed by one of the Mata's earliest (American) disciples. The San Ramon centre is actively involved in promoting the Mata and her Mission in the USA. There are also more informal Mata Amritanandamayi '*satsangs*' or spiritual gatherings in several foreign countries where lay devotees come together for regular programmes of ritual, meditation and worship. The finances for the MAM's institutional empire come from the generous contributions of devotees and disciples of the Mata across the world.

The Mata, even though she does not belong to any renunciatory order herself, has in her turn instituted and nurtured an order of renouncer-disciples who engage in spiritual questing under her tutelage and guidance. In the ashram or spiritual retreat at Amritapuri in Kerala, where the Mata resides through most of the year when she is not on her periodic tours of Mission branches in India and abroad, she grooms these spiritual aspirants, both male and female, for a life of spiritual striving. For an indefinite period from the time they first enter the ashram, these aspirants are exposed to the many rigours of austere ashram life when the Mata and her senior disciples closely observe their conduct. When they finally 'qualify' for formal entry into spiritual life, they take what is called the *brahmacharya diksha*, a rite formally initiating them into *brahmacharya*, the life of an ascetic. With this initiation, they enter the status of *brahmacharis* and *brahmacharinis* (male and female ascetic spiritual aspirants respectively), are given new names, and are required to wear yellow as a mark of their spiritual status. *Brahmacharya* entails a life of austerity and celibacy, the severing of family ties, and complete surrender and unquestioning obedience to the Mata. A *brahmachari(ni)* who, after years of austerity and spiritual practice, attains spiritual enlightenment (in the Mata's reckoning, for she is believed to be the sole arbiter in these matters), undergoes a further initiation, the *sannyasa diksha*. This ritual, where the individual is required to perform his or her own funerary rites, now confirms him/her as a *sannyasi* or *sannyasini* (male or female renouncer).[9] The renouncer's status is marked by saffron clothing. The activities at the ashram headquarters follow a clear hierarchy of command. *Sannyasi(ni)s* are higher up in the hierarchy than *brahmachari(ni)s*. The latter are higher up than new entrants undergoing initial probation.[10] The highest authority of course is the Mata herself, and all important decisions pertaining to the Mission are made in consultation with her.

The first of the Mata's disciples to be given *diksha* was initiated by a monk belonging to the Ramakrishna Math.[11] This disciple then initiated others. The initiation rituals, the system of probation, and the two levels of ascetic life – first as *brahmachari*, and then as *sannyasi* – all follow the pattern in the Ramakrishna order. There are, as I shall discuss in Chapter 4 below, several points of correspondence between the Mata Amritanandamayi and Ramakrishna Missions. Most important is the ethic of *seva* or selfless service that informs the activities of both organizations. Alongside *bhakti* or devotion, the MAM places very great emphasis on selfless service as a path towards spiritual growth. In fact the entire organizational apparatus of the Mission is sustained and managed precisely on the strength of the *seva* inputs of its adherents, both lay devotees and renunciate disciples. Much of this *seva* is directed towards the devotional glorification of the Mata, and takes myriad forms, ranging from monetary contributions to the MAM, to the channelling of non-monetary resources, including physical effort and time, even social influence and political clout, towards the cause of the Mission's expansion and publicity.

An important act of *seva* on the part of the Mata's lay devotees is the setting up of a Mission centre or branch in their town or city as an expression of their adoration for, and worship of, the Mata. Devotees come together, form a *seva* committee, and, with the permission of the Mission headquarters, take on the onerous task of collecting funds to finance the purchase of land and the construction of the ashram building. This project often takes several months, if not years, to complete. Once the local branch has been set up, the Mata appoints one of her *brahmachari(ni)* or *sannyasi(ni)* disciples to head it and oversee its activities. This disciple organizes weekly ritual, discourse, and prayer sessions at the ashram branch[12] which the local devotees attend. (S)he also presides over such projects as building a local Brahmasthanam temple, an Amrita Vidyalaya (school), or an orphanage, using the resources (money, influence, labour) that devotees place at the Mata's disposal.

Institution building and expansion is an important means by which the Mata seeks to further her professed 'mission' in the world. The contributions of devotees and disciples in terms of financial and other resources are, in turn, indispensable in furthering these institution building efforts. In the case of her middle-class devotees in India, their privileged place in Indian society gives them a unique advantage in rendering the kind of services that the MAM requires. Their educational qualifications, material wealth, occupational skills, social connections, influence in important political and business networks, all go a long way in providing the MAM with exactly the kind of resources it needs to facilitate its institutional expansion and growth.

The Mata's urban 'middle-class' devotees

The majority of the Mata's devotees in India are Hindu, English-speaking, educated, well-to-do urbanites in white-collar employment (many in the newer and more prestigious occupations involving high-tech skills and comparatively high earnings).[13] They include government officials, lawyers, doctors, teachers, college lecturers, journalists, managers in multi-national corporations or in smaller private concerns, computer software personnel, engineers and scientists. These individuals, by their own reckoning, belong to the much-talked-of, yet somewhat nebulous and indistinct category that has come to be known as India's 'middle classes'.

There are no clear markers to indicate the precise occupational ranks, income levels or educational achievements that define the middle classes as a separate and distinct category. Yet India's 'middle classes' are the subject of much discussion and debate in the popular Indian press, as well as in academic writings on India. These 'middle classes', though small in size in relation to the rest of the population, are widely said to comprise, in absolute terms, a sizeable constituency of 90 to 100 million, that is, 9 to 10 per cent of the country's total population of just over a billion.

In the existing literature on present-day India, there are relatively few ethnographic studies of what it means to be 'middle class' in the contemporary Indian context. What we do have is extensive historical literature on India's colonial intelligentsia (an important constituent of the 'middle classes' of the late nineteenth and early twentieth centuries), who have been seen as disproportionately important in contributing to the rise of 'modern' nationalist ideologies and political organizations in the colonial period.[14] The category that is today recognizable as India's 'middle classes' has swelled considerably since the days of colonial rule. In the early-to-mid twentieth century, the main constituents of the 'middle classes' were primarily cosmopolitan anglophone intelligentsia in the liberal professions, as well as business and commercial groups.[15] After Independence, and particularly in the closing decades of the twentieth century, there have been many new recruits to the 'middle classes' owing mainly to the growth of Indian industry, and the liberalization of the Indian economy in the early 1990s. Industrialization and liberalization opened up new opportunities in India's business and service sectors, led to rising incomes, and increased the purchasing power of upwardly mobile persons in urban India who benefited from these new developments. Significant numbers of wealthy farmers also spread their networks of interest into the commercial and service sectors, and joined the ranks of the middle classes. In the 1980s and 1990s, media and business attention came to focus on India's expanding middle classes and their 'insatiable propensity to consume'. At international forums they emerged as a key selling point for India, bearing testimony to India's economic progress, and promising a vast potential market for foreign investors.[16]

India's 'middle classes' have also been an important focus of recent commentaries on the resurgence of Hindu nationalism in India since the 1980s. Many such commentaries posit a direct correlation between the expansion of the middle classes since the 1980s, and the rise of Hindu nationalist forces in the same period. Though this study is not one more addition to the voluminous literature that has emerged in recent times on Hindu nationalism, it does, through an exploration of 'Hindu' middle-class religious experience, re-examine important assumptions upon which some of this literature is premised.

Most of the devotees of the Mata I met in the course of my fieldwork readily identified themselves as members of India's 'middle classes'. Among them were persons descended from the older middle-class intelligentsias of early and mid-twentieth century India, as well as newer recruits to this category, mainly first or second generation migrants to India's metropolitan cities. It is true for most of these individuals that, as Béteille (1991a) argues, the ideology of meritocracy has, to some extent, displaced that of ascription. Thus their social and economic status derives not from their place in a given caste hierarchy,[17] but from their capital, credentials and expertise.

These persons see a good education as vital to ensure their economic mobility and access to global opportunities. They try to secure for their sons and daughters entry to prestigious schools and universities, even if it means paying a 'capitation fee' to enter.[18] These serve as springboards to educational opportunities in the USA, UK, Canada and Australia. Many of my informants already had sons and daughters studying in universities abroad where they sought to cultivate an international professional identity and gain access to business and professional opportunities worldwide. These individuals place education at a premium not only because of its value as a means to upward mobility, but also because of its symbolic value. Education serves as an important status marker, distinguishing those with an English-medium education in a prestigious school or university, from others who may have received instruction in Indian regional languages and who lack the resources to seize higher and better opportunities in the educational and professional fields.

Consumption patterns too are central to the construction of social identity and status among my informants. Most of them revealed a keen awareness of consumer items available in the market. To them shopping is a prime occupation to fill leisure hours. Individual orientations to shopping vary drastically from one family to the next. Those at the lower end of the income scale such as government officials and university lecturers generally appear anxious to shop at places where they can bargain and get goods at the lowest possible prices. Others more flush with money, especially young managers and software experts in well-paying multinational companies, are often concerned more with prestigious brand names than with cost cutting, and prefer to shop at the more expensive and exclusive shopping centres and arcades.

This predilection for consumerism is inextricably linked with the transnational connections of the urban middle classes. Theirs is a world of accelerated flows of capital, technology and information across countries, modernized telecommunications and globalized consumption and lifestyle patterns. The economic liberalization of the 1990s, which brought an influx of foreign consumer goods, as well as access to foreign television through satellite transmission, exposed the country as never before to global economic and cultural influences. This is reflected in the consumption patterns of India's urban middle classes, which conform increasingly to certain 'globalized' standards, though not to the exclusion of local cultural sensibilities. Brand products such as Barbie dolls and Nike sportswear, television soaps like *Santa Barbara* and *NYPD Blue*, fast-food centres like Pizza Hut and Burger King, are all part of their everyday world, just as are 'ethnic' eating places, chic Indian boutiques and popular Indian-language television serials.[19] As Pinches (1999) rightly points out, consumer items operate for most individuals as principal signifiers of social status and achievement. There are thus certain 'positional goods' (ibid.: 32) that separate the urban 'elites' from the less advantaged – these include cars, often in the latest models, expensive dwellings, clothes with designer labels, meals bought at expensive restaurants and modern fast-food centres, expensive holiday package tours, recreational facilities and mobile phones.

This consumer culture is evident equally in less tangible spheres of urban middle-class life, most notably that of religious preference. The urban environs of contemporary India provide fertile ground for the mushrooming of religious and spiritual groups, whose wares range from discourses on scriptural Hinduism to meditation techniques, stress-relief and relaxation methods, and techniques of spiritual and physical healing. They attract adherents from the more affluent sections of society who, as I noted before, can contribute towards the growth and publicity of these groups and their leaders, either through donations in cash and kind, or through the circles of influence that they command in the higher echelons of local business and political circles. Individuals often participate in more than one such organization and derive the benefit of perceived spiritual growth and healing, and a sense of keeping up with their peers in matters not just of material, but also spiritual wealth. 'Spirituality' comprises an important element in drawing room conversations in most urban middle-class households. Long, involved discussions on the latest spiritual wares available, or animated comparisons between different gurus and between diverse meditation and healing techniques, are all commonplace in the everyday social interactions of these individuals. The transnational links of these middle classes, as I noted earlier, are reflected in the religious and spiritual organizations to which many of them attach themselves. Most such organizations, like the MAM, command an international presence, and connect devotees worldwide not only through institutional networks, but also through such modern means of international communication as electronic mail and the Internet.

The urban middle-class devotees of Mata Amritanandamayi are thus actors in a global market seeking to enhance their educational and career opportunities to gain upward mobility. They are consumers of luxury goods, participants in competing worlds of consumerism dominated by lifestyle patterns of the affluent West. They are people circulating across geographical spaces and distances both physically and through their familiarity with revolutionized media and communications systems. Such a 'universal' and 'cosmopolitan' image, however, is only part of the story. The other part relates to ties with the local and particular, and to definitions of what it means, in particular contexts, to be Indian. Thus it is with reference to both axes, the universal and the particular, the global and the local, that the self perceptions of India's urban middle classes must be considered.

The appeal of modern gurus to India's urban middle classes

Several scholars studying modern transnational guru organizations originating in India have noted their particular popularity among India's urban middle classes. In seeking to explain this phenomenon, they invariably point to a perceived void of one kind or another in the lives of these urbanites which results from their supposedly 'unsettling' encounter with modernity, and which they purportedly seek to fill by participating in a guru faith. According to this argument, the lives of these urban middle classes are characterized by a sense of rootlessness, alienation and anomie (Varma 1998). First, it is argued, they have lost their anchoring in traditional Indian social support systems such as joint families, village communities and caste networks, and find themselves adrift in the inhospitable and alienating environment of India's towns and cities which are 'singularly deficient in institutions of community interaction' (ibid.: 139). They are therefore in search of a sense of belonging, security and anchoring in new and alternative communities. Second, succeeding generations of urbanites see themselves as having increasingly 'lost touch' with the values, traditions, and belief systems of previous generations. Third, the argument goes, they also encounter, in urban India's modern environment, changes of an unprecedented nature, with which they find themselves incapable of keeping pace, and whose very rapidity and scale they find traumatic and stressful. The uncertainties and anxieties that accompany this fast pace of change leaves them hankering after the imagined certitudes and securities of a more 'stable' past.

It is in such a climate of uncertainty, rootlessness and alienation, it is argued, that religious ideologies, organizations, and leaders come to be looked upon by middle-class urbanites as ideally suited to fill the void in their lives. Membership in religious and/or spiritual organizations provides a refuge against the impersonal social structures of a modern urban environment. By invoking the certitudes and simplicities of an idealized past, guru-faith bolsters the individual's capacity to face up to the uncertainties of fast-paced city life. As a repository of ultimate 'truths', guru-faith puts the individual back in the centre of a social and moral order grounded in absolute values. This is the line of argument we encounter in recent studies of such modern gurus in contemporary India as Sathya Sai Baba (Swallow 1982)[20] and the popular proponent of Sahaja Yoga, Mata Nirmala Devi (Kakar 1984).[21] Given the ability of gurus and guru-organizations to effectively address the very problems encountered by India's middle-class urbanites, it is only logical (it is argued), that modern India should witness a spate of guru-centred religious faiths and organizations among these sections of its population.[22]

The constituencies from which Sathya Sai Baba, Mata Amritanandamayi and Mata Nirmala Devi draw their followers overlap to a considerable extent. Thus many of the devotees of Mata Amritanandamayi whom I interviewed were, for instance, either simultaneously also devotees of Sathya Sai Baba and/or Mata Nirmala Devi, or had been so at some point in the past before shifting their loyalties to Mata Amritanandamayi. My findings based on fieldwork among devotees of Mata Amritanandamayi cast doubts on some of the claims and assumptions made in these earlier studies regarding the sense of 'lack' experienced by middle-class urbanites in India.

None of the Mata's devotees whom I interviewed appeared to 'miss' a sense of community in their urban environment. Most of them claimed to share close ties with members of their extended family, either resident in the same city, or geographically dispersed yet closely in touch through modern means of communication. For many, their immediate 'social circle' comprised acquaintances from similar socio-linguistic and caste backgrounds, relatives, friends from the educational institutions where they studied, colleagues at their work place, or even neighbours. Many were members of groups like social clubs, caste associations and neighbourhood welfare committees. India's modern urban environment, as these persons experienced it, was not, it appeared, the breeding ground for alienation, isolation and anonymity that previous scholars have made it out to be. Some of my informants claimed they preferred not to socialize extensively simply because their commitments at home and in the workplace left them little or no time. In the course of their everyday lives these people saw little or nothing of their fellow devotees, and preferred to keep things that way. Others, mostly retired persons or elderly housewives with plenty of time on their hands, who did socialize with fellow devotees, saw this socializing as complementary to already existing social networks of which they were part. Many were introduced to the Mata by their friends and relatives, and they in turn were instrumental in bringing their friends and kin to the Mata's fold.

Similarly, none of these persons expressed any anxiety about 'losing touch' with their religious traditions. All of the devotees I met, almost without exception, claimed to have gained their early orientation to religious faith and observance from their parents and grandparents. A significant number of my informants claimed they had felt dissatisfied with the 'mechanical' and 'ritualistic' religious observances and 'blind faith' of their parents, and had sought greater 'meaning' in their own religious lives. This 'meaning' they found by seeking guidance from a guru like the Mata, by listening to discourses and sermons delivered by religious scholars, and/or by acquainting themselves with Hindu philosophical and/or religious texts and commentaries. Others who had not been actively searching for meaning of any sort, claimed to have found this meaning almost serendipitously, through a chance encounter with, and subsequent surrender to, their guru. Rather than worry about 'losing touch' with existing traditions, most of the Mata's devotees were concerned about the 'meaninglessness' of traditional faith and practice as they had known them, and sought to replace these with a more informed, meaningful and reflective approach to religion.

It is certainly true for most of these persons that they have encountered (and continue to encounter), in the course of their lifetime, large-scale transformations in the objective conditions of their existence owing to the acceleration in transnational flows of capital, technology and information following India's economic liberalization, the modernization of India's telecommunications, the opening of new educational as well as career opportunities, and the growing preference for modern lifestyles. It is these objective transformations, as Miller (1994) rightly argues, which finally transform the sense of change in the modern world from something constant and gradual to something accelerating exponentially, and which create an overwhelming sense of the compression of time and space (ibid.: 65–6). It would be incorrect to assume, however, that this change is experienced by the entire range of India's middle classes as overwhelmingly stressful, traumatic and alienating. On the contrary, most of the devotees of Mata Amritanandamayi whom I encountered were individuals who had benefited vastly from the changing conditions in India's political economy, and who had done well for themselves by seizing the education and job related opportunities that had come their way. For the majority of these individuals, their experience of the unprecedented pace and scale of change in modern India's urban environment has resulted not so much in a sense of despair and failure, as in the hope of increasing possibilities and multiplying opportunities. Most importantly, it has meant a growing awareness of multiple choices in every sphere of life, including that of religion. This awareness of the diverse opportunities available to them, and the recognition of individual choice as key to negotiating life in a 'modern' world, are centrally important to understanding why significant numbers of India's educated middle-class urbanites are attracted to modern gurus like Sathya Sai Baba and Mata Amritanandamayi.

The religion one encounters in many of contemporary India's high profile modern guru organizations is most importantly a religion of choice. It is this, I argue, that makes participation in these organizations particularly attractive to sizeable sections of India's educated middle classes. There are three crucial and closely related elements central to this notion of choice. First, choice means *personal freedom* to create for oneself a religious life conducive to one's particular individual tastes and dispositions. Religious affiliation comes to be seen not as a require-ment, but as an option, 'one among a range of possible loyalties freely chosen and freely left' (Vanaik 1997: 101). Questions of religious selfhood assume a reflective character, where 'the case for free choice and complete revisability of religious identities . . . [is] accepted and respected' (ibid.). Second, choice also means *self-authorship* of a highly personalized form of religious faith. Religion in this sense is no longer rooted in past traditions and handed down in a taken-for-granted way from one generation to the next; it is instead personally constructed by the individuals concerned to suit their specific inclinations and requirements (Bruce 1998; Wallis and Bruce 1992). In constructing this personalized religion, the individual makes selections from a wide array of elements that he or she encounters in his/her religious environment. Third, this individual construction of one's religious life represents an *internalization of faith* such that it is inner spiritual striving and self-fulfilment that

14

become central to religious life rather than the affirmation of shared community orientations, affiliations, aspirations and identities. Guru organizations such as the Mata Amritanandamayi Mission and the Sathya Sai Mission offer their own particular repertoire of religious elements for devotees to choose from, without binding them to a long-term commitment to the respective organizations, or demanding their allegiance to a rigidly defined set of beliefs and practices.

Scholars studying new religious movements, or indeed new religious 'organizations' in the West have often commented on how many such organizations, especially those originating in India (as also elsewhere in the East), tend to focus more on the private and individual aspects of religious life (self-authorship and self-fulfilment) than on the public and collective (fostering a sense of community).[23] It is remarkable that similar observations have not been made by scholars studying the same organizations in their home (Indian) environment. Perhaps the tendency to overlook the private, individual and interiorized aspect of modern guru-centred religious organizations in India has to do with the intellectual legacy bequeathed by scholars like Louis Dumont, which tends to see lay Hindu society as composed not so much of individuals as of castes, families and other social groupings which subordinate the individual to the imperatives of the collective. Be that as it may, what scholars have observed for the Western following of modern transnational guru organizations from India is in fact equally true of Hindu adherents in India. The religious faith that many such organizations foster in their largely urban, educated middle-class Indian following is of an individual, private and inward-looking variety that is concerned not with community identities but with individual self-fulfilment.

Hindu selfhood and modernity

Questions about modernity and how it is experienced by middle-class urbanites in India have important implications for our understanding of Hinduism and Hindu selfhood in the contemporary world. Commentaries on Hindu selfhood define it in widely varying terms, depending on which aspect of the diverse traditions encompassed under the misleadingly singular term 'Hinduism' they identify as constituting its 'essence'. In most cases, the tendency has been to portray Hindu selfhood as diametrically opposed to its Western counterpart. The binary oppositions that define these conceptions of Hindu and Western selfhood are based largely on notions of a dichotomy between tradition and modernity, such that the Hindu self, defined as rooted in 'tradition', is contrasted with Western selfhood, the quintessence of 'modernity'.

Early studies, which looked primarily to ancient scriptures for an understanding of Hinduism, saw Hindu theodicies of salvation as constituting its core. These theodicies of salvation are preoccupied first with what is perceived as the inexorable karmic cycle of birth, death and rebirth, and second, with the all-important ideal of *moksha*, or release from this cycle, upheld as the ultimate Hindu spiritual goal. Many early Hindu philosophical traditions describe the pursuit of this goal as leading away from worldly engagements to a state of increasing inner quietude and mental and emotional detachment from everyday realities. It was easy to infer from this that Hinduism is primarily an other-worldly, mystical religion, and therefore that Hindu selfhood, as an ideal-type, is other-worldly and mystical in its orientation. For Max Weber (1958b), Hinduism's other-worldly mysticism explained why modernity struck roots not on Indian soil (or anywhere in the East for that matter) but in the West where Protestantism's inner-worldly asceticism provided conducive ground for the spirit of capitalism, and concomitantly modernity, to flourish.[24]

More recently, the French scholar, Louis Dumont, drew attention to India's social organization, and its supposedly all-pervasive caste hierarchies, as constituting the quintessence of Hinduism. From his study of Hindu social organization, Dumont (1965a and 1965b, 1980) inferred that hierarchy and holism lie at the heart of Hindu selfhood. Dumont contends that Hindus value not equality (as in the modern West) but hierarchy as the fundamental organizing principle of their life-worlds. Hierarchical ranking, based largely on the separation between the pure (sacred) and the impure (mundane/organic) informs every aspect of Hindu social life and Hindu self-perceptions. He also contends, most importantly, that Hindus have no identity separate from the collectivities, most importantly the caste categories, to which they belong. Agency is attributed to these collectivities and not to the individual; indeed in Dumont's view Hindus have no conception of the individual,[25] except outside the social domain, in the figure of the renouncer (Dumont 1970). Collective solidarities, as well as interdependence between, and holistic identities within, collectivities, Dumont argues, are the cornerstones of Hindu self-perceptions. In the absence of individual freedom, free will and independent agency, (traditional) Hindu society with its hierarchical social structure provides a neat contrast to the individualism, personal agency and egalitarian ethic of the (modern) West.

Still more recently, commentaries on Hinduism have tended to focus almost exclusively on the resurgence of Hindu nationalist forces in India since the 1980s. Stressing the distinctiveness of Indian selfhood, scholars such as Ashis Nandy (1985, 1990, 1997) and T.N. Madan (1987a, 1997) explain the rise of Hindu nationalist forces in India in terms of a presumed 'incompatibility' between Hindu selfhood and modernity. The 'Hindu' self, in this scheme of things, is uniquely religious in its orientation, lacks the cognitive capabilities necessary for Western rationality, and is unsuited to Western-style political institutions and Western forms of capitalism. Here too the argument is that present-day Hindus suffer from a sense of alienation and defeat as a result of the legacy of India's colonial experience and their own exposure to post-colonial modernity.[26] The upsurge of Hindu nationalistic sentiments in the present is then seen as an angry response to this sense of alienation, and as a backlash against modernity and its related ideological impositions.[27]

These commentaries on Hindu selfhood and modernity, while they each focus on a different aspect of Hindu world-views and traditions, share some key characteristics. First, they each define Hindu selfhood in the singular, vastly simplifying Hinduism and reducing it to a single 'essence' rather than acknowledging the multiplicity in philosophies, beliefs, practices and customs that in fact constitute Hindu worlds in all their diversity.[28] Second, the resultant 'essentialized' Hinduism is posited against modernity and the modern West, which too are reduced to simplistic essences. Modernity in this scheme of things is treated as a monolithic conceptual category, the result of a historical process under-stood to unify Western notions of selfhood into something uniquely non-traditional and distinctive. The encounter between Hindu tradition and Western modernity is then envisaged as an encounter between incompatibles, where the result can only be one of two things – Hinduism's assimilation of modernity and its world-views, or Hinduism's rejection of modernity, the latter leading to antagonism, confrontation and violence.

In contrast with essentializing and oversimplified notions of the Hindu self posited by those seeking to establish its distinctiveness, this study explores selfhood not as a 'given' but as a 'construct'. My aim here is to examine the processes whereby individuals construct their 'Hindu' selves in particular ways and in particular contexts. The building blocks of such self-construction are often the diverse philosophies, values, beliefs and world-views with which these individuals become familiar through their exposure to various 'Hindu' contexts and traditions.[29] Crucial to the process of self-construction, as I see it, is the choice and agency individuals exercise in making their selections from these traditions, and often in combining these with what they see as 'modern' attitudes and orientations. My attempt here is to treat modernity not as scholars tend to understand the term, but as my informants themselves come to define it as they engage individually and severally with their immediate and disparate real-life experiences. Instead of perceiving modernity as something which persons *assimilate* or *reject* in its entirety, this study explores processes whereby individuals *construct* 'modernity' in their imagination and thereby *negotiate* its conditions. Devotion to a guru is often one of the means by which individuals come to terms with modernity's pulls and pressures. In the case of devotees of Mata Amritanandamayi, this is indeed the case. This study therefore rejects the idea that modernity is incompatible with the Indian self, and that there is in fact 'no scope for compromise between the old and new' (Nandy 1990: 79). Instead, it asks how attachment to a popular modern-day guru, Mata Amritanandamayi, facilitates individuals' negotiation of their selfhood, and indeed of modernity itself.

The conclusions I draw from this study do not apply to all 'Hindus' in a wider sense. What I am attempting to do here is simply to draw attention to one of the multiple ways in which Hindus interact with and negotiate modernizing, globalizing and other far-reaching influences in their lives. All too often academic scholarship zeroes in on any one dominant trend in society, in India's case the resurgence of Hindu nationalism, and typifies it as the quintessential 'Hindu' response to modernity and change. While in no way discounting the significance of Hindu nationalist developments in India in recent times, I seek here to draw attention to other parallel developments that are, in my view, equally significant if we are to understand contemporary Hindu worlds in all their diversity. In this connection, I turn now to a brief discussion of recent developments in anthropological theorizing on 'modernity', which are crucial to the present study.

The anthropology of 'modernity' and 'modernities'

Modernity as a conceptual category in the social sciences and humanities has undergone several radical changes in the course of the last three to four decades. Early understandings of modernity as a Western model of 'progress' and 'development' were challenged with the onset of postmodernist thinking, which criticized the assumptions of Western thought, questioned the desirability and legitimacy of 'modernity', and exposed the politics of domination and oppression that lay behind Western conceptions of 'modernity', 'truth' and 'rationality'. In the early days of postmodernist theorizing, some scholars tended to see the postmodern as making a radical break with the modern, and anticipated that post-modernity would spell the end or death of modernity. Others, however, perceived postmodernity not as that which replaced or succeeded modernity, but instead as that which represented the culmination or apogee of modernity itself. This latter understanding has dominated much of the recent scholarship on the subject, with scholars emphasizing continuity, rather than rupture, between modernity and postmodernity. Postmodernity is thus seen as an aspect of modernity itself – the modernity of late capitalism. 'Modernity', in turn, far from being the obsolete conceptual category that early postmodernist theorists had predicted, remains central to current theorizing in the social sciences and humanities.

Nowhere is this more true than in anthropological scholarship where there has been a recent spate in ethnographic studies of modernity. There has, however, been an important change in the way anthropologists perceive modernity. Rather than perceive the Western model as the one singular and definitive 'modernity', anthropologists now see this as one among many possible variants of modernity. Western modernity, as it spreads across the globe, theorists now argue, assumes many different forms, in different socio-economic, historical and cultural contexts. There are thus 'modernities' in the plural rather than 'modernity' in the singular. The notion of 'multiple' or 'alternative' modernities suggests that there is no unilinear, universal and homogeneous path to 'progress' and 'development'. Global processes are shaped through their interaction with local contexts, and the result of such interaction is diversity and multiplicity.[30]

This kind of conceptual pluralism, however, has its own share of problems. If there is a multiplicity of 'modernities' across the world, what is it that all of these share in common that qualifies them all as 'modernities' in the first place? In attempting to answer this question, recent theorists have tended to try and complement an understanding of modernity in terms of objective socio-economic conditions, with one that takes into account cultural orientations and subjective dispositions.[31] Knauft (2002: 18), for instance, in his discussion of 'alternative modernities', defines modernity as 'the images and institutions associated with Western-style progress and development in a contemporary world'. The desire to become modern, as Knauft rightly points out, is not simply an academic projection. Images and institutions of so-called progress and development are extremely powerful forces today, and inform people's thinking across the world. This is not to suggest, however, that people everywhere receive these images and ideas in homogeneous ways. Modernity instead becomes a contested category, such that notions of development and progress are no longer taken for granted as following the Western model, but are negotiated differently in different socio-historical and economic contexts through selective appropriation, opposition and redefinition. This approach facilitates the study of 'alternative modernities' in a way that engages the global with the local, and features of the political economy with cultural orientations and dispositions. Far from being a static category, consisting of certain fixed essences, modernity becomes instead a process shaped by the agency of the persons negotiating its meaning. It is such an understanding of modernity that runs through the following pages of this book.

Approach, sources and methodology

This study is based on extensive fieldwork among the devotees and disciples of Mata Amritanandamayi. The first phase of my fieldwork was conducted over a period of twelve months in India, from mid-1997 to mid-1998, partly in Kerala, the state of the Mata's origin and where the Mission has its headquarters, and partly in Delhi where the Mission operates a local unit of the organization and commands a sizeable following of local devotees. Following this I spent several weeks conducting fieldwork in London, during and after the Mata's visit there in July 1998. This first phase of fieldwork was completed as part of my PhD programme at the University of Cambridge, UK. After the completion of my PhD, I revisited my fieldwork site in India in July 2001, meeting up with some of the devotees in Delhi and Kerala whom I had met and interviewed three years previously. This second phase of fieldwork was vital in providing important insights into changes in guru devotion over time, and devotees' self-perceptions of their own spiritual growth under the Mata's guidance, or in some cases, their progressive disenchantment with the Mata's brand of spirituality.

The starting point for my fieldwork in 1997 was the local ashram branch in Delhi, where I met the resident *brahmachari*, the ascetic disciple of the Mata in charge of the MAM's Delhi affairs. This *brahmachari* arranged for me to get in touch with local devotees, who in turn introduced me to fellow-devotees known to them, and so the network of contacts grew. After the first few months of fieldwork in Delhi, I moved on to Kerala where I spent several weeks in the Mata's ashram headquarters in Amritapuri. There I met more of the Mata's ascetic disciples and lay devotees, those resident in the ashram, as well as others (Indians and foreigners) visiting from different cities across India and abroad. While in Kerala my fieldwork also took me beyond the ashram headquarters to the Mission's ashram branches in Trissur, Kochi, Kozhikode and Palghat. In each town, as in Delhi, I managed, with the help of the local ashram authorities, to establish contact with devotees and spend time with them learning about their religious lives, their faith in the Mata, and their involvement in the MAM's activities. I also visited some of the educational and charitable enterprises of the MAM, located in Kerala as well as in the neighbouring state of Tamil Nadu.[32]

The method used for fieldwork and data collection included intensive interview sessions both with the Mata's lay devotees and with her renouncer disciples. These were conducted in an informal style, where interviewees described their experience of the Mata, explained the extent of their involvement with the Mata Amritanandamayi Mission, and commented on its various aspects. These devotees and disciples, though they were from diverse regional and linguistic backgrounds, were mostly fluent in English. Most of my interviews were therefore conducted in English. A small number, however, were carried out in Malayalam (the language spoken in Kerala) and in Hindi. Translations provided in the text are my own. My fieldwork in London provided me with a rare opportunity to interview the Mata herself. My interviews extended also to people outside the circle of devotees and disciples, to social and political activists, journalists, and casual observers, even critics, of the Mission, who often made valuable contributions to my understanding of the Mission and its following. I also interviewed a sizeable number of foreign devotees, both at Amritapuri in Kerala and in London, and got from them a sense of how non-Indians perceive India, Indians, and the faith propagated by the Mata.

Apart from informal interviews, participant observation of the Mission's activities, enabled through many weeks spent at the ashram headquarters in Kerala and several days at the ashram branch in Delhi, was the other main methodological tool adopted in this study. This entailed participating in ashram life, in the Mission's rituals and daily practices, attending sermons and *bhajan* (prayer) sessions, engaging in common *seva* (service) activities in the ashram, and getting to know about the life of a devotee not so much as a researcher but as a fellow participant. Besides conducting interviews and engaging in participant observation, I also analysed the publicity material generated by the Mission. I examined the Mission's websites, viewed the video cassettes and CDs produced by Mission volunteers, and scanned the voluminous publications and promotional pamphlets generated by the Mission. I also examined articles in newspapers and other publications which contained references to the Mata.

My relationship with the devotees was a complex one. From the point of view of the Indian urban middle-class devotees of the Mata, I was visibly one of them, owing to my own middle-class upbringing in Delhi, immediately apparent from the way I dressed, spoke, addressed my interviewees, and conversed with them about a range of themes of mutual interest from TV soaps to options in the educational field. Some of my

21

interviewees enquired at length about my PhD programme in the UK, which I had embarked upon a year before. Many attached a certain prestige value to higher education abroad, and expressed great curiosity about life as an Indian student in the UK. They quizzed me about chances of obtaining scholarships at universities abroad, reasons why I had selected this particular topic to research, and my own perception of the Mata. Most devotees were hospitable and friendly, and many went out of their way to help me with my research, offering to introduce me to other devotees, escorting me to local MAM sites, and arranging to keep me informed about developments in their local MAM branch, often seeing these acts as expressions of *seva* or selfless service, in keeping with the Mata's precepts.

My familiarity with the social context of these individuals – Indian, Hindu, urban, educated and middle class – helped to ease me into my fieldwork setting. I had worries, however, right from the outset, about how they would receive the fact of my largely irreligious upbringing, and my total absence of faith in the Mata. I made no attempt to hide my lack of faith from devotees and disciples, and presented my interest in the Mata and her Mission as largely impersonal and academic. In the course of my fieldwork I discovered that this lack of faith did not present as much of a problem as I had feared. Several devotees anticipated that in the course of my fieldwork I would inevitably be overcome by the Mata's magnetism and find myself drawn into her fold. When this did not happen they concluded that perhaps the time was not yet right for me to secure the protection of a guru, and that perhaps I had not achieved the spiritual maturity necessary to appreciate the bounty of the Mata's grace. Devotees saw their faith largely as the result of their immediate and personal experience of the Mata's divine qualities, and they were more than ready to concede that this faith could have no meaning for one who had not had a similar experience. In this respect some devotees saw my research approach as fundamentally misguided. They said it was futile to try to understand the Mata through my mental faculties. In order to appreciate her, these devotees told me, I must 'let go' of my powers of reasoning and learn to rely on the intuitive powers of my heart. They were emphatic in their assertion that the Mata cannot be understood, she must be experienced. Others attributed their own experiences of the Mata's divine grace to a matching of chemistries between guru and devotee. The absence of such experiences in my case indicated that perhaps my chemistry did not match well with the Mata's, and that some other guru might prove to be the right one for me.

A central paradox in my research became apparent to me in the course of my fieldwork. Here was I, an Indian, located at a British university, trained as an anthropologist in a Western scholastic tradition, researching an Indian guru organization which in its turn addressed a multicultural audience, and writing about this faith for a largely Western or Westernized readership. Researching in a globalized context meant that I grew increasingly aware of the shifting alterities in my role as researcher. I became extremely conscious of the tenuous nature of insider/outsider divisions that operated in my fieldwork setting.[33] Indian devotees of the Mata, for instance, often saw me as an insider vis-à-vis non-Indian devotees because of some notion of a shared 'Indianness'. At other times they tended to view me as an outsider, by virtue of my being a non-devotee. Non-Indians likewise slotted me differently at different times, sometimes sharing confidences with me about what they disliked about Indian devotees of the Mata. I was in their view too 'Westernized' to count as an Indian. At other times, I was very much an Indian in their perspective, and my questions about their attitudes towards Indians elicited the uncomfortable and guarded responses of a team player wary of betraying his or her 'side'.

Writing about a transnational guru organization for a transnational readership had one other important aspect to it, which came to my notice early in my research. In response to a letter I wrote in early 1997 to the Mission authorities in Kerala seeking permission to study their organization, I received an encouraging reply from a senior *sannyasi* in the Mata Amritanandamayi Mission. He wrote:

It is indeed fortunate to know that youngsters like you are seriously taking an interest in research and study of the anthropology of Indian religious evolution. This will help in exposing to the world, the hidden treasures in the cultural heritage of our country. Amma and the revolution brought about by Her various service oriented activities in the diverse fields of society, stands as a living evidence to the fact that the religion of India, which is the most ancient one (Sanatana), has always remained a unique but dynamic path to the truth which knows to revitalize itself from time to time as obvious from the advent of Mahatmas like Amma.[34]

I realized how my research and subsequent publications based on it could easily feed into the MAM's programme of ever-greater publicity and propaganda for the Mata and her Mission. I was often asked the uncomfortable question of whether I would present the MAM in a positive or negative light. Luckily, my informants seemed not to worry too much about the potential consequences of negative publicity; with their abiding faith in the Mata they found it easy to discount any possibility of lasting damage to the Mata's reputation. This was convenient for me, yet I still worried about the implications (positive or negative) of my research findings for the Mission and its adherents. I drew some consolation from the fact that, when I returned to my informants in 2001 and explained to them the main arguments in my recently completed PhD thesis, they appeared not to find anything objectionable in the outcome. In university circles in the UK, where I talk about my research on the Mata to audiences often previously unaware of her existence, I suppose I must inadvertently contribute towards publicity for the Mata. This book too will contribute to making the Mata known to more people, even though publicity for the Mata is not even remotely the aim of this exercise.

The chapters that follow examine in detail the main themes set out here. Chapters 2 and 3 examine devotees' initial encounter with the Mata, the distinctive features of this guru, and her spiritual teachings and prescriptions. Chapter 4 explores the process whereby devotees choose Mata Amritanandamayi, from among a multiplicity of gurus in India, as the object of their devotion. Chapter 5 examines the ways in which devotees engage with the teachings and practical recommendations of the Mata. Chapter 6 studies the ways in which devotees sustain and legitimize their faith in the Mata. Chapter 7 deals with the global context in which the MAM operates, and explores the interaction between the Mata's Indian and Western devotees as it takes place at the MAM's headquarters, the Mata's spiritual retreat at Amritapuri in Kerala. The concluding observations in Chapter 8 then draw together the various themes explored in preceding chapters. It sums up the findings of this study and draws inferences about how modernity and notions of Hindu selfhood come to be constructed in this modern guru's fold.

2

ENCOUNTERING THE MATA

For most devotees, their initial encounter with Mata Amritanandamayi occurs at her public appearances during her annual visits to the thirty-odd ashram branches of the MAM scattered all over India. My own initial encounter with the Mata was at one such public appearance in Delhi in 1996. It was in February of that year that I first learnt of Mata Amritanandamayi's intended visit to Delhi, from advertisements announcing her arrival that had begun to appear in the Delhi editions of several of India's mainstream newspapers. Soon there were posters on display in shops, on roadside hoardings, at bus stands and along the brick walls lining Delhi's roads, bearing the Mata's smiling visage and setting out the schedule of the public programmes that she would conduct in the capital city.

The first of the Mata's public programmes that I attended, in March 1996, was held in the venerable environs of Delhi's Constitution Club, a venue routinely hired out for expensive marriage ceremonies and receptions, press conferences and seminars, and located in the heart of Lutyens's New Delhi, with its neat wide roads lined by imposing buildings dating back to the Raj. The crowds that had collected in the club grounds on the appointed day numbered two to three thousand. A festive *pandal* (a colourful tent-like shelter commonly erected at public celebrations of marriages and religious festivals) had been set up at one end of the compound. Inside, men and women were seated on the floor in separate groups before an empty stage decorated with flowers, and with a large framed photograph of the Mata placed at the centre. At least half a dozen microphones were positioned at different points on the stage. Loud music, recordings of *bhajans* (prayer songs) in praise of the Mata, blared from the giant speakers facing the audience.

To one side of the enclosure was a row of stalls doing brisk business; the items on sale included the Mission's publications, photographs of the Mata, and trinkets such as pendants, bracelets and rings bearing the Mata's photograph in miniature or with her name inscribed on them. On sale also was a range of 'Amrita[1] herbal products' (soaps, oils and incense), and audio and video cassettes, the former mainly recordings of *bhajan* sessions led by the Mata herself, and the latter bearing such titles (in English) as 'Around the World with the Divine Mother' and 'Amma's 40th Birthday Celebrations'.

The audience appeared to be a cross section of Delhi residents from different regional and linguistic backgrounds. I could discern strains of Hindi, Malayalam, Tamil as well as English in the din around me. There appeared to be an even mix of devotees from the southern and northern states of India, and a number of foreigners (Americans and Europeans) as well. A few of the foreigners and Indians were clad in white, saffron or yellow. These, as I later learnt, were ascetic disciples of the Mata, their spiritual status in the organization marked by the colour of their clothing. They were busy making last-minute preparations for the evening's programme.

It was well past the scheduled time of the Mata's arrival when there was a stir at one end of the enclosure. Many in the audience gravitated towards that end in apparent anticipation of the Mata's arrival. Presently a tall red and gold ornamental umbrella came into view, a piece of ritual paraphernalia of the sort traditionally associated with royalty. It was held aloft by a disciple of the Mata. As the crowds parted, the Mata became visible under the umbrella, striding purposefully into the enclosure and up onto the stage – a short, dark, plump figure in a white sari and a white long-sleeved blouse. Her movements were unhurried. She sat herself down on the carpeted floor at the front of the stage. She gazed for a while at the audience with her hands folded before her, then closed her eyes.

The stage was now beginning to fill up with her disciples – men and women clad in saffron, yellow and white. They sat behind and on either side of the Mata. After them came a long line of politicians, many of whom I recognized as prominent figures in India's, particularly Delhi's, political scene. A local devotee, whom I recognized as a member of the Indian parliament from Kerala, and belonging to the Hindu right-wing Bharatiya Janata Party (BJP), introduced the Mata to the audience. He described in reverential tones her childhood, the early manifestations of her divinity, the miracles she had performed, and the activities of the Mata Amritanandamayi Mission. Each of the politicians delivered a speech in turn,[2] eulogizing the Mata and describing in glowing terms her compassion, and the social service activities and charitable endeavours she had organized in many parts of the country. Much of this followed the typical format of public functions in India with the speeches, the tones

26

of reverence and glorification, and the *pandal*, all contributing to a recognizably familiar air of festivity and felicitation.

After the long sequence of speeches, the Mata opened her eyes. She embraced each of the politicians before they departed quietly, leaving the stage to the Mata and her disciples. She then addressed the audience in Malayalam in a soft husky voice. A young man translated her speech into Hindi. The Mata's discourse was in very simple language, devoid of the Sanskrit terms and abstractions commonly found in spiritual discourses by gurus. She dwelt on the travails of everyday life. She spoke, in homely and intimate terms, about problems in the job market, marital problems, inter-generational conflict, and the pressures of life in the present age. Inner strength and humility, she asserted, are the prerequisites for coping with external pressures. She spoke of the value of love, of patience and compassion, and exhorted her audience to overcome the self-centredness and egotism which, she stressed, lay at the root of all sorrow and pain.

After the discourse was a *bhajan* session. All those on the stage joined in. There was tabla and harmonium accompaniment.[3] The *bhajans* were in praise of different gods in the Hindu pantheon – among them Ganesh, Ram and Sita, Krishna, and Saraswati. Some were familiar tunes, commonly rendered at devotional gatherings, while others, as I later discovered, were exclusive to the MAM repertoire. The Mata and one of her disciples, a man in saffron with long flowing hair who played the harmonium, led the singing. They would sing a line and then repeat it so that the others could join in. The singing was lively, with the tempo of each *bhajan* reaching a crescendo before it came to a halt and a new *bhajan* began. The audience participated enthusiastically, clapping to the beat and repeating the lines after the Mata.[4] She herself sang rapturously, swaying to the music, occasionally raising her hands above her head in a gesture of supplication, and calling out to Krishna in a loud and plaintive tone of yearning and love.

The *bhajan* singing continued for an hour and a half. At the end of it, there was a lull, and then suddenly the members of the audience scrambled to their feet and moved away to the periphery of the enclosure. With great speed, two long queues, separate for men and women, formed on either side of the stage. Each queue was cordoned off, with volunteers pushing people into line and restricting their movement. This was in preparation for the last item in the evening's programme – *darshan*[5] or receiving the Mata's embrace individually. Once again the recorded music started up. I hastily joined the queue for women and awaited my turn.

The Mata sat at the edge of the platform and as individual devotees stood before her she took them in her arms and embraced them warmly. I saw men and women break down and sob in her arms while she held them tenderly and whispered in their ears. I felt shaken and uneasy. The Mata's embrace, I realized, came as a climax to the profusion of emotions and impressions that I had experienced in the course of the evening's programme. The melodious and highly charged *bhajan* session that preceded the embrace, the effect of many voices singing in unison, and the unexpected changes in tempo, had all served to excite the emotions and create a mood of anticipation and awe. Now, as I stood in the queue and saw devotees ahead of me break down and cry in the Mata's arms, I caught myself wondering whether the same would happen with me. Was there something about the Mata that triggered off these volatile reactions when one was in her embrace?

As I neared the stage, a volunteer organizer hurriedly instructed me to hold my hands down and my head high, physically forcing me into the right posture of receptive deference to the Mata. I was roughly pushed towards her. She clasped my head and whispered 'my child' in Malayalam. Then she held me away from her and gave me a long searching look. Something was thrust in my hand. I was pushed away. I emerged from the throng of people near the Mata feeling unsteady on my feet and happy to breathe freely again. I discovered I held a small packet in my clenched fist. It contained a boiled sweet. This was the Mata's *prasad* (sanctified substance).[6] I came away from the Club grounds and the highly charged atmosphere, my ears ringing from the loud devotional music blaring from the loudspeakers behind me.

The power of the embrace

Interviews with devotees revealed that the most distinctive feature of the Mata, and, as far as they are concerned, the most compelling, is the intimate and personal nature of her interaction with the audiences at her public programmes, where they experience her embrace as a moment of emotional upheaval and catharsis. The Mata's mode of interacting with devotees is unlike that of other gurus and godpersons in India. No other guru in Hindu devotionalist traditions in India is known to make a practice of ritually embracing devotees individually in order to convey his or her love for them. The embrace is novel for two reasons. It is unconventional because of the numerous socially-recognized restrictions on physical contact between people, particularly between men and women.[7] In the Mata's case, she embraces men and women alike. Besides, physical contact between guru (or god) and devotee is usually known to be an expression of inequality between the two. Devotees touch the guru's feet, thereby acknowledging their lowly status compared to that of the guru,[8] or alternatively, they prostrate themselves on the ground before the guru, and the guru bestows her blessings by placing her hand briefly on the devotee's head. The Mata, by embracing devotees individually, appears to do away with such extreme forms of inequality, and seems instead to reinforce the metaphorical mother–child relationship, with its key motifs of surrender and love, that is implied, but seldom *physically* expressed, in other devotionalist traditions.[9]

After my initial *darshan* of the Mata, I was often asked by devotees whether I had 'experienced' anything during the embrace. I was unsure about the import of this question and did not know how I was expected to answer it, until it became clear, in the course of interviews, that for most devotees this embrace, and what they had 'experienced' at that moment, were the trigger factors that had led them to accept the Mata as their guru and 'surrender' to her 'divine' love. The question as to whether I had 'experienced' anything was a leading one, and my answers, I discovered, indicated to my interrogators whether I was a potential devotee.[10] Devotees described their own experience of the embrace in terms of a sudden unaccountable rush of feeling, a point of high tension causing them either to break down and cry, or feel an unparalleled joy, which they sought to recapture in subsequent meetings and *darshans*.[11] A north Indian devotee who first saw the Mata in 1995 when she came on her yearly visit to Delhi, described the initial meeting in vivid terms.

I had not seen Amma before that and I had just read a little about her, seen her pictures . . . I saw the posters all over so out of sheer curiosity I said, let us go. We (a friend and I) went. We went and we heard the discourse, the *bhajans*, everything, then people queued up for the blessings. Slowly we headed towards Amma. When my turn came she hugged me. My god, it was such a tremendous feeling. From head to toe it felt like some current was passing through me, and it was beautiful. You know, like divine intoxication. I took the *prasad* and *vibhuti* [sacred ash] she gave me. I could feel there was a smile on my face, I was so happy, and even when walking it was like one was really intoxicated. I was not talking to anybody. I wanted to be by myself. I sat down there for a while, and then came home. Somehow, a few days later, by god's grace, it was arranged for us to meet her again, privately. . . . We lost our way and were late reaching the appointed place. When we reached there, Amma was waiting. She lifted me onto her lap and hugged me. It was like a cloud burst. I just cried and cried and cried. I don't know what happened but I just couldn't control the tears.

Most devotees, while describing their initial experience of the Mata's embrace, express their utter surprise and bewilderment that the embrace should have triggered such a violent surge of emotions. Mostly they are unable to account for their bouts of weeping in the Mata's arms, and attribute it to some extraordinary effect of the Mata on them. What they 'experienced' in the Mata's arms during their first encounter, and what they feel repeatedly at each subsequent *darshan*, is this unaccountable emotional catharsis, and this, for most individuals, establishes unequivocally that there is 'something' about the Mata – that this is no ordinary mortal but somehow, unique, extraordinary and 'divine'.[12]

Devotees, in describing their emotional upheaval in the Mata's embrace, tend to treat it as a spontaneous reaction to 'divine' love. The emotional upheaval is something that 'happens' to them, 'overwhelms', even 'paralyses' them. Their emotions are seen as an uncontrollable force, which overtakes them and leaves them surprised and bewildered. This experience is then attributed to the divine agency of the Mata, in the presence of whose powers they find themselves helpless and lost. Though devotees stress the spontaneity of their emotions, it is easy to see how several factors come together in the course of the evening's events to culminate in an overflow of emotional feeling. I have already noted how the mood of anticipation and expectation created by the *bhajans*, and the sight of others in the queue breaking down in the Mata's embrace, all build up to an emotional high-point which is neither entirely spontaneous nor separable from the particular environment in which these individuals find themselves. In addition to these factors is the expectation on a devotee's part that contact with a truly 'divine' or spiritually enlightened 'other' must entail extraordinary experiences. The embrace in turn grounds these expectations and emotions in its very physicality. The bodily sensation which the embrace evokes is an essential trigger to the emotional upheaval that follows.[13]

For some devotees, their initial experience of the Mata goes beyond the emotional upheaval experienced during the embrace. They recollect their first meeting with the Mata as a moment when she also changed their lives in inexplicable and miraculous ways. A male devotee described to me how, on account of a heart problem, he had lost the capacity to move his left hand. He had despaired of ever recovering its use. On his first meeting with the Mata, however, she happened to stroke his hand and, hours later, he suddenly found he could move his hand once again. Another devotee, an old woman, described how she had been in search of a guru ever since her previous guru had 'quit this life'. She had been unable to find a guru who appeared to be 'right' for her. When she first went to see the Mata, it was out of the hope that the Mata might prove to be the guru she longed for. As she awaited her turn for the Mata's embrace, she agonized mentally over the futility of her search so far. When her turn came the Mata appeared to read her thoughts when she said, 'Child, your search has now ended. Do not despair. Amma is here for you.' The old woman burst into tears and wept uncontrollably in the Mata's arms.

Yet another devotee, the personnel officer of a fertilizer company in Alwaye, Kerala, who had long suffered debilitating bouts of insomnia and mental depression, had this to say:

> The Mother was receiving the devotees one by one and I heard some people remarking about her spiritual power. 'She can do all the things which God can do', some devotees said. While receiving *prasad* from the Holy Mother, I told her about my problem which I felt even God could not solve. 'Mother, I am a person suffering from tremendous mental depression. For the last 15 years I have been suffering from insomnia and cannot sleep even one hour at night. Due to lack of sleep, my face has turned black and dull. I have become very weak as well. Many nights I have sincerely called and prayed to God to give me sleep. All my prayers have ended in vain.' The Holy Mother smiled at me and affectionately smeared some sacred ash on my forehead. She did not utter a word. I returned home when Mother left the place.
>
> It was midnight when I had my supper after which I felt very tired. It was 12:30, but as sleep was beyond my imagination, I simply lay down on the cot. I opened my eyes when I heard my servants calling me . . . I was shocked when the servant boy told me that it was 9 o'clock in the morning. Fortunately, it was a Sunday and I didn't have to go to work. The boy served me a glass of tea, yet I was unable to keep my eyes open. Effortlessly I again went back to sleep . . . It was like a dream . . . From that day until today, I am getting good sleep. It is all due to Mother's blessings.

For the first devotee, the miracle of recovering the use of his hand; for the second, the wonder of the Mata having read her mind and answered her question; and for the third, the miraculous cure of his insomnia, was the ultimate proof that the Mata possessed extraordinary powers of omniscience and omnipotence.

Who is the Mata?

The initial experience of the Mata's 'extraordinariness' is usually followed by a burning curiosity to know more about her and to meet her again. Who is this Mata? How does one account for her extraordinary powers? These are questions to which devotees urgently seek answers. After their first *darshan*, newcomers at these public programmes often look for books and other literature on the Mata to satisfy their curiosity. One of the books selling briskly at the stalls in the Constitution Club, I noticed, was the Mata's biography. I too picked up a copy of this text, which I discovered was the single 'official' version of the Mata's life story published by the Mata Amritanandamayi Mission.[14] This text was originally published in Malayalam in 1986 but has since appeared in translation in several other languages, including English, French and Hindi. The version of the text that I picked up was an English rendition by Swami Amritaswarupananda, the Mata's chief disciple and the Vice President of the Mission. This was its seventh edition and had already sold, according to printing history, 22,000 copies between 1988 and 1996.

The Mata's biography covers a span of 27 years, from the time of her birth to the establishment of her ashram in 1981. She was born on 27 September 1953, to a poor and low-caste family at Parayakadavu, a fishing village in south Kerala's Kollam district. Her parents named her Sudhamani. Her only formal education was up to the fourth standard of the local primary school, after which she was made to stay home to shoulder burdensome domestic chores. The biography says that Sudhamani's childhood was extremely troubled. Her dark complexion marked her out from the rest of her family, and led to her being ill-treated by her parents and siblings,[15] who put her to work as a servant in the household.

For most people, the main motivation for reading the biography, I discovered, was to find confirmation of what they already believed or wanted to believe – that the Mata was endowed with supernatural powers. This they found in abundance in the biographical narrative. She is described there as one who exhibited extraordinary characteristics right from her infancy.[16] She entered the world with a smile on her lips, and learnt to walk and talk at an amazingly early age. Even as a youngster, the biography tells us, she displayed an unaccountable longing for the god Krishna,[17] and spent most of her time in meditation, ecstasies, trances and prayer. Her family and neighbours mistook the young girl's strange mystical behaviour for signs of insanity. She would sing songs expressing a deep longing for Krishna, burst into tears, and spend many hours each day in apparent contemplation of her beloved god. The highpoint in her life came at the age of twenty-one when she came to 'identify' herself with Krishna.[18]

It was during a Wednesday evening in the month of September 1975 that certain events occurred which would later mark the beginning of a fresh chapter in the annals of India's spiritual history. The little one [Sudhamani] . . . was in her usual sublime mood and the melodious tune of a devotional song was heard on her lips. As [she] passed the entrance gate of the neighbouring house . . . Sudhamani came to an abrupt halt. She had overheard the final verses of the Srimad Bhagavatam[19] being read out in the courtyard of this house. The reading had come to an end and the devotional singing was just beginning.

Sudhamani stood there captured by the moment and appeared to be intently listening to the singing. Suddenly her mood changed dramatically . . . the little one ran to the spot and stood in the midst of the devotees who were gathered there. Over-whelmed with divine bliss, her identification with the Lord overflowed into her external being transforming her features and movements into that of Krishna himself! . . . The devotees, for most part, believed that Sri Krishna had come there temporarily in the form of this village girl in order to bless them.[20]

Soon after this initial identification with Krishna, the biography tells us, Sudhamani was seized with a desire to behold the goddess Devi.[21] An initial vision of the Devi triggered an unquenchable longing for oneness with this form of divinity. Months of penance followed, and culminated in a dramatic union with the 'Divine Mother'.

Sudhamani's anguish reached a pinnacle . . . In her own words: 'Each and every pore of my body was wide-open with yearning, each atom of my body was vibrating with the sacred mantra, my entire being was rushing towards the Divine Mother in a torrential stream . . . ' In unspeakable agony she cried out, 'O Mother . . . here is Your child about to die drowning in unfath-omable distress . . . this heart is breaking . . . these limbs are faltering . . . I am convulsing like a fish thrown on shore . . . O Mother . . . You have no kindness towards me . . . I have nothing to offer You except the last breath of my life . . . ' Her voice became choked. Her breathing completely stopped. Sudhamani fell unconscious . . .

> The Divine Enchantress of the Universe, the Omniscient, the Omnipresent, the Omnipotent Being, the Ancient, Primal Creatrix, the Divine Mother, appeared before Sudhamani in a living form dazzling like a million suns. Sudhamani's heart overflowed in a tidal wave of unspeakable Love and Bliss. The Divine Mother benignly smiled and, becoming a Pure Effulgence, merged in Sudhamani.[22]

Following the Mata's identification with the 'Divine Mother', the biography says, she came to realize that her life on earth was intended for a specific purpose.

> One day Sudhamani heard a voice within her say, 'My child, I dwell in the heart of all beings and have no fixed abode. Your birth is not for merely enjoying the unalloyed Bliss of the Self but for comforting suffering humanity. Henceforth, worship Me in the hearts of all beings and relieve them of the sufferings of worldly existence.'[23]

This then became the central mission of the Mata's life on earth. The biography enumerates numerous miracles that the Mata performed around this time, which served to legitimize her claims to divinity. These range from instances where she cured incurable diseases, or brought the dead back to life, to those where she predicted or averted misfortune, read devotees' minds and granted boons, and blessed childless couples with offspring.[24] After identifying first with Krishna and Devi, the Mata, according to her biography, went on to transcend the particularisms of these deities and soon realized her innate ability to identify with any chosen deity at will. The biography describes Mata Amritanandamayi as a '*purna*' (full or complete) avatar.[25] 'The word 'Avatara' [or avatar]', it explains,

> means coming down or descent. A Purna Avatara is the descent of the nameless, formless and immutable Supreme Energy assuming a human form and manifesting infinite power without any limitations. The intention of such a One will be to restore and preserve righteousness (dharma) and uplift humanity by making it aware of the higher Self.

Following the Mata's realization of her identity as an avatar, she began to stage periodic Krishna *bhava darshans* when she appeared before fellow-villagers dressed as Krishna.[26] Soon after, she began to appear in

Devi *bhava* as well, apparently defying all gender categorizations in her self-definition. During her early Devi *bhava darshans* the Mata appeared as a fierce and wrathful goddess, wielding a trident and dancing before her devotees as one possessed.[27] In the early 1980s, she ceased to appear in Krishna *bhava*, and the trident-wielding Devi gradually came to be replaced by the more benign, smiling and composed Devi we see today, whom devotees take to be the embodiment of compassion and love.[28]

Her reputation as an avatar and miracle worker soon spread and she began to attract large numbers of people from well beyond the confines of her village, who went to her in the hope of miracle solutions to their problems. In addition to miracle seekers, she also attracted a small band of spiritual aspirants who sought her out as their guru. The earliest among these were Nealu, an American, now the head of the San Ramon MAM centre in California, Gayatri, an Australian woman and one of the first female disciples to receive *sannyasa diksha*, and Balu, a youngster from Kerala who is now the Vice President of the MAM Trust in India. These individuals, and in due course other spiritual aspirants, both Indian and foreign, came to settle down at the Mata's native village looking to her for guidance in their spiritual questing. In 1981 an ashram was officially established in Parayakadavu, and in the same year, following the suggestion of one of her disciples, Sudhamani assumed the name Mata Amritanandamayi. The Mata Amritanandamayi Math and Mission Trust came to be registered as a public charitable trust, to 'put into practice the Holy Mother's teaching [that] "SERVICE TO HUMANITY IS OUR DUTY TO GOD"'.[29] The Mata became the chairperson and managing trustee of this institution, and some of her earliest Indian ascetic disciples came to constitute the board of trustees.

Following the establishment of the Mata Amritanandamayi Math and Mission Trust, MAM branches came into being first within Kerala and then elsewhere in India. Abroad, the first ashram centre at San Ramon in California came to be established largely through the efforts of Nealu, who campaigned extensively to promote the Mata and her message in the US. Subsequently ashram centres were set up in France and Reunion Island. Her tour schedules both within India and abroad expanded progressively, with ever more countries being added to her itinerary. With money pouring in as donations from devotees and disciples, the Mission directed its activities towards charitable, educational and medical ventures which were progressively grander in scale. The most recent of these, the management, computer science and engineering colleges in Coimbatore, Tamil Nadu, as well as the Amrita Institute of Medical Sciences in Kochi, Kerala, are extremely high profile establishments which provide services of a quality comparable with the best educational and medical institutions in the country. In the view of devotees, the development of the Mata's Mission from its humble origins in her native village to the transnational and high-profile establishment it is today, bears ultimate testimony to the Mata's inherent divinity and the miracle-working powers that they believe she, as an avatar, must wield.

The phenomenon of the avatar-guru

Clearly it is of singular importance to the self-representations of Mata Amritanandamayi that she claims to have been incarnated on earth as an avatar in order to fulfil a particular divine mission. In defining herself as an avatar with a mission to fulfil, Mata Amritananadamayi draws upon known symbols and meanings in Hindu traditions. Indeed the concept of the avatar is one with which most Hindus are familiar. Scriptural as well as popular understandings of avatars define them as divine incarnations whose life on earth is intended to address a specific worldly need or problem. The supreme Hindu god, Vishnu, is believed to have incarnated himself on earth at various times in the course of human history to address specific earthly needs.[30] In the popular Hindu religious text, the *Bhagavad Gita*, Krishna, who is believed to be one of Vishnu's ten avatars, claims that whenever the world should experience a decline of *dharma* or righteousness, he will incarnate himself in earthly form in order to destroy the evil threatening the world order, and to redress the imbalance between right and wrong. It is this conception of the avatar that appears to inform her devotees' understanding of the Mata's claims.

While the concept of the avatar is itself not new, and while it is also not unusual to find devotees make claims on behalf of their gurus regarding their presumed avatar status, the phenomenon of a guru making this claim on his or her own initiative is a relatively new and noteworthy development in the Hindu world.[31] The most popular of modern India's spiritual leaders to make a similar claim is Sathya Sai Baba. Sai Baba's rise to prominence in the 1940s as a popular avatar-guru from Andhra Pradesh in south India pre-dates that of the Mata by nearly four decades.[32] His 'mission' as an avatar, he claims, is to restore *satya* (truth), *dharma* (duty or righteousness), *shanti* (peace) and *prema* (love) to the world.[33]

The phenomenon of the avatar-guru addresses a crucial issue at the heart of much of the discussion and debate surrounding renunciation in Hindu traditions – this is the apparent contradiction between the otherworldly quest of renouncers and their involvement in the affairs of the world.[34] Both Sathya Sai Baba and Mata Amritanandamayi appear to conform to the ideal of a renouncer in several respects. They are both believed to be single, celibate and to lead austere and ascetic lives, apparently transcending caste and other social distinctions. Their claim to have been incarnated on earth as avatars in order to fulfil particular divine missions serves most crucially to eliminate any tension between the ideal renouncer's other-worldly orientation and his/her engagement with the affairs of this world. As avatars incarnated in this world to fulfil particular missions, these gurus are not only justified in their engagement in worldly matters, they in fact derive their legitimacy from this engagement (Warrier 2003b). In other words, in order to justify their claims to be avatars, they must back these claims by actually appearing to fulfil their self-declared mission through active engagement with the world. An important element in the avatar-gurus' endeavours to 'fulfil' their earthly missions is the setting up of institutional organizations towards that end. The Mata Amritanandamayi Mission has close parallels in this respect with the institutional establishment headed by Sathya Sai Baba, the Sathya Sai Mission, with its network of branches and centres, schools, colleges and hospitals. The size and spread of the avatar-gurus' spiritual empires, and the strength of their following, establishes their authenticity as avatars, and legitimizes their professed mission on earth.[35] This constitutes one of the most significant features of these avatar-gurus, marking them out as a modern force driving contemporary change in global Hinduism.

Unveiling divinity

In the view of her devotees, Mata Amritanandamayi's Devi *bhava darshans* are today the most important demonstration of her divine status as an avatar-guru. These are understood to be episodes when she affords them a glimpse of her 'true self' by appearing in her *bhava* ('divine mood') as Devi or goddess. The last day of the Mata's visit to any city is usually set aside for Devi *bhava darshan*. Newcomers who have had her *darshan* once and have been sufficiently moved by their encounter to want to see more of this guru, often make haste to catch up with her on the last day. On this occasion, the *darshan* is markedly different from the one described at the beginning of this chapter. This time devotees behold the Mata not in her usual white attire, but as Devi or goddess, resplendent in a colourful silk sari, a crown on her forehead, a flower garland around her neck. A disciple of the Mata performs an *aarati* (a ritual offering of light) in worship of the Devi, moving a multi-wick lamp in a circle before her. The *darshan* takes place to the accompaniment of melodious and plaintive *bhajans* (either live or recorded) in supplication to the goddess.

As for the regular *darshan*, here, too, devotees go up to her and she embraces them individually. The Devi *bhava darshan* starts at about six or seven in the evening, and continues through the night and into the early morning hours of the following day. At about five or six in the morning, when the last devotee has had *darshan*, the Mata rises from her seat. She stands for a while beaming at the devotees and holding flower petals in her hands. She sways from side to side gently and then as the *bhajans* reach a crescendo, she throws the flowers at the audience. This is a big moment for the devotees. This for them is the bounteous Devi standing before them in all her glory, almost like a calendar picture come alive[36] and showering upon them her divine grace in the form of fresh, fragrant flowers. If the flowers happen to fall over their heads they consider themselves individually blessed. The *bhajans* then cease and the *darshan* is over.

Devotees understand the Mata's Devi *bhava darshans* as episodes when the Mata 'unveils' her true self as a goddess, and gives them a glimpse of her supreme divinity. They believe that by revealing a little more of her divine self to them, she makes immanent and comprehensible what is otherwise transcendental and abstract, and thus helps them to 'approach god'. These revelations are moments when the Mata makes her devotees aware of her godliness, which manifests itself as something wholly different from the everyday mundane world. Each time the devotees are confronted by the same mysterious act – the manifestation in their midst of something which they perceive as belonging to a wholly different order, a reality that does not belong to their everyday worlds.

The Mata's Devi *bhava darshan*, where she actually dons the finery of a goddess in order to appear much like standard oleograph representations of goddesses in popular religious traditions, is without precedent in India's more well-known Hindu devotionalist styles. Though *bhava* itself is a familiar concept in certain devotionalist traditions, the Mata defines this concept in an entirely novel way.[37] *Bhava*, in some of the more well-known *bhakti* traditions in eastern India, notably in Bengal (see McDaniel 1989), refers to episodes of ecstasy and trance, and of madness, passion and chaos, where mystics have been known to be transported into states where they are no longer in control of themselves. These are understood to be states of direct experience of the divine which are natural and spontaneous, and are marked by freedom and transcendence. The Mata's *bhava darshans* are far removed from these states of ecstacy and trance. Unlike these mystics, she claims to be completely in control of herself during her *bhavas*. Rather than spontaneous states of chaos, her *bhavas* are ritualized states when the Mata systematically and deliberately dons the garb of a goddess, in order to reveal her divinity to her followers.

The Mata's biography explains the import of the *bhava darshan* as follows:

> Bhava Darshan is the manifestation of different Isvara Bhavas or Divine Moods by an Incarnation of God according to the wishes of the devotees . . . These Bhavas manifested by Incarnations [take] place only on certain occasions to fulfil a particular end, especially in response to the ardent desire of their devotees. Moreover, they . . . last only for a short time. The Holy Mother Amritanandamayi manifests the Divine Moods three nights a week lasting for periods of 10 to 12 hours depending on the number of devotees present for Darshan. As far as the Holy Mother is concerned, this is her way of serving humanity, plunged as it is in the deep quagmire of worldliness . . .
>
> During the Holy Mother's . . . Devi Bhavas she brings out that which is within her . . . in order to bless her devotees. The Holy Mother once said regarding the same, 'Mother is not manifesting even an infinitesimal part of her spiritual power during the Bhavas. If it were to be manifested as it is, no one could even come near!' She continues, 'All the deities of the Hindu pantheon, who represent the numberless [sic] aspects of One Supreme Being exist within us. A Divine Incarnation can manifest any one of them by mere will for the good of the world . . . Devi Bhava is the manifestation of the Eternal Feminine, the Creatrix, the active principle of the Impersonal Absolute'.[38]

The Mata's *bhava darshan* may be understood in terms of the ritual consecration of images in Hindu temples, and their regular worship through puja. Consecration of a temple image entails infusing it with sacrality through the performance of particular rituals by specialists. Preston's (1985: 9) observations regarding the creation of the sacred image in Hindu temples are pertinent here.

> Sacred images are products of the human imagination – they are constructed according to systematic rules, and then they are infused with sacrality and kept 'alive' by highly controlled behaviours intended to retain the 'spirit in matter' . . . Somehow the mystery of the invisible becomes more intense and awesome in the attempted act of its creation. This is the substance of revelation – an unveiling of the deity through the construction of its image, and then the discovery, each time anew, that the image is but a phantom of a larger reality beyond human grasp.

The outstretched hand gropes in the darkness to touch something
forever beyond its reach. The mystery is in the reaching and the
eternal frustration of never completely finding.[39]

Just as the consecration of an idol serves to unveil the deity through
the construction of its image, in the Mata's case, her self-proclaimed
divinity, which is already contained within her person, is unveiled through
her Devi *bhava*. It is in order to facilitate the revelation that she attires
herself in the finery of the goddess. The *aarati*, or service of light with its
ritual waving of the sacred flame before the deity (here the Mata, while
she sits resplendent in her goddess regalia), appears to reinforce divinity's
embodiment in physical form. In anthropological studies of Hindu rituals
of worship, puja, and particularly its culmination in *aarati*, is understood
as a moment when the worshipper seeks to identify with the worshipped,
and god and man merge in 'an intangible display of incandescent light
and fragrance' (Fuller 1992: 73). It is a symbol of what Fuller (ibid.)
describes as the 'quintessentially Hindu idea' that divinity and humanity can mutually become one another, despite the relative separation
between them that normally prevails in the mundane world. In the case
of the *bhava darshans*, this idea of merger is brought into much sharper
focus through the physical embrace that follows the initial *aarati*, when
the Mata, as goddess, welcomes devotees into her arms, and lavishes
her love and grace on each one individually. As is the case with temple
pujas, in the case of the Mata's *bhava darshans* too, the devotee's contact
with the divine is momentary and fleeting. So is the *bhava* itself, and has
to be revived every time anew by the Mata, who, in donning the finery of
the goddess, unveils her divinity and makes it accessible, temporarily,
to the waiting devotees.

The divine embrace

Love and divinity, these then are the two key elements that individuals
experience in the course of their initial encounter with Mata Amritanandamayi. The Mata's worldly mission, conceptualized as an offering
of love to humankind,[40] is encapsulated in her embrace – a simple,
intimate and, for devotees, extremely poignant, gesture. This contact with
the Mata clearly has a strong emotional impact on the devotees. Why do
devotees find the embrace so emotionally unsettling? The Indian middle-
class devotees of the Mata, I argued in Chapter 1 above, are mostly people
who have done well for themselves by seizing opportunities in modern
India's business and service sectors and are conscious of their position of
privilege in a rapidly expanding and changing socio-economic milieu.

They come from diverse social backgrounds, but common to them all is the respect which they express for individual freedom, opportunity and choice, vital factors that have helped them achieve their present positions of privilege. They are proud of their own, and their children's, educational qualifications and career achievements. It would seem reasonable to expect that these people should be self-assured and confident in their privileged social location. Yet the tearful scene that I witnessed at the Constitution Club belied all such expectations. Why do these people weep so in the arms of the Mata?

From the accounts of devotees, it appears that most of them first seek out a guru when they come up against major crises in their lives such as severe health problems, family discord, financial trouble, physically and emotionally crippling accidents, alcoholism and drug addiction. At such times, the first channels of help are the systems of expertise intrinsic to modern society such as the medical and legal establishments. These systems, while they do offer rational, professional and standardized means of support, are, however, unable to provide the personalized support and assistance that most individuals crave. Weber (1958a), the most pessimistic of the commentators on modernity, lamented the modern world's increasing reliance on these systems, which he saw as detrimental to the fulfilment of the psychological and emotional needs of individuals. Giddens (1990:27) echoes these sentiments when he points out how trust in abstract systems provides for the security of day-to-day reliability, but by its very nature cannot supply either the mutuality or intimacy which personal trust relations offer. Relying on abstract systems, he asserts, is not psychologically rewarding in the way in which trust in persons is.

This is where a guru like the Mata holds out the promise of relief and reassurance. Persons in distress come to hear of her through well-meaning friends and neighbours who urge them to seek the Mata's blessings and alleviate their distress. They often go for their first *darshan* of the Mata when she visits their city or locality. In contrast to the cold, impersonal nature of modern professional institutions, what they discover in the Mata's embrace is a ready appreciation of their emotional needs, and an outlet for expressing their raw emotions. Their violent sobbing and profuse weeping in the Mata's arms often by itself has a therapeutic effect on these individuals. Many experience this as an 'unburdening' and as a sense of immense relief. As children of a divine mother, her devotees are often able to recover in her arms a childlike sense of security and protection, which they say they crave in an increasingly impersonal and uncontrollable world.[41]

Most individuals who go to her to secure relief from a pressing problem return with the knowledge that the Mata has made a resolve, *sankalpa*, on their behalf, that has the power to change the course of their lives and solve their problems. Some of them go on to experience an improvement in their immediate conditions which they see as proof that the Mata is no ordinary mortal, but that she is divine and possesses extraordinary powers. Devotees believe she has the power to ease their worldly suffering by working miracles in their personal lives. The biography cites numerous instances of her devotees having had miraculous experiences of her loving ministrations. Nearly a hundred pages (almost a third of the book) are descriptions of devotees' experiences of the Mata's 'divine' love. For newcomers, these stories are of immense significance. Those who believe they had an extraordinary experience at the first meeting with the Mata find confirmation of it in these accounts. To others who have a problem that needs solving, or a wish that has remained unfulfilled, these intimations of the Mata's miracle-working abilities gives hope. These hopes and expectations reach a high-point when newcomers see the Mata in her Devi *bhava*, and receive an embrace directly from the goddess. This, for many, is their most over-powering experience of the Mata, when her 'divine love' subsumes them in its sheer immediacy and spectacular grandeur.

By displacing other deities and living in the world as a self-proclaimed goddess, Mata Amritanandamayi thus makes devotionalism's goals of proximity to the divine and of god-realization that much more immediate and accessible.[42] She also make this devotion a highly intimate and personal experience for the devotee. Indeed it is noteworthy that despite the size, scale and geographic spread of her spiritual empire, Mata Amritanandamayi succeeds in establishing individual ties with each and every devotee. In this, the revolutionized means of communication and technology available in the modern world are a crucial factor facilitating the avatar-guru's accessibility to devotees from across the world. Modern means of communication and transport, and their effect of having 'shrunk' the world, are thus centrally important for the success of this avatar-guru's mission on earth, and indispensable to her popularity and appeal, a theme I take up in the following chapter.

3

AN AVATAR WITH A MISSION

Mata Amritanandamayi's self-definition as an avatar as well as her definition of her purpose or mission in the world are both set in a context of 'modernity'. In this chapter I explore the way in which modernity is officially constructed in the Mata Amritanandamayi Mission. The modern world, in the Mata's scheme of things, is a place of suffering. This suffering is brought about by certain crucial imbalances in modern world-views and lifestyles. The Mata's aim is to redress these imbalances and thus alleviate suffering. She is in this sense a 'modern' avatar with a special relevance to the contemporary world. From a devotee's point of view the Mata's construction of modernity provides, most importantly, a *conceptual framework* within which to understand their problems and also to locate their selfhood as 'modern' individuals. Not only this, the Mata, through her ritual and other prescriptions, also provides them with a clearly defined *course of action* which, she promises, will help redress the 'modern' imbalances in their personalities and life experiences.

Suffering in the modern world

Crucial to the Mata's self-representation as a divine avatar is the idea that she has 'descended' to the earth in order to fulfill a particular mission. An undated pamphlet, entitled *Divine Mother Mata Amritanandamayi Devi and Her Mission*, published by the Mission, dwells at length on this theme.

> To the people of this age, bereft of a living faith, their hearts thirsting for pure love, Amma has come as a torrential shower of Divine Love. Ever established in the unbroken experience of Supreme Truth, She accepts everyone as Her own Self. Taking suffering humanity upon Her lap, soothing their pain and giving

them hope, She dispels the darkness from their hearts and leads them on the path towards perfection and everlasting joy.

Throughout two decades of tireless service, Amma has personally counselled and consoled millions of people from all walks of life and from every corner of the globe. Mother wipes their tears with Her own hands and removes the burden of their sorrows. The personal touch, warmth, compassion, tenderness and deep concern She shows everyone, the spiritual charisma, innocence and charm which come ever so naturally to Her, are all unmistakably unique.

The purpose of the Mata's descent, in this scheme of things, is to alleviate human suffering in the modern world. Why then is the world suffering? The Mata's answer to this has both a soteriological dimension, deriving from traditional Hindu understandings of suffering and salvation, and a 'modern' dimension, that has a particular and immediate relevance to the contemporary world.

The Mata uses the Hindu doctrine of karma and rebirth in order to explain human suffering.[1] According to the karma doctrine as the Mata expounds it, individuals pass through a series of lives in a cycle of births and deaths. One's deeds (karma) in previous lives determine the quality of subsequent lives. To secure release from the cycle it is necessary to rid oneself of the effects of bad deeds, *prarabdhas* (burdens) of past lives. It is also necessary to refrain from indulging one's *vasanas* (harmful attachments or 'tendencies' in this life) which only contribute to the further accumulation of *prarabdhas*. *Vasanas*, and the *prarabdhas* that accumulate because of them, are seen as the cause for the suffering of humanity. One's spiritual aim must be to eliminate these. Such a quest must culminate in 'release' from this cycle and the ultimate union of the individual *atman* or soul with the universal *brahman*, the 'cosmic essence'. This is the attainment of *moksha* or salvation, understood as the ultimate objective of an individual's spiritual search.[2] The Mata explains this soteriology thus:

> Child, the impressions created by the actions performed in the previous births are manifested in this birth. These inherited tendencies decide the course of action during this lifetime. What we should do is to exhaust them while doing spiritual practices and avoid adding new ones . . . The first *vasana* in a *jiva* (individual soul) is God-given. From that arises karma (action). From those actions arise new *vasanas*. All these *vasanas* accumulate as latent tendencies inherited from the

previous birth and bring forth a new birth. This cycle will go on spinning like this. Liberation from *samsara* (the birth–death cycle) is possible only through attenuation of the *vasanas*. All spiritual practices like *satsang* (companionship with great souls), chanting the Divine Name, meditation etc., are helpful for weakening the *vasanas*.[3]

This spiritual quest, and its culmination in *moksha*, is represented symbolically in the MAM in the form of an unusual *pratishtha*, or sanctified image, enshrined within the Brahmasthanam,[4] a temple unique to this organization. Within each Brahmasthanam (abode of *brahman* – the supreme consciousness or divine essence), the *pratishtha* comprises a four-sided block of stone bearing the image of a different deity on each side. The first three sides bear the forms of Devi, Shiva and Ganapathi respectively; on the fourth side is carved the image of a serpent. The Mission's literature on the Brahmasthanam explains this as follows:

> In addition to representing the principle of unity in diversity, the four images can be seen to symbolize various stages of an aspirant's spiritual path. The image of Devi represents Parashakti, the supreme power of god, by whose grace we are initially brought onto the spiritual path. The image of Shiva represents that non-dual aspect of the Supreme that purifies aspirants of their sins and bestows renunciation and discrimination. The image of Lord Ganesh represents that aspect of God that removes the obstacles on the aspirant's path, and the serpent represents the Kundalini Shakti, the serpent power lying dormant in the Mooladhara (root) chakra, which is awakened by one's spiritual practices and ultimately rises to the Sahasrara (crown) chakra, to join with the Absolute, culminating in Self-Realization.[5]

The MAM literature on the Brahmasthanam describes the institution of the temple as a 'practical instrument for realizing the divinity that is innate in every individual'.[6] At each Brahmasthanam, the consecration of the idol, or *prana pratishtha*, is conducted by the Mata herself. Through this act, the Mata is believed to transfer her own divinity to the image and thereby divinize and energize it. Daily pujas serve to maintain this energy within the image, and the Mata's yearly visits to the temple and special pujas she conducts during annual temple festivals are believed to re-energize and revitalize this power.

The soteriology described by the Mata is by no means unique to the MAM. It is merely one more variant of a larger body of belief in karma, afterlife and *moksha* (salvation) which, in its myriad forms, informs Hindu religious life in diverse contexts.[7] However, in her teachings the Mata goes on to give this soteriology a particularly contemporary relevance. She identifies certain 'negative tendencies' (*vasanas*) which she perceives as distinctive of modern lifestyles and attitudes, and which result in sorrow. These *vasanas* are first, humankind's insatiable material desire, second, the extreme selfishness of the modern world, and third, its excessive preoccupation with rationality and the intellect. In her 'dialogues with devotees' in the MAM's *Awaken Children* series, the Mata explains the deleterious effects of the *vasanas* of the present day, and the agony that humankind suffers as a result. About the effects of material acquisitiveness, she says:

> [People in the modern world] want to enjoy life. But the only problem is, they have the wrong idea of 'enjoying life'. Real enjoyment of life depends on relaxation, not on tension. Yet most people . . . are very tense most of the time. Men are not able to spend any peaceful moments with their wives and children. They are more worried about their work, their business, their status in society and about what others will think or say about them. They are always worried about one thing or another. They want a new house, a new car, a TV, or a new relationship. A person engrossed with life in the world always wants some new thing. He is fed up and bored with old things. He can never be satisfied with what he has. He thinks that new things will make him happy. His mind is always set on what he does not have. He is always living either in the past or in the future, never in the present, and he runs after everything he craves. He goes on acquiring and possessing. He has no time to enjoy, to relax and be in the present. So finally, he collapses. This is what happens to most people in this so-called 'modern society' – be it in the East or West.[8]

The solution to this problem, and the Mata's self-proclaimed mission as an avatar, is to awaken people 'spiritually' and launch them on a quest for spiritual achievement. The spiritual quest is perceived as a journey leading away from the attractions of the external world towards a greater realization of one's 'inner wealth'. In contrast to the transient pleasures of worldly attachments, the Mata describes the beauty of spiritual wealth thus:

Children, spirituality is the real wealth. Spirituality is the inner wealth which helps one to renounce all outer wealth, through an understanding of the meaninglessness of external riches. It is the wealth which helps one to become 'wealthier than the wealthiest'. It is the realization that God alone, the Self alone, is the real wealth. Spirituality is the wealth that helps us have a healthy approach to life.

Children, once you know your essential nature, the entire universe becomes your wealth. In that supreme state you have nothing to gain or lose. Having given up all attachment you become ever established in the state of supreme detachment . . . you can smilingly give up even so-called precious objects and still feel content and peaceful. Spirituality is inner wealth which makes you feel content. Once you attain that state, you have nothing else to gain or lose. Once you acquire that inner spiritual wealth, you start living in fullness. Externally you may not be wealthy at all, but internally you are rich and full. You realize that you are the master of the entire universe. You become the master of water, air, earth, and ether, sun, moon, stars and space. Everything in the universe will be under your control. Therefore, children, try to become a master, not a slave.[9]

Besides obsessive materialism, another of the many problems of modern society, as the Mata sees it, is its excessive preoccupation with the intellect, and with scientific rationality, that is, with matters of the 'mind' as opposed to those of the 'heart'. In her exposition, the world of the present appears cold and dry, and depleted of all emotion and affect.

In the modern age, human minds are dry. Too much reasoning has spoiled the contemporary mind. People use their intellects for everything. They have lost their hearts and their faith. Beauty lies in the heart. Beauty lies in faith and faith dwells in the heart. Intellect or reasoning is necessary, but we should not let it swallow the faith in us. We should not allow the intellect to eat up our heart. Intellect is knowledge, and knowledge is ego. Too much knowledge means nothing but a big ego. The ego is a burden, and a big ego is a big burden . . . Presently the intellect predominates and there is not enough love. Therefore, we must strive to empty the intellect of useless thoughts and fill the heart with love. That is the solution for all distress and confusion of modern society.[10]

The Mata not only sees the modern world's excessive preoccupation with the intellect as one of the reasons for humanity's suffering, but also criticizes science and technology for their failure to deliver results that can alleviate suffering.

> Science has developed its areas of enquiry immensely, but still there are many things which the human intellect cannot understand; there are many things which cannot be explained by scientific facts. Even though science has attained previously unimagined heights of achievement, isn't the universe still a mystery? Though it has grown wonderfully, science has not yet grasped even an infinitesimal part of what the universe really is. Isn't it true that science has totally failed to make human beings happy and peaceful? Has science with all its great achievements been able to make humanity more humane? All the technological developments and scientific advances that we have achieved result from our rational thinking; they are products of the intellect. But predominance of the intellect has destroyed the quality of life. It has destroyed love, faith, and surrender to a higher goal in life. It has only helped to inflate the ego, and the vanity of the ego has become a stumbling block for us.[11]

Her tirade against science and rationality, the Mata explains, is not so much an attack against the scientific world-view itself, but against what is seen as the modern self's 'excessive preoccupation' with this world-view. Asked by a devotee whether she is 'dead-set against science and intellectual thinking', the Mata clarifies her position as follows:

> Son, Mother is not against science and intellectual thinking. Mother is not trying to say that science has completely ruined us, nor is She trying to say that intellectual thinking is useless. Science and the intellectual quest have brought about great achievements for the entire human race; there is no doubt about that. But what Amma wants to convey is that we human beings should not give importance to science and rational thought to the exclusion of everything else. They have their place. Keep them there.[12]

Elsewhere she says:

> You can choose both head and heart. There is no problem in this, but there should be a balance, for if you choose logic and

rationality alone, you are in trouble . . . Remember the choice is yours. Use your discrimination [sic] and choose . . . Mother is not trying to dismiss science or logic totally. Mother is only trying to point out the dangerous tendency of the modern age to give too much importance to reason and logic, totally ignoring love and faith, qualities which unite the human race.[13]

The Mata's concern here is with what she sees as the growing exclusivism of modern individuals. The modern world's preoccupation with science and rationality, she argues, leads to an exclusivist stance vis-à-vis the world, that closes the mind to other facets of human existence, most significantly, the realms of faith and experience. In stressing complementarity rather than conflict between different world-views, the Mata is what we may, following Tambiah[14] (1990: 104), refer to as a 'pluralist'. The pluralist, Tambiah points out, far from being anti-scientific, accepts the sciences at full value. The pluralist's typical adversary is the monopolistic materialist or physicalist who maintains that one system, physics, is pre-eminent and all-inclusive, such that every other version must eventually be reduced to it or rejected as false or meaningless. The Mata's real enemy too, as I noted before, is not scientific rationality itself, but rather the modern world-view that sees scientific rationality as the only legitimate way of perceiving and ordering the world to the exclusion of all else.

It is to counter this monopolist position that the Mata encourages the revival of faith. Modern individuals, as per the Mata's teachings, should harness the capabilities of science and technology to enhance the quality of their lives,[15] but must not rely on these forces to the exclusion of all else. Beyond the comprehension of the intellect and scientific rationality lies another sphere, that of the heart, of faith, intuition and 'experience', which they must tap into, according to the Mata, in order to give their lives the meaning and wholeness that the scientific world-view by itself fails to provide. Through the Mata's self-proclaimed mission on the earth to reinfuse the world with love, she promises to counter the 'dryness' of modern minds by bringing about an awakening, in her devotees, of the emotional sensibilities and experiential powers lying dormant within their hearts.

A third and crucial problem with modern society, in the Mata's scheme of things, is its selfishness. She strives to counter this selfishness by presenting herself and her Mission as a shining example of selfless service to society, infinite compassion, and love for all. According to the promotional literature of the Mission, the MAM was founded 'in order to disseminate the message of spirituality, Universal Love, and selfless service to humanity, which shines through the life and teachings of the Divine Mother, Her Holiness Mata Amritanandamayi Devi'. The purpose of the Mata's life is described as 'serving suffering humanity'. 'Just as an incense stick spreads its fragrance as it burns itself out,' one of the Mission's many promotional pamphlets explains, 'Amma wants to give Herself to others. Amma's only wish is that Her hand should always be on someone's shoulder, caressing and consoling them and wiping their tears. Amma's whole life is an offering to the world.'

To sum up the Mata's message, then, the modern world is a place of sorrow and suffering because of the imbalanced and skewed nature of the modern individual's engagement with the self and the world. Imbalances in lifestyles and attitudes are, in her view, a crucial and highly damaging feature of 'modernity' as it manifests itself in contemporary times. Modern individuals are excessively materialistic, rational and egocentric to the detriment of complementary and 'balancing' aspects of their lifestyles and personalities – those of spirituality, faith and affect, and selflessness and compassion. It is important to note here that the Mata, while advocating a restoring of 'balances' in the modern world, does not attack the objective conditions of 'modernity'. Thus such objective factors as revolutionized science and technology, modern modes of production and consumption, and the spread of mass communication and media systems do not by themselves present a problem in her scheme of things. What she does attack is what she sees as humankind's lopsided engagement with these conditions, such that in a world dominated by rationality, materialism and personal ambition, people tend to lose sight of spirituality and faith. She therefore advocates a revision of modern attitudes and orientations, so as to restore a sense of balance between opposites, such that materialism is complemented by spirituality, rationality by faith and emotion, and egotism by selflessness

How does the Mata expect to achieve her goal of redressing the imbalances of modern personalities and world-views? As a first step towards fulfilling her mission, the Mata enfolds people from different walks of life in her intimate embrace. This embrace is often presented in the Mission's promotional literature as a life-transforming experience for the recipient. This is the point at which the Mata 'hooks' individuals (to use devotees' own expression), before going on to work a transformation in their lives and personalities. Once they enter her fold, the Mata encourages devotees to follow certain ritual and spiritual prescriptions which, she claims, are intended to revive the realm of the heart, faith, and the emotions, 'dissolve' egotism, and, in the long term, lessen the suffering of the practitioner. The Mata also encourages devotees to engage in small acts of social service or *seva* which, she claims, will serve to erode their egotism and selfishness. Most important in all of this, however, is not the precise observance of her prescriptions but the cultivation of what is understood to be an attitude of 'surrender' to the guru.

Spiritual and ritual practice

The Mata recommends simple ritual practices which, she promises, will secure the practitioner's material well-being and spiritual enhancement, ends which, significantly, she sees as mutually complementary rather than conflicting. Their observance, the Mata tells devotees, brings about a gradual elimination of *prarabdhas* and *vasanas*, and this results in the practitioner's well-being not just in the short term but also in the long term. In the short term, these practices are expected to alleviate suffering by improving the practitioner's material conditions, and by warding off illness and other kinds of misfortune. In the long term, they are believed to effect a change in the practitioner's personality and attitude, infusing his/her life with spirituality, faith, and an attitude of emotional surrender towards the guru. This in turn is believed to secure happiness and contentment, and enhance the practitioner's progress towards spiritual salvation.

The ritual practices she recommends, though they draw upon traditional Hindu symbols and meaning systems, are noteworthy for their innovativeness and novelty. By mixing and combining traditional symbols in ingenious ways, the Mata effectively weaves together a meaning system that promises to address devotees' problems in an immediate and expedient manner. In several respects, her ritual prescriptions are self-consciously modern, an aspect which devotees greatly appreciate, and a point to which I will return later in this chapter. In what follows, I take up each of the Mata's ritual prescriptions in turn.

A major concern in the MAM has to do with the influence of planets on individual destinies. Malefic planetary influences on one's life are believed to lead to pain and suffering. The Mata therefore recommends the practice of rituals which will counter these influences. Central to her recommended system of rituals is a special type of puja based on astrological calculations which, the MAM literature claims, is unique to the Brahmasthanam temple. The special puja, which the Mata calls the '*samooha grahadosha shanti puja*' or the 'congregational puja for countering the influences of malefic planets', is a key feature of the Mata Amritanandamayi Mission and attracts thousands of participants. The following passages from an undated MAM pamphlet entitled *The Brahmasthanam: An Epoch Making Temple*, are noteworthy for their emphasis on the 'proven' efficacy and practical relevance of the new form of worship.

> Astrologers have observed that in most cases, sorrowful experiences such as accidental deaths, financial difficulties, marital problems and other difficulties of life, manifest in a person's life primarily during the periods of transit and conjunction of the planets Shani (Saturn), Rahu (fragmentary planet) and Chovva (Mars), in that person's astrological chart ... Amma has dedicated Her life to dispelling the sorrows of mankind, and has personally listened to the woes of millions of people over the last two decades. While seeking a solution to the miseries of the people, Amma had a divine vision of the Brahmasthanam temple, and a new mode of worship specifically designed to counteract the malefic influences of Shani, Rahu and Chovva. Amma experimented with the practicality of this new form of worship by studying the experiences of thousands of people who came to Her for guidance. Those who performed the rituals and pujas She recommended achieved excellent results in every case, successfully averting the misfortunes predicted in their horoscopes. On the other hand, a majority of those who did not perform the prescribed rituals fell prey to the unfortunate experiences their horoscopes foretold. Thus, after establishing the effectiveness of these new pujas, Amma founded the first Brahmasthanam temple, in Kodungallur [Kerala] in April 1988, where the congregational pujas, which now form an integral part of the schedule at each Brahmasthanam temple, were performed for the first time ...

> Even if one is not currently undergoing a period of malefic planetary influence, these pujas are very beneficial, giving both spiritual and material upliftment ... Thousands of devotees have found their lives uplifted and transformed by participating in these pujas. Indeed, a steady stream of reports have poured in, testifying to divine experiences received, such as miraculous escapes from accidents, cure of chronic ailments, solutions to financial and marital problems, blessings of childbirth, employment gained, and other personal blessings.

It is clear from the above passages that in the Mata's scheme of things the authenticity of a ritual is predicated upon its efficacy as an appropriate means to a desired end. The claim that the Mata prescribes rituals after 'experimenting' with them to ascertain their 'practicality' bolsters her image as a modern-day, goal-oriented avatar determined to fulfill the task she has set herself of easing the suffering of humanity.

Identifying malefic planetary influences, and performing corrective rituals to eliminate these, is commonplace in Hindu religious practice.[16] The corrective ritual is usually performed by a Brahman temple priest on behalf of the client, and these pujas are traditionally performed on an individual basis. In both these respects, the Mata's version of this ritual is novel. Not only does she do away with priestly mediation, instead allowing individuals to perform their own puja by following her instructions, she also organizes it as a collective affair where many destinies are supposedly set on course at once. The instructor is no priestly figure but the Mata herself, whose authority as ritual officiant derives not from any scriptural sanction, but from her self-proclaimed 'divine' status as an avatar.

My first experience of a congregational puja was in March 1996, soon after I had my first *darshan* of the Mata. On the appointed day, at the newly-constructed Brahmasthanam temple in an affluent suburb in the outskirts of Delhi, I joined hundreds of people gathered to participate in a puja intended to counter the malefic influences of the planet Shani (Saturn). The puja, extensively advertised in the mainstream daily newspapers, was ticketed at the rate of 50 rupees per head. The participants were seated on the floor in long rows along the temple compound, with the puja paraphernelia – a lamp, camphor, water, incense, blades of grass and clarified butter – laid out on the floor before each one. Television screens positioned at strategic locations showed the Mata on a platform at one end of the compound, where she sat draped in a white sari, ready to preside over the ritual proceedings. The puja itself was simple, and the Mata led us through its various stages step by step. An important part of the puja was the chanting of the Lalitha Sahasranama, the thousand names of the goddess Lalithamba, an ancient Sanskrit devotional composition, and a key component in the Mata's symbolic repertoire.[17]

For individuals unable to attend these congregational pujas, however, there is the option of having the corrective ritual performed on their behalf by the Mata's ascetic disciples at the ashram headquarters. The Mission's website lists the pujas that can be thus performed at the ashram on behalf of clients. It provides details regarding the specific benefits to be derived from each kind of puja, and sets out the fees for each. These mail-order pujas are a centrally important feature of the MAM's ritual repertoire, particularly attractive to non-resident Indians and other devotees overseas, who can derive the satisfaction of having performed the necessary puja even without being physically present during its observance.

The MAM's congregational pujas are held once every year, when the Mata visits each of her temple sites in different parts of India to mark the anniversary of the idol installation. The central feature at the anniversary celebrations or Brahmasthanam *mahotsavams*, is this collective puja, which draws more and more participants every year, and serves as an important means of publicity and propaganda for the guru. Apart from these large-scale public rituals personally conducted by the Mata, she also recommends simple daily spiritual practices for her devotees to observe at home, which too, she promises, will yield both material and spiritual benefits to the practitioner.

The first of these is the *manasa* (mental) puja, which defines worship not in terms of specific ritual acts and observances but in terms of the performer's attitude of surrender. This puja is remarkable for its simplicity – there is no paraphernalia required for its performance and the entire ritual is a mental exercise rather than a physical effort. There is neither a concrete idol to which the puja is dedicated, nor any of the usual ritual objects (lamps, clarified butter, camphor, water) to aid in the ritual performance. During *manasa* puja, the devotees conceptualize their favourite deity in their minds. They then take their deity through a series of steps in an attitude of utter adoration and devotion. They (in their imagination) bathe the figure, dress it up in beautiful clothes, adorn it with precious jewels and ornaments, savour its beauty, offer it *manasa pushpam* – flowers from the heart (or, the heart itself as a flower of offering), feed it, perform an *aarati* (ritual offering of light) before it, circumambulate it, and then conclude the puja with some prayers and Sanskrit verses. After the completion of the puja, the deity is 'returned' to its place in the devotee's heart.[18] Each devotee has the freedom to conceptualize the puja and even the deity according to his or her imagination, and the puja, while it can be conducted collectively, retains a highly personalized and individual flavour that makes it particularly appealing to devotees.

Besides puja, *dhyana*, or meditation, is also recommended by the Mata as an important item in one's daily spiritual practice. She defines meditation as the constant and loving remembrance of god. She advises devotees to perceive god as a beloved entity – a father or mother or a lover, and to think of this entity constantly, trying always to feel his or her presence, grace, compassion and love. To assist in this effort at concentration, the Mata recommends the chanting of the mantra, referred to as *japa*. The mantra is usually a string of words or sounds repeated in order to aid concentration in meditation. The mantra is not a prayer, but 'a kind of sound form of the deity it embodies' (Parry 1985: 209). It is believed to be potent and powerful and capable of bringing about changes in the chanter's mental and emotional state.

Studies of religious sects in India led by renouncer gurus show the signal importance of mantras in initiating neophytes into a given lineage or tradition of renouncers. This initiation is the mantra *diksha*. The guru whispers the mantra in the disciple's ear, and with that the disciple is ushered in as one of the group. All members of a given devotionalist order share the tradition's mantra, but it remains unknown to outsiders. The mantra in a guru–*shishya* (teacher–disciple) lineage or *sampradaya* serves to distinguish insiders from outsiders and bind the insiders together in a common bond of knowledge and practice.[19] The practice within the MAM however differs from this format.

The Mata gives mantras to her devotees on request. These are not all the same mantra. Each devotee receives a different mantra depending on his or her choice of favourite deity. This could be any of the deities in the Hindu pantheon, or even the Mata herself, or, in the case of non-Hindu devotees, other venerated figures such as Christ or the Virgin Mary, whose name comes to be incorporated within the mantra.[20] The purpose of the mantra here is not to bind the devotees together in an esoteric knowledge of one mantra exclusive to the group, but to establish individual and separate links between each devotee and the Mata, and to aid in the devotee's spiritual endeavours by helping him/her focus, through mantra *japa*, on the favourite object of his/her devotion. In this, the Mata marks a radical departure from the beliefs and practices of known guru *sampradayas* or orders, where the guru conventionally binds devotees in common worship to the order's central deity. The Mata instead allows for heterogeneity, plurality and individual preference within her fold, not only in the matter of the object of devotees' worship but also, as we shall see in the following pages, in the mode in which they choose to engage in this worship.

The Mata, in one of the MAM publications, explains the concept of *mantra* to her disciples. She says:

> Children, when Amma gives you a mantra, She sows a seed of spirituality within you. She transmits a part of herself into your heart. But you have to work on it. You have to nurture that seed by meditating, praying, and chanting your mantra regularly, without fail. You have to be totally committed.[21]
>
> The natural way to get yogurt is by adding a spoonful of yogurt to warm milk. Having added the culture, you let it stand for some time, and thus, all the milk is transformed into yogurt. In the same way, Amma has transmitted part of Herself into you. Now you have to 'let the milk stand' – you have to attain a state of inward stillness by constantly repeating your mantra and

doing other spiritual practices. Your entire being will thus be transformed and you will then realize your divine nature.

Not all devotees choose to receive a mantra from the Mata. The ones who do, chant it ritually during certain times of the day. They aspire to an ideal state where they would unconsciously chant the mantra with every breath they take. With constant practice, devotees believe, the chanting itself must become second nature to the individual, and the mantra must come to him/her spontaneously without any conscious effort. For most devotees, however, this is a distant ideal. Chanting the mantra, devotees believe, gives them increasing mental concentration and stills their mind so that it gets a respite from constant worry and worldly distractions. The Mata describes the mantra as the 'oar of the boat' in which the individual seeks to 'cross the ocean of life and death'. She describes it as the instrument one uses to cross the *samsara* (world) of one's restless mind with its unending thought waves. Through the stillness that the chant cultivates in their minds, it is believed, devotees will gradually achieve the inner state required for the Mata to effect the intended spiritual transformation.

Like the chanting of the mantra, chanting the different names of a given deity (usually in Sanskrit) is also believed to exert a positive effect on the devotee. The *naamavali* (string of names) used extensively in the MAM's ritual practice is the Lalitha Sahasranama (LS) which, as I mentioned earlier, is often recited during congregational worship. Devotees, however, are encouraged to recite, as part of their daily spiritual practice, the names of whichever deity they find most appealing.[22] Several such ancient Hindu devotional compositions, dedicated to different deities in the Hindu pantheon, are commonly in use in my informants' households. In each such composition the particular deity is addressed by different names in Sanskrit. Each name describes one or more aspects of the deity in the most glowing and eulogiztic terms. Besides the Lalita Sahasranama (thousand names of the goddess Lalitamba), there are, for instance, the Hanuman Chaalisa (dedicated to the monkey god, Hanuman), the Vishnu Sahasranama (thousand names of Vishnu), and the 108 names of Shiva. The daily chant is seen as a means of inculcating an attitude of love and surrender in devotees, and preparing them to accept life's joys and sorrows as god's will. As with the mantra *japa*, here too the belief is that the ritual chanting of the deity's names will imperceptibly transform the devotee. A person regular in its observance, according to the Mata, will gradually gain union with *brahman*.

The value of weeping

The Mata thus prescribes a limited number of simple and systematic practices for the well-being and spiritual growth of her devotees. In her ritual prescriptions, however, what the Mata emphasizes is not so much the precise detail of individual ritual practice, but the practitioner's mental attitude while performing each ritual. She tells her devotees to perform these rituals in an attitude of complete surrender, profound love for the deity, and extreme humility. They must try to achieve a mental state of abject helplessness, where they cry out to the deity in utter longing and despair, and plaintively seek divine help to see them through the travails of this life. Devotees usually play up this emotional aspect of the ritual, and, during *dhyana*, *japa* and puja, shed copious tears of love and longing, beseeching the deity for release from their worldly burdens.

This emphasis on the devotee's emotional attitude while performing rituals has been noted in ethnographic accounts of other Hindu devotionalist traditions.[23] According to the belief surrounding ritual acts of worship, cultivating an appropriate mental state towards the deity intensifies the results of that worship. By expressing, through ritual, feelings of selfless and overwhelming love for, and also helpless surrender to, the deity, devotees hope to taste the rare joy of proximity to, and momentary communion with, the divine. The dominant emotion that the Mata encourages her devotees to cultivate during puja is that of a child crying in longing for its parent, and it is by cultivating this emotion vis-à-vis the object of worship, that devotees are encouraged to enhance their devotional sentiments.[24] Crying, in the Mata's scheme of things, is intended to reawaken the emotional sensibilities believed to lie dormant within each individual, and thus to revive the domain of the heart,[25] of the emotions, and of faith. This is an important part of the Mata's self-proclaimed mission to reinfuse the world with love, and to counter the 'dryness' of modern minds. Weeping in the course of ritual performance is believed to 'dissolve' egotism, eliminate *vasanas*, and thereby prevent the further accumulation of *prarabdhas* which create suffering and misfortune. She therefore encourages her devotees to cry in longing for their chosen deity.

> Children . . . try to pray till your heart melts and flows down as tears. It is said that the Ganges[26] purifies whoever takes a dip in it. The tears which fill the eyes while one is remembering god have tremendous power to purify one's mind. These tears are more powerful than meditation. Such tears are verily the Ganges.[27]

An essential component of this emotionalism is of course the devotees' initial weeping in the arms of the Mata when she enfolds them in her 'divine' embrace. The Mata's embrace is believed to serve as an important catalyst for the flow of emotions. However, most devotees experience the embrace only rarely, either when the Mata visits their city or when they visit her ashram in Kerala. At other times, they are advised to perform the rituals recommended by the Mata. These, it is believed, can similarly draw out their emotions, cause them to weep, and thereby soften their hearts.

Entry into the Mata's fold, and the observance of her prescribed rituals, thus launches devotees on a journey of the heart, where their life comes to be defined increasingly in terms of cultivating emotionalism. By encouraging them to weep in supplication to the deity, she claims to sensitize them to an aspect of their being that is founded not on 'dry' intellectual reasoning but on faith and affect. In observing their daily rituals, devotees now see themselves as engaged in a project of priming the heart, reviving the spheres of emotion and faith, and cultivating openness and humility. To this end, they learn to give their emotions free rein and to value weeping as 'cleansing activity' that will remove the blockages of the heart and enhance their receptivity to the Mata's all-emcompassing love and compassion.

According to the Mata, women are better equipped to embark on the spiritual journey than men. Women, in her scheme of things, are more emotional than men, and they are closer in touch with their hearts than men. Women are also more compassionate, selfless and capable of great sacrifice. For all these reasons, the Mata claims, women constitute the spiritually stronger sex. Even while making such conventional and essentializing generalizations about women, the Mata also takes the rather unconventional step of defying age-old notions about female impurity. She encourages women to observe rituals such as the chanting of the Lalitha Sahasranama even during their menstrual periods, an injunction that violates one of the most sacrosanct of Brahmanical Hinduism's pollution taboos. In an even bolder statement, she inducted for the first time in 1998, her female disciples as priestesses into the Brahmasthanam.[28] The Mata goes some way (though never the entire distance) in challenging traditional gender discrimination in India. By valorizing emotionalism, faith and the realm of the heart, she appears to devalue masculinity (stereotypically associated with the mind, rationality and the intellect) as a system of prestige. This is not to say, however, that she in any way challenges patriarchy as a system of dominance in Indian society or the world at large.[29]

Growing spiritually through *seva*

Like ritual, *seva*, or 'selfless service to humanity', is another key component of the spiritual practice of Mata Amritanandamayi's disciples and devotees. It is also, as I noted in Chapter 1 above, the central principle upon which the entire institutional empire of the Mata Amritanandamayi Mission is founded. *Seva* in its broadest sense simply means service. It could be service directed towards society, towards an individual, towards one's parents, towards god, or towards one's guru. The word has Sanskrit roots and appears in several Sanskrit-derived Indian languages. In specific social and historical contexts, the notion of *seva* assumes particular meanings and orientations. The notion of guru *seva*, or service to one's guru, for instance, is much elaborated and refined in several Hindu devotionalist traditions and determines the precise nature of guru-*shishya* (disciple) links in each (Babb 1987; Juergensmeyer 1991). The same is true of *seva* to particular deities as part of their worship in temples (Bennett 1990; van der Veer 1988). *Seva* as humanitarian service was practised as early as the late nineteenth century by ascetics in the Swaminarayan tradition (R.B. Williams 2001). This ideal of *seva* was later popularized by Swami Vivekananda, and has informed the spiritual striving of the renouncers of the Ramakrishna Mission (Beckerlegge 1998, 2000a and b; Sen 2000; Gupta 1974) since the early part of the twentieth century.

Common to all these different meanings, however, is one key idea which distinguishes *seva* from other kinds of action. The ethic of *seva* hinges centrally on the notion of 'selflessness'. *Seva* as an ideal-type is service rendered impersonally and selflessly, not with the expectation of reciprocity, reward, protection or patronage. Ideally it is rendered anonymously, as a service intended for the good of the beneficiary and not for enhancing the reputation of the benefactor. *Seva* thus rendered counts as meritorious action for the one who renders it. This understanding of *seva* as an ideal-type, though clearly distinct from actual patterns of behaviour, does however serve as a yardstick against which those rendering different kinds of *seva* come to be evaluated (Mayer 1981).

Mata Amritanandamayi prescribes selfless *seva* as an indispensable component in the spiritual practice of her devotees and disciples. *Seva* in the MAM is not understood specifically as *seva* to the guru, to god or to humanity. Yet what comes to count most commonly as *seva* in the MAM are services directed towards its upkeep, promotion or expansion. The upkeep of the MAM entails the everyday running of its several institutions and involves devotees in *seva* directed towards their smooth day-to-day operation and management. The promotion of the MAM requires actively striving towards garnering publicity for the Mata, and organizing campaigns to raise awareness about her and her teachings and to win her ever more devotees. The expansion of the MAM entails planning for the establishment of new institutions, raising funds for these new ventures, and working towards their successful completion.

All such service, provided it is rendered without expectation of reward, is seen as meritorious activity. *Seva* in the MAM's scheme of things helps 'burn up' the cumulative ill effects of 'negative karmas' in previous births, and hastens the individual's progress towards ultimate release from the endless cycle of birth, death and rebirth. *Seva* is considered particularly relevant in the modern age as an effective counter to the selfishness, egotism and mindless acquisitiveness seen as characteristic of modern consumerist societies. This idea is particularly appealing to the Mata's more affluent devotees who, by rendering small acts of *seva* to the Mata and her Mission, derive the satisfaction of enhancing the spiritual element in their lives and accumulating spiritual merit, thus counterbalancing the negative karmic effects supposedly accruing from material acquisition. An important act of *seva*, for these devotees, is the donation of money or property to the MAM. The value of these donations may vary greatly between different donors, yet any financial contribution, however big or small, is welcomed by the MAM, and the act of donating is seen as immensely beneficial to the donor.

A 'modern' face of spirituality

The Mata's teachings as well as her ritual prescriptions have a self-consciously 'modern' aspect. First, of course, her message identifying the 'ills' of modernity, her advocacy of a 'balanced' approach to modern conditions, and her self-professed mission to alleviate the sufferings of a modern world, situate her in a distinctively 'modern' context. It is important to bear in mind, most importantly, that the Mata does not in any way campaign *against* 'modernity'. She advocates neither a rejection of 'modernity' nor a return to traditionalism. Instead, she identifies what she considers certain crucial imbalances in the modern world, which, if redressed, can alleviate human suffering and make life in modern times more comfortable.

A second crucial factor that establishes the Mata as a 'modern' guru is the decisively goal-oriented aspect of her spiritual and ritual prescriptions. Most of her prescriptions have an underlying means–end logic which is usually explained in great detail in the numerous pamphlets and printed guides produced by the Mission. In the Mata's scheme of things, the authenticity of a ritual is predicated upon its efficacy as an appropriate means to a desired end. Thus 'traditional' ritual practices have little value of their own if they fail to yield the desired results. Indeed in several respects she marks a radical departure from what is popularly understood to be Hindu 'tradition'. For instance, as I noted earlier, she does away with the age-old convention of caste-based priesthood in the temples run by her Mission. She also flouts gender conventions and admits female disciples into priesthood. Much of the publicity material produced by the Mission carries the claim that the Mata prescribes rituals only after experimenting with them in order to ascertain their practicality. This instrument–rational approach to ritual observance is presented, in the Mission's promotional literature, as evidence of the Mata's 'modern' approach to religious belief and practice.

A third feature that marks the Mata out as a 'modern' guru is her self-professed respect for variety in the matter of her devotees' spiritual preferences. Rather than take her followers through a common regimen of spiritual practice, she allows them the freedom to make choices between her various spiritual prescriptions and follow only those that suit their particular temperaments and inclinations. None of her spiritual recommendations are compulsory for lay entrants to her fold, nor are they intended to be observed to the exclusion of spiritual practices that individuals may have picked up from other sources and found benefi-cial. Devotees thus enjoy considerable autonomy and freedom to engage with the Mata's spiritual recommendations in whatever manner they choose (a point I take up in Chapter 5 below). This once again reinforces the Mata's self-definition as a guru with a 'modern' approach to religion who follows a free, flexible and open attitude in the matter of religious observance.

In addition to this, there are other crucial factors relating to the way the Mata Amritanandamayi Mission is set up, organized and managed, and the Mata's message conveyed to devotees across the world, which establish it as a 'modern' enterprise, at home in a world of revolutionized technological and communication systems. The high-profile management, engineering and computer science institutes set up by the Mission, and its professedly state-of-the-art multi-super-speciality hospital in Kerala, contribute to this image of the Mission as a modern establishment. So also the extensive movement of MAM personnel and media images across the MAM's transnational spiritual landscape. Indeed given the vast size and spread of the Mata Amritanandamayi Mission, it is impossible for devotees to be in close and constant physical proximity to their guru all or even most of the time. In the absence of frequent one-to-one interactions between guru and devotees, the organization relies exten-sively on modern media and communication systems, as well as on the large-scale movement of people across spatial boundaries, for forging and sustaining guru–devotee bonds across time and space. These twin factors of media and migration, as Appadurai (1996) argues, 'impel and compel' the work of the imagination, transforming the everyday subjectivities of devotees across the globe, and facilitating the generation of a geographically scattered 'community of sentiment' centred around the figure of the Mata.

The movement of persons across the MAM's transnational landscape takes a variety of forms. There is usually a high volume of traffic of ascetic disciples across the Mission's network. Disciples are frequently sent on tours of branches and centres across the world to organize a spiritual workshop here or deliver a religious sermon there. Those posted at field locations are often recalled to the headquarters and others sent out in their place. It is common practice for disciples at field locations to visit the Amritapuri ashram and spend time in the company of the Mata when she is in residence in Amritapuri. Most importantly, the Mata's visit to all major MAM branches, which takes place at least once a year if not more often, affords the disciples posted at the various locations a chance to consult her about the activities at their respective sites. Besides the Mata's ascetic disciples, her lay devotees also travel frequently, often going on spiritual journeys and pilgrimages to the Mata's spiritual retreat in Kerala. In the winter months between December and February, the bulk of this traffic comprises foreign devotees of the Mata travelling to India to spend time with their guru. At other times, Indian devotees and pilgrims flock to her ashram, either individually or in groups, in the hope of seeing her and securing her blessings.

Alongside this extensive movement of persons across the globe, the MAM's vibrant media network gathers up its various branches and personnel into a single and far-reaching web of communications. The MAM's electronic network comprises mainly webpages managed by different groups of devotees and disciples across the world. The most important of these, www.ammachi.org, produced and maintained by disciples in the USA, and www.amritapuri.org, maintained by disciples at the ashram headquarters in Kerala, provide a wealth of information about the Mata, the Mission, its various activities, main events at the Amritapuri ashram, and the travel schedules of the Mata and her senior disciples. Mission branches at different locations often maintain their own webpages and also produce newsletters for limited circulation within local devotee circles. In India the MAM circulates a spiritual journal, the *Matruvani*, which now appears in several different Indian languages besides English. This journal is meant both for the spiritual nourishment of devotees and as a means for securing new entrants into the Mata's fold.

The MAM also produces other printed material, ranging from pamphlets and posters to books, either about the Mata or containing her teachings. Besides this, CDs on her and her Mission, video recordings of such events as her travels abroad or her birthday celebrations in her native village, as well as MAM diaries, calendars, trinkets, scented soaps and incense sticks, all go towards providing different modes by which devotees scattered across the globe can, at least symbolically, keep in touch with the Mata.

Media and migration, and the transformed subjectivities resulting from these, facilitate what Appadurai (1996) describes as an 'experiential engagement with modernity' which is unprecedented in its intimacy and immediacy. In the case of the Mata Amritanandamayi Mission, it is perhaps apt to say that the collective imagination of devotees and disciples, created and sustained through the circulation of persons and media images, facilitates their intimate and immediate engagement with the modern form of spirituality propagated by the Mata. This spirituality is founded on a particular understanding of modernity as constructed by the guru, and on a particular set of ritual prescriptions which she recommends, which are directed at cultivating a 'selfhood' better equipped to engage with the imperatives of modernity in a mature and balanced way.

Conclusion

Modernity, as it is constructed within the Mata Amritanandamayi Mission, appears not merely as a set of objective transformations (indus-trialization and urbanization, technological and scientific advancement, revolutionized communications), but more importantly as a set of dispositions or orientations towards these conditions, which make for a skewed lifestyle lacking balance and holism. The Mata encourages devotees to engage with the objective conditions of modernity in a judicious and discerning way, and not get so excessively preoccupied with them that they lose a sense of perspective or 'balance' in their lives. The loss of perspective, and the resulting imbalance is, in her reckoning, the cause of much of the sorrow and suffering of the modern world. In striving to alleviate modern humanity's suffering and sorrow, she seeks to restore the realm of the heart in a world of 'dry minds', and to reinfuse the modern world with love. Towards this end, she prescribes spiritual and ritual practices aimed at cultivating spirituality, emotionalism, and faith in the lives and personalities of her followers.

This particular construction of modernity undergirds the shared understanding and orientation of the Mata's devotees scattered across the globe. In the first place, this collective imagination reinforces the Mata's identity as a 'modern' guru who respects the imperatives of modernity and is familiar with its demands and pressures. Second, it provides frames of reference by which to understand sorrow and suffering. The Mata's teachings, while drawing upon popular Hindu soteriologies of suffering and salvation, give these a uniquely contemporary relevance, identifying certain 'imbalances' and depletions in the contemporary world, supposedly caused by a skewed engagement with the conditions of modernity. Third, it addresses a notion of an 'ideal' modern self, defined in terms of a restored balance and harmony in modern lifestyles and personalities. And finally, her ritual and other prescriptions provide devotees with tangible means by which they can, if they so choose, supposedly alleviate the suffering in their immediate lives, as well as bring about long-term transformations in their 'modern' personalities, such that they can lead more balanced, better-integrated and happier lives. It follows then that religious selfhood, as it is constructed in the Mata's religious discourse, and conceptualized in the collective imagination of her devotees, is seen not as a given, but instead as malleable and revisable, and predicated upon the spiritual and other choices individuals make in their daily lives. The cultivation of an ideal selfhood, as per this understanding, entails not a rejection or assimilation of 'modernity', but a considered negotiation with its conditions, such as to achieve optimum results in one's personal life – a theme we will encounter again in the remaining chapters of this book.

4

CHOOSING TO SURRENDER

Earlier in Chapter 2, I discussed the way in which newcomers, in the course of their initial encounter with the Mata, receive a taste of her 'divine' love and, attracted by the unique and personalized style of the Mata's interaction with them, enter her fold. Not all the individuals who sample the Mata at her public *darshans*, however, become her devotees. Those who do are aware that the Mata is merely one in a host of gurus crowding India's spiritual landscape, each of whom has his or her distinctive style of engaging followers. These range from slick, modern healers in business jackets and ties, to wild sadhus with matted hair and ash-smeared bodies. The spiritual wares they offer include discourses on scriptural Hinduism, meditation techniques, stress relief and relaxation methods, specialized ritual prescriptions intended to effect specific outcomes, and methods of spiritual and physical healing. These persons are a visible presence on television, in the myriad journals and magazines on religion and spirituality readily available for public consumption, at websites maintained by spiritual groups, and in advertisements in the print and electronic media announcing a guru's spiritual discourse here or a prayer session there. Pamphlets and newsletters, posters, audio tapes and video cassettes circulate widely to provide potential devotees with a sampling of the available choices.[1]

From the point of view of guru-seekers, this variety and diversity is an important and immediate reality with which they are forced to contend in the course of their spiritual quest. In such a context, it becomes imperative to ask how individuals make sense of the bewildering variety that they encounter in the world of gurus and guru organizations. Why do devotees of Mata Amritanandamayi select her from the vast array of gurus available for their spiritual gratification? How do they conceptualize relationships between the Mata and other gurus, and negotiate their often multiple guru allegiances?[2] These are some of the themes I explore in this chapter.

Recognizing one's guru

The preceding questions about guru choice become doubly problematic given the climate of doubt and distrust that often clouds guru-seeking. Guru-seekers, while they revere and respect so-called 'holy' persons, at the same time regard these figures with extreme suspicion and unease. The fear that a guru may not be 'genuine' is one that nags even the most trusting, and this unease is borne out by the numerous stories that circulate through local gossip channels, or are prominently publicized in the mass media, about gurus being exposed as con-men (and women) with criminal connections, using their spirituality as a facade for making money, or sexual predators using the mask of their celibacy to run clandestine sex rackets.[3] The Indian film industry, with its mass appeal and pervasive influence over the public imagination, often fans these doubts and fears by portraying gurus as crooks and libertines who exercise clout in the highest circles of power and who cannot, therefore, be brought to book easily for their criminal activities. How then do those individuals who choose to enter the Mata's fold as devotees satisfy themselves that she is 'genuine'? And, again, why do they choose her rather than any other guru figure as the object of their veneration and devotion?

The language of guru recognition and choice, I learnt through interviews with the Mata's devotees, is highly nuanced. One does not 'choose' one's guru. There is no personal agency involved in 'choosing' or 'selecting' one's guru; instead, the guru 'appears' before one and one simply comes to 'recognize' her as the intended guru. 'When you are spiritually ripe enough for the guru', devotees explained, 'the guru will herself appear before you and take you in hand'. One devotee described the Mata as the 'divine angler' who had him 'hooked'; another described her as a 'cosmic magnet' who attracted devotees as magnets attract iron filings.

Yet others attribute the recognition of one's guru to an intuitive knowledge which cannot readily be explained. One devotee described how he had met a range of gurus in a desperate search for the 'right' one. None of the gurus had inspired his confidence. It was only when he met the Mata that he finally felt he could 'surrender' himself to her, and that too not at the first meeting but after several meetings. This devotee compared his search for the right guru to the search for one's life partner. 'You can't describe it', he said. 'It is only when she comes before you that you know she is right.' In either case, he asserted, this knowledge is based not on reason or logic, but on such factors beyond the pale of reason as faith and instinct. Some devotees described this knowledge in terms of certain 'vibrations' that one senses in the presence of the right guru.

Others described it in terms of a matching of chemistries between guru and disciple. Not every guru's chemistry matches with yours, they explained to me, and you are lucky if you happen to find the one who resonates with your being and personality.

This same 'intuitive' knowledge, according to devotees, enables one to discriminate between a genuine guru and a fake one. One devotee described it thus:

> There is this very familiar feeling around a true guru or a genuinely self-realized soul. When you get to the person, there is this quality that you recognize immediately. It is like when you go into a garden and you know that there are roses. You go there and you smell the flowers and you know they are there. You don't even need to open your eyes to find out you are in a garden of roses.

Though devotees deny all conscious choice in selecting the Mata as their guru, their narratives, describing their initial impressions of her, point to several vital factors that implicitly go into guru assessment and choice. These factors are manifold, and are accorded different degrees of importance by different individuals. It is interesting that the very factors which attract some devotees to one guru turn others away, because of their conflicting interpretations and assessments of the guru's personality and style. Be that as it may, it appears from their narratives that most devotees do have a conception of what a guru ought to be like, and it is when the Mata matches their expectations and preferences that they become willing to enter her fold as devotees.

Intimacy of the embrace

For most persons, the critical factor in their choice of a guru is of course the guru's perceived efficacy or otherwise in solving their immediate problems. Persons who seek out a guru in the hope of specific outcomes are more likely to attach themselves to the guru if, during their initial meeting(s) with the guru, their immediate needs are met, their personal crises resolved and their anxieties allayed. In the Mata's case, her personalized style of interacting with devotees itself goes a long way towards meeting their needs for reassurance. Devotees consider the embrace to be unparalleled in terms of its beneficial effects on the recipient. In most Hindu devotionalist traditions, it is believed that the mere sight, or *darshan*, of a guru or even the image of a god, leads to the transfer of certain beneficial essences and qualities from the 'divine' entity to the beholder. In the Mata's case, the beneficial effect, devotees believe, is magnified because of the physical contact that she establishes with each devotee. One devotee, a young woman in Delhi who runs her own employment agency, explained this in terms of electro-magnetic rays and 'scientific' principles.

> There is a scientific principle guiding gurus, you see. Around a human being there is a field of electro-magnetic rays. A golden hued field called the aura. You can enlarge your aura by concentrating, meditating . . . The larger the aura, the better for you. It is your body's strength, your resistance to diseases, your mental capacity, financial stability, success in all ventures. If you have negative qualities in you – hatred, anger, jealousy, lust – your aura will dissipate. Also, if someone touches you, you lose some of your aura to that person. Gurus concentrate, meditate on their favourite deity. Their aura goes on increasing. Not only do they increase it, they maintain it. They have erased their negative tendencies . . . But even they cannot afford to let anybody touch them. If they do, they lose some of their strength. So they keep their distance. They allow *darshans*, no touching.
>
> In India we see any number of gurus. Nobody ever touches. No one allows you that much freedom or access. They always keep you at a distance . . . [Whereas Amma is different.] If you observe Amma closely, you will find her whole body vibrates. She oozes aura. Her aura is unlimited. No matter how much she gives, there is no end to it. If a person approaches her even for a tenth of a second, and touches her, all the person's *prarabdha* [karmic burden accumulated from past lives] gets burnt up. Beyond that Amma hugs and kisses you. That way you cannot imagine the extent of benefit to yourself.

For most devotees, the intimacy of her embrace is the most compelling aspect of the Mata. This intimacy, as I mentioned in Chapter 2 above, is entirely unconventional, as it flouts all restrictions on physical contact between members of the opposite sexes, and challenges the norm of hierarchy that usually characterizes the relationship between guru or god, and devotee. Not surprisingly, it is precisely the unconventional nature of the Mata's love that renders it highly suspect in the eyes of sceptics. For non-devotees who have had her *darshan* and come away unimpressed, the physicality of the embrace is often one of the factors that decide them against the Mata. Receiving an embrace from a woman is, for many, an uncomfortable experience, especially if the recipient is male. This kind of perception is laden with sexual undertones, and these sceptics often dismiss the embrace as an act by which, consciously or unconsciously, both Mata and devotee seek sexual gratification.[4] Devotees, on the other hand, emphasize the maternal aspect of the Mata's love, and seek to justify what is otherwise a highly problematic aspect of their relationship with their guru by idealizing her status as divine mother. They regard as narrow-minded and perverse those who see sexual undertones in the Mata's loving embrace.

Austerity and selflessness

Devotees of the Mata tend to be very sceptical about gurus who openly demand donations and services from their devotees. Any hint of personal aggrandizement on the guru's part is seen in a negative light, and it is often those gurus who are seen to lead austere lives, and who appear selfless in their engagement with devotees, who carry maximum credibility in devotees' perceptions. Devotees of Mata Amritanandamayi stress what they see as the 'selfless' and altruistic nature of her love. This, they claim, is evident in the long hours of her *darshan* sessions. These often last up to twelve hours, when the Mata tirelessly meets devotees, never pausing for a break. This, for them, is the self-sacrificing mother, caring only about her children and paying no heed to her own needs for rest and quiet. Her biography claims that this self-sacrificing spirit was evident right from her childhood, when she would feed the poor in her village and herself go hungry, or tend to the sick and dying, sparing no thought for her own comfort and well-being.

Even though the Mata today heads a vast institutional and financial empire, leads a comfortable life as a guru commanding international fame and recognition, and receives generous donations from wealthy devotees across the world, her followers often claim that there is little she herself stands to gain from the success of her Mission. Her own lifestyle, as they see it, remains austere and indeed full of hardship, since she is constantly straining to ease the suffering of others. This for many, is the sign of a genuine guru, who works not for personal aggrandizement but for the good of the world. It is of no consequence, for these devotees, that the Mata, once a poor fisher girl, now travels in a Mercedes Benz or by jet to visit devotees across the world. It does not count that she has devotees milling around her most, if not all, of the time, anxious to do her slightest bidding. In fact her material conditions have improved dramatically in the course of the MAM's growth and spread, but it is not this, but rather the Mata's 'selfless sacrifice' in the cause of the world's well-being, that devotees invariably seek to highlight. An important index of this sacrificing motherly love, in devotees' views, is the array of charitable ventures that the MAM has initiated for the welfare of society. These they see as evidence of the Mata's commitment to 'social service', her altruism and philanthropy, which constitutes for them an important basis for her legitimacy as a 'genuine' guru. Sceptics, on the other hand, once again question the Mata's legitimacy precisely on the grounds of the MAM's visible affluence, which they perceive as contradictory to the ideals of asceticism and austerity associated with 'authentic' gurus.

Approachability of the Mata

The Mata, according to her followers, impresses people by her approachability and the openness in her demeanour. The way in which she interacts with devotees, listens to their woes and addresses their problems, they claim, is such as to make them feel comfortable in her presence. Rather than feel intimidated by her, devotees claim to experience their entry into her fold as a kind of home-coming. The natural ease, graciousness and familiarity with which the Mata treats her devotees, confirm their belief that she is all that she claims to be. She does not need to 'show off' her powers, or impress them with her superiority, they say, because she is so secure in the knowledge of her own divinity.

I myself had occasion to view this 'simplicity' at close quarters when I sought permission to interview the Mata during her visit to London in July 1998. The Mata's visits to London are a yearly affair, and part of her annual tours of MAM centres in India and abroad. On this occasion, she was to meet devotees at South London's Battersea Grand Hall, the first of a series of her five or six *darshan* sessions in the course of her three-day stay in the city. Here, unlike in India, there were no separate queues for men and women. Still, two queues had formed in the centre of the hall. One, I was told, was for regular *darshan*. The other was meant for people who wanted not merely an embrace, but, more importantly, answers to pressing questions regarding their personal life, career changes, health problems, financial constraints and the like. An English woman, a disciple of the Mata whom I had earlier interviewed in India in 1997 and who was now accompanying the Mata on her 'world tour', suggested to me that if I wanted to interview the Mata, I might join the 'question queue' and try my luck.

Nearly half of the five or six hundred devotees present that morning were non-Indians. Some were Sri Lankan Tamils, but the majority were Europeans, some British, others from France, Germany, Italy and one or two other countries in Western Europe. One of her senior disciples stood by the Mata's side to translate devotees' questions (which they asked in English) into Malayalam, and the Mata's answers into English.

Well before it was my turn to ask questions, I managed to tell this disciple the reason for my presence in the queue. He recognized me, from my days spent in fieldwork at the Mata's ashram headquarters in Kerala, as the 'young researcher' who was attempting to study Mata Amritanandamayi. When my turn came, he introduced me to the Mata. She greeted me with a winning smile. She held a devotee in her arms as she looked in my direction. Throughout the question and answer session, she continued, without interruption, to receive devotees in her embrace one after the other, even as she replied to my queries with a readiness and spontaneity that I found disarmingly attractive.

I asked my questions in my somewhat unpractised and occasionally unidiomatic Malayalam, but she appeared to follow them easily enough. I had prepared a list of questions, and I did not expect that I would have time enough with her to ask them all. She, however, seemed in no hurry to terminate the session, and appeared to pay no heed to the impatient line of devotees still awaiting their turn to seek solutions to the problems that troubled them. I asked my first question hesitantly, fearing that she might find it rude and tactless. 'Are you god?' To my surprise, this was greeted by a loud guffaw from the Mata. She then turned to her disciple and said, in tones of utter amusement, 'Did you hear what she just asked? Am I god?' There was more laughter, before the Mata finally looked me in the eye and said indulgently, 'Child, what can I say? What is *your* conception of god?' I was unprepared for this counter question, and therefore replied only with a bashful smile before I proceeded to ask my other questions. The entire exchange was notably casual and friendly. In all, I spent about twenty minutes in close proximity to the Mata. I watched from close quarters her unhurried, indulgent way of dealing with those who came to her, and the readiness, spontaneity and apparent sincerity of her gestures and speech. Neither pedantic, nor the least reticent, she came through almost exactly as her devotees had described her to me – a person remarkable for her simplicity and apparently unaffected warmth.

Most devotees had had prior experiences of other gurus, and saw the Mata's approachability and spontaneity as an important factor distinguishing her from the others, and enhancing her personal appeal. One devotee in Delhi, Kishore,[5] employed as a manager in a private firm, contrasted the Mata's style of relating to people with what he had encountered at the Divine Life Society in Rishikesh in north India.[6]

It wasn't as though I thought the gurus at Divine Life Society were fake. It is the cleanest organization, but . . . the whole orientation is philosophical. The emphasis is on intellectual striving. Here [in the MAM] it is more from the heart. There is love . . . You feel it is your home . . . Everyone is so loving. You don't feel you are an outsider. Your concept of a guru changes after you come here. Amma is so practical. She comes down to your level, wherever you are. She understands our mental level. And we understand her . . . In the Divine Life Society, you feel hesitant to go forward and talk to them. They are in their own intellectual worlds . . . In Amma's ashram, you feel part of the whole thing. You don't feel like coming away.

A strikingly large proportion of the devotees I interviewed drew parallels between the Mata's personality and that of Ramakrishna, the well-known nineteenth-century guru from Bengal, whose hagiography and teachings have been popularized through much of India by his disciples. The Ramakrishna Mission today has branches in many parts of India, and engages lay persons in many of its charitable and spiritual activities.[7] Most of the Mata's devotees appeared familiar with the activities of this organization and claimed to know about the mysticism of Ramakrishna from the voluminous literature that now exists about him. Ramakrishna too, devotees told me, reached out to people in the simple and spontaneous manner which they appreciate in the Mata. What devotees applaud in both gurus is their intense love, directness and emotional fervour in dealing with lay persons.

Simplicity of the guru's teachings

Another important criterion guru-seekers often use for choosing between gurus is the style of their religious discourse. Some prefer the extremely simple and spontaneous discourse of gurus like Mata Amritanandamayi, who captures her devotees' imagination with her simple stories, anecdotes and parables. Here again, devotees often draw parallels with Ramakrishna, who is believed to have revealed the most profound truths by means of simple anecdotes drawn from everyday life.[8] The Mata conveys her teachings in a very direct and often emotionally charged manner, speaking in her mother tongue, Malayalam. Devotees then translate her speech into other languages. She avoids the Sanskrit terms and abstractions commonly found in spiritual discourses by gurus.

The Mata's devotees whom I interviewed were almost unanimous in deploring the highbrow, and jargon-rich discourses of many of India's contemporary gurus. Non-devotees, on the other hand, often find the Mata's style overly childish and simplistic and prefer the spiritual discourses of other more erudite gurus like the late Chinmayananda.[9] The content of Chinmayananda's speeches derived more often than not from ancient Sanskrit texts and provided the guru's interpretation of particular verses and passages in these texts. His discourses tended to be far more intellectually demanding and often even obscure in comparison with the Mata's simple oratory.

Underlying devotees' appreciation of the Mata's simple teachings is their conviction that what the Mata conveys through her discourse must have its basis in India's ancient texts and scriptures. It is a known fact that the Mata has had no formal (or informal) training either in Sanskrit or the scriptures. Yet devotees presume that the Mata, as a self-realized and therefore 'enlightened' ascetic, must have spontaneous access to the wisdom of these ancient texts and that she must, in her discourses, convey the gist of their contents in her own highly personalized style.[10]

For the Mata's devotees then, the language in which she communicates her wisdom is both simple and profound. Alongside their regard for the simplicity and contemporary relevance of the Mata's message is a great reverence for Sanskrit and for the contents of the scriptures. This reverence stems not from a personal knowledge of the Sanskrit scriptures but from a vague sense of their greatness and glory passed on from earlier generations.[11] In the modern age, when individuals lack the time or inclination to try and glean for themselves the wisdom contained in the ancient scriptures, the Mata (devotees believe) provides quick and easy access to their contents. This wisdom, they hope, will in turn help them to cope with the trials of their everyday lives.

Lack of display

Gurus who are glamorous, pretentious, or intellectually arrogant, who seek to project themselves in order to impress the public, and who woo devotees by means of spectacular display, are, I gathered from my interviews with devotees, to be treated with circumspection. Genuine gurus do not seek to impress because they do not need to; their personality, their actions and their graciousness speak for themselves. Devotees lay much store by what they describe as the 'lack of display' in the Mata's self representations. This assertion comes as something of a surprise, given the extravagant display at her Devi *bhava darshans* where she dresses up as a goddess claiming thereby to reveal her innate divinity. When I asked devotees about the apparent contradiction here, many explained that these *darshans* were intended not as an opportunity for the Mata to display her own powers, but as a reminder to devotees that they must follow the path of spirituality. In this connection they invariably cited a passage in the Mata's biography where, in response to a devotee's question as to why she wears the 'costume' of Devi, the Mata says:

> It will help people to remember what Bhava is. Child, each attire is important in its own way. We are naked when we are born. Later, according to each country and social custom, people adopt different kinds of dress. Whatever the dress, the person is the same. In this age people give much importance to dress. Mother will make this point clear through an anecdote. One man was cutting down a tree which was growing by the side of a road. Another man who happened to see him doing this said, 'Don't cut down that tree! It is wrong to do so, it is against the law.' The man not only refused to stop cutting but also scolded him severely. The person who tried to prevent the hooligan from cutting the tree was a policeman. He departed but soon returned in his official dress. Even from a distance the mere sight of the policeman's cap was enough to make the hooligan flee without looking back. See the different impact created when he came in ordinary and then official dress. Therefore, special attire is needed to teach ignorant people.[12] Likewise, the costumes of Krishna and Devi Bhavas. Some people who still feel dissatisfied even after talking to Mother for hours will feel fully content after conversing with her only for a couple of seconds during Bhava Darshan. They feel peaceful after having told all their worries directly to god.[13]

Devotees, when citing this passage, invariably highlight what they see as the Mata's self-deprecatory tones in comparing her 'divine' attire to a mundane police uniform. It is this self-deprecation and humility that devotees consider central to the Mata's personality, and which are in fact vital to their perception of her 'genuineness'. Self deprecation, in this scheme of things, is a crucial virtue by which, paradoxically, the Mata succeeds in bolstering her claims to extraordinariness. It is interesting that in the passage quoted above, the Mata does not undermine her own divinity. Instead she reinforces it, suggesting only that the outer vestments are in fact an indication of what lies within.

Devotees see the same lack of display in their manifold experiences of the Mata's miraculous interventions in their lives. They lay great store by what they describe as her 'subtle' way of working miracles. She is no exhibitionist, they assert proudly, and she does not display her divine powers in full public view in order to convince people of her extra-ordinariness. Instead she works subtly and quietly, intervening in their lives and transforming them silently without any drama or fanfare of any sort. One devotee described it thus:

> This is what I like about her – that she doesn't display all these powers. She says she knows only Malayalam. To my driver she spoke in Hindi, to my friend she spoke in English, to one tenant here she spoke in Bengali. The foreigners say she has spoken to them in the foreign languages . . . [14] If she were to speak openly and display her powers maybe I would find her less convincing. Because I don't like any display. The other day some mahatma was speaking on television. He said, we are such small people, the moment we do something we want to broadcast it to the world and say, this is what I have done. Whereas the creator of the world just created the world, then he stayed out of it. He doesn't come down to tell you, 'I did it'. So only a creator can remain like that without saying 'I did it'. That's what I like about her.

Another devotee described the Mata's 'demonstrations' that she was 'ordinary', as something that went far beyond even the extraordinary. In his view, the Mata's real achievement was that she could do so much without ever resorting to display and exhibitionism. 'In Amma's case,' he said, 'whenever people tell me of some miraculous happening, I'm always sceptical. I think, now why would Amma demonstrate it like that? She has no need to.'

Devotees' emphasis on the lack of exhibitionism in the Mata's style of miracle working reflects Parry's (1994: 258) observations on the problematic relationship between the laity and the ascetic (in this case the guru) in the matter of miracle working. What is problematic here is not so much the miracle working itself as its brash display, which devotees regard with suspicion since, in their view, truly accomplished ascetics, or authentic avatar-gurus, should not have to display their powers; yet without this display, there is no 'proof' that these persons are indeed what they claim to be. The Mata gets around this problem by means of her 'subtle' style of working miracles. This is particularly important given the visibly conspicuous miracle working of the other extremely popular contemporary avatar-guru, Sathya Sai Baba, whose miracles comprise the materialization of ash, as well as other objects like watches, diamond rings, and cameras, in the course of his *darshan*. Sceptics see this as the cheap conjuring tricks of a magician and several devotees of the Mata express their reservations about the Baba precisely because of this open and brash display. This is a point I shall take up again later in this chapter.

Egalitarianism

It is important for devotees that the Mata does not discriminate between people of diverse religious faiths and backgrounds but instead welcomes them all equally into her fold. It is also important for them that, within her Hindu following, she does not make any distinction between people of different castes. The Mata's own 'low' caste status appears of no consequence to her Indian devotees except to vindicate their belief in her extraordinary powers. In their view, no 'ordinary' mortal could have thus risen meteorically, as she did, from poor, low-caste village origins to the stature of an internationally famous spiritual leader. The majority of her devotees, because they are people from the educated professional classes in India's towns and cities, are also from the 'upper' castes since it is primarily those of higher caste origins who have benefited most from the opportunities available in India's service and professional sectors. However, the Mata does have 'low' caste devotees as well, many of them the beneficiaries of her charitable ventures. These individuals too are received warmly in the Mata's embrace. In her religious discourses, the Mata is silent on the issue of caste, neither challenging it, nor acknowledging its presence.

One of the most remarkable stories that circulates among devotees illustrating the Mata's openness to all and her refusal to discriminate between people has to do with a poor 'low-caste' leper, Dattan, who went to the Mata's ashram in Kerala to seek refuge there. The narrative describes how when she saw him, the Mata folded him in her embrace, and how, over several months, she 'treated' him by sucking his sores clean. Devotees often cite this story to illustrate how the Mata is beyond all distinctions of high and low, rich and poor, and strong and weak, and how she loves all equally, unconditionally and without discrimination.[15] These perceived attributes of the Mata, then, are of immense importance in her devotees' reckoning.

Some of the devotees I interviewed described caste considerations as largely irrelevant in their everyday lives. Kishore (whom I introduced earlier in this chapter in connection with his experience of the Divine Life Society) was emphatic in his assertion that caste was of no consequence in his personal life. Both he and his wife were insistent that they would not have been devotees of the Mata had they noticed that she in any way discriminated between persons of different castes. Kishore recalled how his grandmother, back in his village in north India, would not allow the ('low caste') local sweepers to come near her. She considered them a polluting influence because of their 'impure' profession. In his own home in Delhi, this devotee said proudly, he did not even bother to ascertain the caste status of the hired helps who came to do the cleaning and laundry. Likewise, he said, caste would not be a criterion determining his children's choice of marriage partners. Vasanthi, a university lecturer in Delhi and a devotee of the Mata, said in response to the caste question: 'I have never believed in the caste system. I have revolted against it especially because my mother believed in it and I reacted violently to her belief. Caste would not, for instance, ever be a consideration in the selection of a groom for my daughter.'[16]

Other devotees, however, were more cautious in expressing their attitudes towards caste. One such individual, a retired government official in Kerala, said: 'I would be a hypocrite if I were to claim that caste is of no consequence to me.' He conceded that caste does not apply at all in the MAM's scheme of things, and appeared to rejoice in this knowledge. The Mata, he said, makes no distinction between Brahmans and non-Brahmans, or even between Hindus and non-Hindus. In his own life, however, he said in tones of acute embarrassment, caste considerations did operate. He admitted that he would consider caste a key criterion in his choice of a suitable groom for his daughter. 'We look for compatibility between partners. We look for common backgrounds. And caste is therefore an important criterion. Not that other castes are inferior or anything like that. It's just that these things take time to change.' Even devotees like this one, who spoke of the relevance of caste in their private lives, were anxious to convince me that they saw the caste criterion only as a parameter for establishing 'compatibility' with other caste members, and not as a ranking principle which graded people in terms of superior and inferior.[17] Many treated caste affiliations as a vestige from the past, and saw it as something that would change with time and lose all relevance in the India of the future.[18]

It follows from the preceding discussion that the intimacy of the Mata's embrace, the simplicity of her teachings, her approachability, the egalitarianism in her world-view, her austerity and selflessness, and the lack of display in her style, are all crucial factors contributing towards devotees' choice of her as their preferred guru, and towards establishing her authenticity and genuiness in their eyes. There are other preference criteria as well that attract at least some devotees to the Mata, and lead them to choose her as their guru. One of these is the size and composition of her spiritual empire. Early in one's interactions with this guru one gets an impression of her vast popularity abroad and the extent of her transnational reach. Her non-Indian devotees, mainly from the affluent nations of the West, as well as her Indian devotees resident overseas, are a highly visible presence at her public programmes. The promotional material on the Mata invariably highlights the size and extent of her following. Besides this, at most of her public appearances, the audience is four to five thousand strong. For newcomers, the size and composition of the crowds is itself an indication that there 'must be something' about the Mata and that she is worth exploring as a potential guru.[19] The relationship between her appeal, and the size of her following, thus follows a circular logic. Just as she attracts a large and diverse following because of her appeal, she also appeals because she attracts a large and diverse following, which devotees see as an indication of her legitimacy and authenticity as an avatar-guru.

For her devotees from Kerala, the Mata's Kerala origins and the fact that she can communicate with them in their native language, Malayalam, enhances her appeal. No other spiritual leader in Kerala is known to have attained the kind of international or even nationwide popularity and recognition that the Mata has earned for herself.[20] Malayalis in India and abroad often attend her programmes to 'check out' the credentials of this fellow-Malayali. Many become her devotees, and many also switch allegiance from other gurus like Sathya Sai Baba to this relatively new and successful avatar-guru from their home state.

Several and diverse factors thus go into a devotee's choice of the Mata as guru. Devotees, however, never refer to this as a 'choice'. Instead, for them, it is an act of 'surrender'. Whereas 'choosing' implies an active selection from among possible guru options, 'surrender' seems to imply a passive submission to a power greater than oneself. Though it is clear from discussions with devotees that they are active agents who make a conscious choice in selecting the Mata as their guru, it is notable that they should invariably seek to represent themselves as passive entities, and deny exercising any personal agency or will in entering the Mata's fold. This crucial contradiction between active individual agency and passive surrender lies at the heart of devotees' construction of their selfhood as followers of the Mata, and is a theme we shall encounter again in the discussions to follow.

Exclusivist and inclusivist orientations in guru choice

The Mata is not always the only guru in her devotees' lives. In terms of their guru loyalties at any given point in time, there are two kinds of guru-orientations commonly observable amongst devotees. I refer to these here as the 'exclusivist' and 'inclusivist' orientations. Exclusivists see their attachment to the Mata as precluding the possibility of simultaneous attachments to other gurus. They find it contemptible to owe allegiance to more than one guru at the same time, or to drift from guru to guru in the hope of tangible rewards. To be a 'tourist of gurus', in their view, is to take an altogether frivolous approach to spirituality. It is like 'digging for water' in not one but several places at the same time. According to this logic, if you dig shallow holes in the ground at several places, you will not find water, whereas if you dig deep in one place, you must, sooner or later, find it. Exclusivists therefore try and remain loyal to their chosen guru. They might still sample the wares of other guru figures and even attend the discourses, prayer sessions and rituals conducted by other guru organizations, seeing such attendance and participation as spiritually meritorious activity. In terms of being 'attached' to a guru, however, they remain exclusively loyal to their chosen one. Only in extreme circumstances, such as the passing away of the chosen guru, or disillusionment with her, will exclusivists consider the option of attachment to a new spiritual mentor.

Unlike exclusivists, inclusivists attach themselves simultaneously to several gurus. Each individual selects his or her cluster of chosen gurus on the basis of personal preferences or practical expediency, and the cluster's composition keeps changing over time, with older attachments yielding place to newer and more attractive ones. Those of the Mata's devotees who fit this description constantly sample the spiritual wares of new gurus, form new attachments, and add to, or discard from, their chosen guru clusters.

Devotees' orientations, whether exclusivist or inclusivist, are usually reflected in the guru iconography with which they tend to surround themselves. Devotees' homes usually bear visible signs of their guru allegiances. The walls of living rooms are adorned with framed photographs and calendar pictures of their gurus, past and present. Often invocations to the gurus, most commonly in Sanskrit, are printed across doorways. Stickers and magnets bearing the visages of the gurus or some related symbol are prominently displayed on refrigerator doors, dashboards and windscreens of cars, and on the surfaces of satchels and brief cases. Most people wear some kind of reminder of their gurus on their person. These include rings and lockets bearing miniature photographs of their gurus, bracelets with the gurus' names carved on the surfaces, or rosary beads that have been blessed by one or the other guru. Many carry photographs of the gurus in their wallets and purses. They surround themselves with books containing hagiographies of the gurus, and compilations of the gurus' teachings. Whereas exclusivist devotees of the Mata usually tend to display only those icons that relate to her, inclusivists often combine iconography from different guru traditions. It is not uncommon to see, in the homes of the latter, photographs of Sathya Sai Baba, for instance, displayed alongside those of Mata Amritanandamayi. Similarly it is not uncommon to discover the odd devotee wearing, alongside a bracelet with the Mata's name carved on it, also a pendant bearing the visage of a smiling Sai Baba.

Related to the issue of devotees' exlusivist versus inclusivist orientations is the question of how they conceptualize relationships between the Mata and other gurus. In drawing comparisons and contrasts between the Mata and the various other gurus whom they may have encountered in the course of their spiritual explorations, devotees most commonly tend to perceive the relationships between them in terms of one of three possibilities: identity, complementarity, or competition. This can perhaps best be demonstrated by exploring the different ways in which devotees of the Mata conceptualize the relationship between her and Sathya Sai Baba.

Some perceive the relation between the two avatar-gurus as one of unity and identity, seeing both as manifestations of the same divine force. A devotee of Mata Amritanandamayi used the analogy of electricity to explain the unity of the divine energy manifest in both gurus:

> The creator may have a billion different forms but the source of energy is all the same. Just like electricity. Whether it lights up a bulb in this house or one in the next, it is all the same. The source that generates this electricity is one.

Devotees of this persuasion may appeal to both gurus equally for divine protection and guidance, and participate equally in the activities of both guru organizations. Alternatively, they may prefer to focus their devotion on either one, in the belief that single-minded surrender to any one chosen guru, rather than devotion to several, is the superior way of disciplining the mind and enhancing one's spiritual progress.

Others perceive the relation between the two gurus in terms of complementarity rather than unity. According to some devotees of Mata Amritanandamayi, there are occasions when Sathya Sai Baba tells particular individuals to approach the Mata rather than him for solutions to specific problems. Devotees often take this to mean that each avatar-guru has a particular area of expertise which the other does not share. Devotees do not venture to speculate on precisely what these 'areas of specialization' are, but hope that in the event that they approach the wrong guru for a particular need, they will be redirected to the 'right' one! Discussions among devotees about the relative merits and limitations of different gurus often centre around speculations as to which guru is best approached for what kind of problem. Some gurus, in this scheme of things, may be most effective as healers of particular kinds of illness, others may be particularly effective in blessing childless couples with offspring, yet others may be most useful in resolving marital discord and/or sorting out financial problems.

Several devotees locate Mata Amritanandamayi and Sathya Sai Baba in a relationship not of identity or complementarity, but one of competition. They see their personalities and/or their teachings as incompatible and therefore find it imperative to make a choice between the two. Some devotees of the Mata, for instance, consider Sathya Sai Baba undesirable as a guru because of his visibly conspicuous miracle working. They see his miracles (most commonly the materialization of various objects out of thin air) as the cheap conjuring tricks of a magician, and, as I noted earlier, express their reservations about the Baba precisely because of this display. This is the point made in a story about the Mata that one devotee narrated to me.

> I heard one story. She was feeding people out of a bucket – in the crowd . . . People kept coming, kept coming . . . and this was a bottomless bucket. And people started saying – Oh! Miracle! Miracle! And she finishes feeding them, and throws down the bucket and says: That's the last time I do that, otherwise I'll have an ashram like Sai Baba.

In this view, the Mata, being 'genuine', does not need to display her supernatural powers in order to convince her devotees, whereas Sathya Sai Baba's miracle display casts doubts on his credibility as an authentic avatar-guru. Devotees of this persuasion who choose the Mata as their preferred guru simultaneously reject Sathya Sai Baba as a potential option.

Sathya Sai Baba of course is only one among the myriad other gurus whom the Mata's devotees encounter in their travels along contemporary India's busy spiritual highway. In making their evaluations of the relationship between these various gurus and the Mata, devotees use different yardsticks, and depending on which yardsticks they use, they perceive differently the compatibility/continuity or otherwise between their own and other guru faiths. As a result of this, boundaries between guru organizations are drawn (and redrawn) differently by different individuals. From the point of view of one devotee, a particular guru faith or organization may appear to be completely distinct from, and incompatible with, devotion to the Mata. From the point of view of another individual, on the other hand, both may belong to the same spiritual complex of which (s)he wishes to be part. (S)he may perceive no clear boundaries demarcating the one from the other and may participate equally in the activities of both. This same individual may, however, perceive a third guru faith as entirely incompatible with the first two and may therefore locate this third entirely outside the limits of his/her preferred guru cluster. These evaluations and guru choices of course are in no sense binding for all time. Devotees' choices change frequently, necessitating a move from one guru (or set of gurus) to other, potentially more satisfying, alternatives – a theme I will further explore in Chapter 6 below.

Conclusion

It is clear from the preceding discussion that though devotees of Mata Amritanandamayi deny personal agency in choosing the Mata as their guru, they are, in fact, active choosers, and their choice does follow from their individual preferences and expectations. I have attempted to show in this chapter how devotees of the Mata, as active 'consumers' in India's teeming spiritual supermarket, are guided by various criteria in their choice of the Mata as their guru and spiritual preceptor. Not all devotees of the Mata attach exactly the same weightage to each of the various criteria discussed in this chapter, but these criteria do, in whatever order of importance, inform their decisions when they choose between the variety of spiritual wares offered by gurus in contemporary India. These individuals display a keen awareness of the various spiritual wares available, many having sampled different gurus before deciding to enter the Mata's fold. In choosing the Mata, they opt for a guru who matches their individual preferences. Choosing the Mata as guru does not mean that devotees necessarily owe their allegiance exclusively to her. Nor does it mean that they cannot change their guru-choice at a later stage. Having chosen her, they then go on to engage with her teachings and recommended practices in different ways.

5

SPIRITUAL PATHWAYS

I demonstrated in the last chapter that guru-seeking for most people entails an active process of choosing and selecting between the different guru faiths and traditions dotting India's spiritual landscape. What happens after an individual has made his or her choice? What are the options available to a devotee once (s)he has selected Mata Amritanandamayi as his/her chosen guru? These are the questions I explore in this chapter. Even after entering the Mata's fold, I shall show here, devotees and disciples are faced with considerable choice – this time with respect to their spiritual practice and ritual observance. Though lay devotees of the Mata exercise far greater freedom in this regard than her ascetic disciples, even the latter do exercise some measure of freedom in following particular spiritual pathways that best suit their temperament.

The path of the renouncer

For those of the Mata's disciples who are formally initiated into ascetic life in the Mata's ashram in Kerala, their spiritual quest entails renouncing their worldly life, and embarking on a life of self denial. The majority of individuals (men and women) who choose to become disciples of the Mata and enter her ashram as ascetic renouncers are young people in their late teens or early twenties. Many come from middle-class families and evidently led comfortable lives prior to their entry into the Mata's ashram. The young ascetics I came to know claimed to have been deeply inspired by the ideal of spiritual seeking. They see their lives as dedicated to the pursuit of spiritual enlightenment, and their every action and every thought is, ideally, geared towards this all-consuming spiritual endeavour. The spiritual quest is conceptualized as a progressive burning up of karmic burden (*prarabdha*) accumulated over this and past lives, and requires that the aspirant desist from all thoughts and actions in the present that could contribute to a further accumulation of karmic burden in the future.

The goal of such self-disciplining and self-mastery, as I noted in Chapter 3 above, is *moksha* or salvation, the soul's ultimate release from the inexorable karmic cycle of birth, death and rebirth.

At the Amritapuri ashram, the Mata puts her ascetic disciples through a strict regimen of daily worship, prayer, meditation and *seva*. They start their day early, assembling in the ashram's prayer hall at 4.30 a.m. to chant the Lalitha Sahasranama. They then attend Vedanta lectures and spiritual discourses delivered by the sannyasis in the ashram. This is followed by a meditation session. Frugal meals are served at the ashram's canteens at fixed times of the day. There is a *bhajan* session in the evening led either by the Mata herself or by her senior disciples which the young ascetics are required to attend. Tuesdays and Fridays are spent in the company of the Mata, when she meets the disciples individually, answers their questions and offers advice, and conducts a joint meditation session in which all are required to participate. Sundays are days of strenuous activity when the ascetics gear up to cope with the thousands of visitors who throng the ashram to see the Mata in her Devi *bhava*.

The single most important activity that consumes most of their time is *seva*, a compulsory part of their spiritual training. They are expected to lead a life not of seclusion and meditation, but one of service to the world. Defining her conception of an ideal renouncer, the Mata explains:

> A *sannyasin* is one who has dedicated his entire life, both external and internal, for others, for the good of the world . . . In order to set an example, a *sannyasin* also should perform actions while living in this world. He should not sit idle saying, 'I have attained the state of actionlessness, therefore I don't have to do any work.' This will set the wrong example that others will follow. Even after attaining the state of perfection, a true *sannyasin* who lives in this world of pluralities will be very dynamic, active and creative on the outside. But he will be totally silent within.[1]

Elsewhere she says, 'If a *sadhak* [spiritual aspirant] does not work, he is cheating the world and cheating God in the name of spirituality.'[2] Asked by a devotee whether a monk, having renounced the world, should engage in material affairs at all, the Mata answers: '*Sannyasa* . . . is not renouncing the world and action. [It] is renunciation of the fruits of action. It is the *dharma* of the *sannyasis* to lead the world.'[3] 'Spirituality', she says, 'is not sitting in a corner with closed eyes. We should be ready to become everyone's servant and also to see all equally. Going out into the world tomorrow, all of you should serve everyone without selfishness.'[4]

And further, she says: 'Action alone cannot take you to the goal. Action performed with an attitude of self-surrender and love is the right path.'[5] The Mata thus advocates an ethic of service that focuses exclusively on action for its own sake, not motivated by personal interest. She tells her disciples not to serve expecting praise or recognition or fame or money. Instead she directs them to focus on the work itself and to derive satisfaction from the knowledge of work done well, with sincerity and to the best of one's ability. This is unmotivated action as an ideal-type.[6] Such action is believed to 'burn up' one's *prarabdhas* and *vasanas* more effectively than ritual observance, and hasten the aspirant's progress towards *moksha*.

Each disciple in the Mata Amritanandamayi Math is assigned specific *seva* duties by the authorities – either the Mata herself or the senior *sannyasis* who manage the affairs of the ashram – and in performing their duties, they are held accountable to the *sannyasi* in charge of their particular area of operations. New entrants to the ashram are expected to prove their dedication and commitment to their spiritual practice by performing satisfactorily whatever duties they are assigned.[7] Most disciples are initially assigned tasks within the MAM headquarters in Amritapuri where they may contribute their daily *seva* in the ashram's computer centre, its accounts section, its kitchens, its stores, its accommodation wing or its press and publications division. Once they have gained some experience, and been exposed to the various aspects of the MAM's operations, they may be assigned to MAM branches and centres across India or abroad, or to its various schools, colleges, technical training institutes and charitable organizations.

Though these ascetic disciples lead closely supervised lives, they still exercise some autonomy in choosing how precisely to deal with the MAM's *seva* regimen, the more so the higher they are located in the institutional hierarchy. *Seva*, in the Mission, is not any one type of activity and does not follow a standardized format for all. Instead, it assumes diverse forms depending on each one's individual skills, capabilities, inclinations and constraints. In rendering *seva*, disciples often display high levels of individual initiative and enterprise. The Mission's 'multi-super-specialty' hospital in Kochi, for instance, is the result of the enterprise, vision and expertise of an Indian doctor previously practising in the USA, who gave up his professional life in order to be able to participate more fully in the Mata's ashram. This doctor assumed charge of the hospital project in Kochi, and through several years' painstaking effort, used his knowledge of medicine and medical institutions to set up the Amrita Institute of Medical Science. Today it is one of the leading medical establishments in Kerala, equipped with the latest facilities for the diagnosis and treatment of a wide range of diseases, and employing a team of highly qualified and well paid doctors from India and abroad.

Similarly, the management and engineering institutes at Ettimadai, Tamil Nadu are the result of the efforts of a young engineer, also an ascetic disciple of the Mata, who, at the time of my fieldwork, had gone on to head this modern educational complex. With single-minded devotion, he worked to realize the Mata's vision of a 'model engineering college' that would excel in what the Mission refers to as 'value-based' education.[8] The computer institutes in Kerala and Tamil Nadu, likewise, are the result of the hard work and enterprise of a computer specialist with a doctorate in computer studies from Bombay's prestigious Indian Institute of Technology, who decided to devote his life to spiritual pursuit under the guidance of the Mata. Clearly *seva*, though it is often seen in the MAM as a kind of 'levelling' activity that erodes the individuality and autonomy of the spiritual aspirant, in fact offers considerable scope for nurturing his/her personal distinctiveness. It provides opportunities for realizing individual capabilities, and relies on the individual potential, enterprise, initiative, aptitude and talent of the Mata's ascetic disciples (Warrier 2003b).

It follows from all of this, that even though the Mata's ascetic disciples renounce their property, their family ties and their careers, in order to enter the Mata's fold as spiritual seekers, their spiritual seeking does not necessarily lead away from the modern material world. Instead their training as ascetics takes place in a modern setting where the acquisition and deployment of modern technical, organizational and managerial skills are seen as an asset rather than a stumbling block along the spiritual path. These individuals thus render their *seva* in a recognizably 'modern' context where subject specialism and expertise are valued. In the Mata's scheme of things, the high profile institutions set up by the Mission exemplify her ideal of a 'balanced' modernity where faith, love and selflessness occupy a crucial place in a modern, competitive and rational context. This ideal is further hoped to be realized in the personalities of her ascetic disciples who, by following the example set by the Mata, are expected to develop into 'spiritually mature' individuals, capable of negotiating the objective conditions of modernity in a 'balanced' way.

The path of the householder

Asceticism and austerity is not the path that the Mata's lay devotees choose to tread. They see themselves as householders with little or no interest in adopting a renouncer's way of life. Their immediate concern, they explain, is not to try and secure release from the cycle of births and deaths. That, they feel, would require an altogether other-worldly orientation for which they are not prepared.[9] Their immediate concerns are more simple – they need the guidance and protection of a guru who will help them tide over periods of crisis in their lives and guarantee them some measure of spiritual well-being. They strive for a peaceful and pleasant life in this world, where they can carry on their duties as householders, all the while informed by a consciousness of their guru's grace. The Mata knows and endorses her householder devotees' disinclination towards an ascetic and austere lifestyle. Whereas she expects rigorous discipline and abstinence from the initiates in the ashram, she addresses her householder devotees differently. To them she says:

> Children, this world is created by the Lord for you to enjoy. No spiritual or scriptural text has ever said that everyone should give up all kinds of worldly enjoyments and engage in constant remembrance of God. No one has said that everyone [should] live in ashrams and become *sannyasins* . . . there are people who can do it and who are determined to do it. Let them follow their path . . .

The Mata's spiritual recommendations are not compulsory for lay entrants to her fold, nor are they intended to be observed to the exclusion of spiritual practices that individuals may have picked up from other sources and found beneficial. Instead the Mata urges devotees to follow whatever practices 'work' best for them regardless of their particular origins. She insists that religion must respect variety in individual temperaments and inclinations and must cater to a variety of tastes and inclinations.

> Religion should be able to satisfy everyone equally without any distinction. Take for example a mother who has ten children with ten different characters. One may be a high-thinking spiritual person, another one a scientist. There might be an artist . . . among them, while another will be . . . doing physical labour. There may also be a rogue or a robber among the ten children. But the mother will consider all equally. While serving food she won't serve the scientist more and the rogue less. She will try to satisfy all equally . . . Children, likewise is true religion. Whatever may be the mental constitution or level of thinking of a person, true religion must be able to satisfy him fully . . . It [must] provide a means to all.[10]

Devotees rejoice in the knowledge that the Mata recognizes the variety in their individual needs, attitudes and preferences. Compared to the Mata's ascetic disciples, these lay devotees enjoy far greater freedom in matters of spiritual observance and ritual practice. Their religious observances are varied, and derive from the wide repertoire that they encounter in urban India's religious complex. These are people who visit Hindu temples, worship gods and goddesses in the Hindu pantheon, and celebrate popular Hindu festivals. Most homes have a family shrine where pictures and idols of different gods find a place, and where the family prays at least once a day. The religious practices of these individuals are, by their own admission, a mix of what they learnt, as children, from their parents and older family members, and what they observed outside of the family through interactions with friends and acquaintances. Often different styles and traditions come together in a remarkable collage, with a distinctly south Indian god like Murugan jostling for space in the family shrine alongside an icon of Vaishno Devi, the north Indian goddess[11] whose shrine is located in Jammu in the Himalayas. Individual family calendars of religious observances accommodate equally rituals and austerities (such as fasting on particular days of the Hindu calendar) that are distinctly region-specific, and others that have come to acquire a more pan-Indian flavour. Individuals and households thus choose from a wide spectrum of religious observances that cuts across geographical boundaries, and make selections that, more often than not, represent eclectic and trans-regional practices.

In many cases, devotees' religious beliefs and practices incorporate items they learnt from other gurus to whom they were previously, or are simultaneously, attached. Devotees particularly appreciate the Mata for not insisting that they discard other gurus' prescriptions when they enter her fold. On the contrary, she often encourages them to continue the meditation and ritual techniques, and especially the chanting of mantras, previously prescribed by other gurus, insisting that every individual should carry on with whatever observances prove most efficacious for him or her. Even after their entry into the Mata's fold, devotees continue to visit temples other than the Brahmasthanam, and attend public programmes conducted by other gurus. All this counts as meritorious activity, and the Mata is not averse to her devotees observing a variety of such practices.

In following the Mata's ritual and other prescriptions, devotees make selections from the range of ritual practices she recommends, and observe only those that suit their temperament and lifestyle. Thus, those who lead busy lives, and see these practices as too time consuming, often prefer to keep their ritual observance to a minimum. This is fully acceptable within the MAM's scheme of things and does not make the devotee any less proximate to the Mata than others who devote several hours every day to observing her ritual prescriptions. Several devotees choose not to engage in any spiritual practice at all, insisting that it is one's mental attitude of surrender to the Mata that really matters, and that these practices by themselves do not amount to much. As free choosers and independent agents working towards their own spiritual development then, devotees enjoy complete autonomy and freedom to engage with the Mata's spiritual recommendations in whatever manner they choose. I cite below the cases of three of the Mata's devotees I met during my fieldwork in Delhi to illustrate this point.

The first is Vasanthi, originally from Kerala, now employed as a lecturer in English literature at the University of Delhi. Vasanthi had been a devotee of the Mata for two years when I met her in late 1997. An articulate and lively individual in her fifties, she lives with her husband, a retired government official, and her son and daughter, in their early thirties, in a middle-class residential complex in east Delhi. The entire family is devoted to the Mata. The second is Nirmala, about the same age as Vasanthi, from the western Indian state of Rajasthan, where she spent much of her childhood and youth. After completing her schooling Nirmala did not go on to attend university but married an army officer and assumed the responsibilities of a housewife. She has travelled extensively throughout India, accompanying her husband wherever his army postings took him. She has two grown children and the entire family is now based in Delhi. The third is Kishore, the manager at a private firm in Delhi whom we encountered earlier in connection with his experience of the Divine Life Society in Rishikesh. Kishore lives with his wife and three young children – two daughters and a son – in a well-appointed bungalow in a relatively new industrial township, Noida, on the outskirts of Delhi. Kishore is originally from Punjab in north India, and claims to have been on the lookout for a guru (prior to meeting the Mata) through much of his adult life. Common to all three individuals is their devotion to, and faith in, Mata Amritanandamayi. However, despite this common guru-affiliation, as I shall demonstrate in the following discussion, the religious orientations of these individuals differ in some important respects.

The first notable difference lies in these devotees' respective attitudes towards spiritual striving itself. Vasanthi claims to have learnt, through her engagement with the Mata, the essence of *sanatana dharma* and the true meaning of spirituality as she had never understood it before. In Vasanthi's scheme of things, spiritual striving must lead the aspirant to a state of complete submission to the divine will and eventually, to ultimate 'identification' or 'merger' with the Mata, whom she perceives as the embodiment of supreme and transcendent truth.

> It took me a long time to come to terms with all this . . . She [the Mata] is not an 'other'. She is ourselves. She keeps saying, when you stand on the bank of a river you think there are two banks. Actually there are no two sides – they are the same. The banks are connected – the water of ignorance is rushing through – which makes you think there are two when actually there is only one. She and I, she and you, are one. The thing is, I can talk about it, but I haven't experienced it. And unless I experience it, I haven't got there. In my daily life I make the same mistakes repeatedly. I think I have to do this or that but actually I am not doing anything. She is doing everything for me. But that surrender hasn't come. It will take years and years . . . In my everyday life very often I forget that I am really her. The relation is like that between a drop of water and the ocean. She is the ocean, we are the drops of water. The drops belong to the ocean, but the drop is not the ocean. Only when it joins the ocean does it become the ocean. Until then we are still drops and we can dry up any minute. Yet we think so much of ourselves.

Vasanthi believes that personal endeavour is indispensable for attaining the spiritual goal. She therefore makes a conscious effort in her everyday life to overcome what she sees as the greatest stumbling block in her path towards spiritual attainment – her egotism and self-centredness. Vasanthi's spiritual striving has, as a result, led to a high degree of introspection and reflexivity on her part where she scrutinizes her every thought and action in the light of what she understands as the Mata's message, and tries constantly to purge herself of what she sees as the spiritually constraining and 'negative' aspects of her personality. Over time, Vasanthi claims to have perceived a spiritual transformation in herself marked by a gradual detachment from material concerns and a growing sense of inner peace and calm.

Nirmala, unlike Vasanthi, believes that householders must not consciously undertake to engage in a spiritual quest of any kind. Her attachment to the guru, she claims, has little to do with personal striving for spiritual attainment. Instead, she looks to the guru for the strength she needs to cope with her everyday troubles. Without a guru, Nirmala said, one is like a 'rudderless raft' with no sense of direction and purpose. The presence of the Mata as a guru in her life, she claims, serves to enhance her 'consciousness of the Almighty'. If this consciousness is forever present in one's mind, and if one nurtures it through daily ritual practice, Nirmala believes the result must be a lessening of one's daily troubles and pain. 'If you have to go through some unpleasantness in this life,' she says, 'you do have to suffer it, but if you have the protection of the guru, the suffering is less.' By sustaining her devotion to the Mata, and keeping up her daily spiritual practices, she hopes she can secure her own and her family's well-being in this world.

In Kishore's view personal spiritual striving is, in the ultimate reckoning, futile. The more one gains spiritually, he believes, the more one is likely to pride oneself on one's gain and the more elusive the spiritual goal becomes. The closer one gets to the spiritual goal, he said, the greater one's chances of slipping and crashing spiritually. Beyond a point, the guru's help is indispensable. He used the analogy of a game of snakes and ladders (a popular board game in urban India) to explain his point.

> One's efforts at attaining *moksha* [spiritual salvation] are like a game of snakes and ladders. Go up a ladder, go down a snake. The higher up one goes, the longer the snakes and the greater the descent. Through one's own efforts one can go as far as the ninety-fifth square. But after that, to get to the goal, the hundredth square, without slipping, is the toughest proposition. That is where the guru can help. Prayers to the guru are the only way. The guru can then bear you across the sea of snakes.

It would appear that Vasanthi and Kishore are agreed on their ultimate spiritual goal – that of attaining *moksha* – but differ in their views on how this goal is to be achieved. Vasanthi relies on personal striving and individual initiative in actively seeking this goal. Kishore on the other hand relies entirely on the guru's grace and prefers to wait passively for the guru to intervene on his behalf. Unlike both Vasanthi and Kishore, Nirmala chooses not to concern herself with questions of spiritual attainment and focuses instead on immediate, this-worldly benefit alone.

Just as these devotees differ in the significance they attach to spiritual attainment and striving, they differ also in their attitude towards ritual. Vasanthi's mother had been a devout observer of daily pujas at the family shrine in her parents' home in Kerala. Vasanthi, however, had rebelled against this observance because she was barred from entering the shrine during her monthly menstrual periods.[12] This was a rule she had found unjust and discriminating, and she had developed an early distaste for all forms of puja. After entering the Mata's fold, she began to observe some of the Mata's ritual prescriptions in the belief that these would enhance her spiritual progress. She now sets aside time every day to engage in the meditational practices recommended by the Mata, and to chant her mantra as well as the Lalitha Sahasranama. When I asked her about the significance she attaches to these devotional chants, she explained to me her belief in the importance of sound.

> When certain vowels and consonants are mixed together in a certain manner, there is a certain impact. When you speak in an angry manner, there are angry vibrations, the whole atmosphere vibrates with your anger. I think that the Sahasranama [the many names of the chosen deity], if chanted correctly, does the opposite – it soothes the mind and calms the atmosphere.[13]

Vasanthi believes that ever since she started her daily practice of chanting the Lalitha Sahasranama, her temper, which, she said, was earlier extremely volatile, has cooled.

Apart from daily meditation and chanting, the only other spiritual practice in which Vasanthi engages is *bhajan* singing. Every evening the family holds a *bhajan* session in their home which neighbours are welcome to attend. The participants, numbering about ten or less, sing devotional songs before a photograph of the Mata. According to Vasanthi, she and the other members of her family have neither the time, nor the inclination, for other kinds of ritual engagements. When I met her, Vasanthi had never performed the *grahadosha shanti* pujas of the MAM, and did not think she would do so in the foreseeable future. She did not attach much significance to astrological calculations and predictions. Her early unease with puja continues to the present, and she prefers not to observe the puja ritual prescribed by the Mata. As a rule she does not worship at temples.

In contrast to Vasanthi, Nirmala claims she cannot do without her puja even for a single day. In her bedroom in her flat in Delhi she has a small shrine where she observes daily pujas before a collection of icons of various gods and goddesses. Among the several paintings, posters and idols of Hindu deities crowding the shrine are photographs both of the Mata and of an earlier guru, now deceased. Apart from her daily puja, Nirmala regularly engages in meditation, using a technique prescribed by her previous guru, and practices *nama japa* and *mantra japa* every day. She feels these practices fortify her internally and give her strength. Nirmala also greatly enjoys visiting temples, shrines and other sacred spots. She has had several opportunities to visit pilgrimage centres and temple shrines across the length and breadth of the country while accompanying her husband on his postings in different parts of India.

When I met her, Nirmala had already performed thrice, in three consecutive years, the *grahadosha shanti* puja organized by the MAM to counter evil planetary influences. She had been told by an astrologer that her life at the time was clouded by the malefic influence of Shani (Saturn), and that her husband had a 'weak Jupiter'. She said she feared the havoc these planets might wreak in her life, and was particularly anxious about her husband's health, since he had only recently recovered from a major kidney complaint. Nirmala had sought the Mata's divine intervention at the time, and it was only the Mata's grace, she felt, and the benefits deriving from her participation in the congregational pujas, that had seen her through the crisis. Apart from her regular prayers to the Mata and the other deities in her household shrine, Nirmala also visits a temple dedicated to the monkey god, Hanuman, situated very near her house. This ritual is of vital importance to Nirmala, for she hopes that offering prayers at the Hanuman temple too might help counter the malefic influences of Saturn in her horoscope.[14]

In the matter of rituals and their observance, Kishore appeared more circumspect than both Vasanthi and Nirmala. 'Ritual', he said, 'is one thing I don't know. I am a total failure at ritual technique.' Right from his early teens, he said, he had been practising his own style of puja. At first this simply meant lighting a lamp at the family shrine twice every day. Sometimes he read from ancient texts such as the *Ramayana* to augment his ritual observance. None of this, he said, had changed even after he entered the Mata's fold. He had received a mantra from the Mata, which he chanted morning and evening when he lit the lamp at the household shrine. 'I suppose rituals are important', Kishore said, 'but I tell you, it is Amma who is most important. No ritual, nothing is required – if you have Amma you have everything. The only thing is, people use this route [ritual practice] to reach Amma's feet. If we take directly to Amma's feet and surrender to her wholeheartedly, none of this, no ritual, no puja, is required.

What is striking in these accounts is the evident diversity in devotees' religious orientations and practices. Different devotees attach different meanings to their ritual and spiritual observances, and thus negotiate their guru attachment differently. Yet, common to all these diverse orientations and practices is a shared idealization of the guru as a divine presence in their lives. Devotees also share a common understanding of the idealized guru–devotee relationship, conceived in terms of the devotee's personal 'surrender' to the guru. Surrender is conceptualized in terms of overcoming one's egocentrism, such that the devotee then becomes infinitely receptive to the guru's 'divine' love.

Seva as spiritual practice

Just as with ritual observance, in the matter of rendering *seva* too, the Mata allows devotees complete flexibility, freedom and choice. No one form of *seva* is considered more meritorious than another, and no *seva* is evaluated in terms of the kind of work done. Devotees believe that the Mata treats all kinds of service equally, the only consideration being that the service should be rendered with utter devotion, humility, dedication and commitment. *Seva* rendered with the expectation of tangible rewards, or with a sense of pride and achievement in the tasks performed, is no *seva*.

The Mata actively encourages the participation not just of her renouncer disciples, but also of her householder devotees, in the MAM's humanitarian activities. Their contributions have been indispensable to the growth and expansion of the Mission. Lay devotees usually render their services at the local ashram branch, where they come together to organize blood donation camps, mobilize food and clothes distribution schemes for the poor, or set up local educational and charitable ventures, such as schools, hospices and orphanages,[15] all under the initiative and supervision of the resident *brahmachari*. Besides this, they attend to numerous administrative and organizational tasks at the branch office, all of which count as *seva*. Some *seva* efforts are sustained over long stretches of time. For instance, the initial plan to construct a building to house the local ashram branch requires concerted and collective effort on the part of a team of committed devotees who work together to raise funds, purchase land, publicize the effort to encourage greater lay participation, liaise with the authorities at the Kerala headquarters, and receive government sanction for the proposed institution.

My fieldwork at the ashram branch in Delhi revealed how modes of *seva* for the local devotees differ widely according to the individual's age, personal commitments, hours of employ in the work place, family composition, personal energy and drive, health and income level. Thus, younger people engaged in full-time employment and with young children to tend at home, do not often spend more than a few hours every weekend on *seva*. Older people, with fewer family commitments, retired from active service, and leading otherwise unhurried lives, often volunteer longer hours of service according to their personal inclinations and aptitudes.

A journalist in his late forties whom I interviewed in Delhi said that his *seva* consisted of a few hours spent every week with the young children at the orphanage attached to the local ashram branch. This journalist lived with his family in a housing complex an hour's drive from the branch. He explained how geographical distance and the pressures of work prevented him from devoting more hours to service at the orphanage. Every Sunday, however, he made it a point to drive to the orphanage where he helped the children with their schoolwork, introduced them to new sport and leisure activities, and often treated them to sweets and savouries that his wife prepared at home. He often visited the ashram branch with his family, and encouraged his two young sons to participate in the local *seva* effort.

Another devotee, a middle-aged housewife, spent far more time in the local ashram branch than the journalist. At the ashram, she spent long hours in the reception room, attending to phone calls and receiving visitors. For her this *seva* was a welcome means of filling up long empty hours each day. This devotee often resided at the ashram for several days at a time in order to avoid the trouble of commuting daily. A third devotee, an elderly woman retired from service as a translator at a language centre in the city, was actively engaged in the affairs of the local Amrita Vidyalaya, one in a chain of MAM schools now operating in more than twenty centres across India. When I interviewed her, the Delhi school had classes only at the primary level, and she and one or two other women were serving as kindergarten teachers for the school's handful of students. Her husband, also a devotee of the Mata, helped with the publication of the Hindi edition of the *Matruvani* printed and published from Delhi.

All these varied activities constitute *seva* in the Mata Amritanandamayi Mission. Much of this *seva* is sporadic and negotiated on a day-to-day basis by devotees according to changing work schedules and personal commitments. The options cover a wide range, and most devotees succeed in finding something suited to their needs, dispositions and constraints. The Mata's middle class devotees are keenly motivated to engage in *seva* activities within the MAM, seeing this as spiritually meritorious activity that must contribute towards cultivating a balanced modern self. Given their position of relative advantage in Indian society, they also have at their disposal the kind of resources (educational qualifications and professional skills, social influence and connections, and indeed material wealth which the more well-off often donate generously to the Mata) required by the MAM. Much of this *seva* is of course directed at the glorification of the guru, and the promotion and propagation of her Mission. The *seva* ethic clearly plays a very important practical function within the MAM, securing the enthusiastic participation of its followers in its institution building and promotional activities, and working as a self-propelling force within the MAM, ensuring its continued growth and expansion (Warrier 2003b).

Signs of spiritual maturation

Devotees claim that the most tangible benefit from their entry into the Mata's fold is that their ritual observances are imbued with greater meaning. Whereas formerly many followed ritual practices blindly without giving too much thought to why they did the things they did, they now locate the significance of their practices within the frames of reference provided by the Mata's teachings. They identify their problems and sorrows as directly related to the conditions of modern day existence, and seek solutions by dedicating their efforts to reviving love, faith and compassion in their everyday lives. Their efforts are directed at attaining a 'balanced' engagement with the conditions of the modern world. The benefits they look for are both immediate and long-term; they look for a lessening of their suffering in their immediate lives, and in the long term they hope to achieve spiritual growth through the curbing of their acquisitiveness, egotism and selfishness.

Not all devotees of the Mata, as I noted earlier, are interested in 'growing spiritually' through their attachment to the guru. Those who are, look out for indications of personal spiritual development under the guru's guidance. Some, like Vasanthi, assume responsibility for their own spiritual growth. Others, like Kishore, see all personal striving as futile, and look to the guru for bringing about the desired change. In either case, when devotees do notice signs of change themselves, they prefer not to take credit for the change, but attribute it instead to the Mata's love and grace. This is a sign that their guru-attachment is working, and that it is yielding the desired results.

The spiritual change which the Mata effects in them, devotees claim, is not sudden and dramatic, but follows a slow, gradual course. The changes are effected 'subtly', and devotees subject themselves to close scrutiny to see where and how they might have changed. There are certain crucial indices by which devotees can measure their own and others' spiritual progress. The most important of these, predictably, is a growing disenchantment with consumerism. Devotees are always keen to detect in themselves a spontaneous move away from a consumerist lifestyle. This, for them, is a clear indication of 'detachment' from the material and the worldly. For Vasanthi, for instance, this shift was evident in her dwindling interest in clothing matters.

> It would be very difficult to say I am totally detached [from the material world]. I couldn't be because then I would have been with her [with the Mata as a renunciate in her ashram]. But I think I am getting partially detached slowly. I am no longer

interested in new saris. Earlier, reopening time for college meant that whether or not I already had saris, I would buy new ones. And all kinds of exclusive things. Now I have no desire for that kind of buying.

Another indication of the change in her personality and her gradual spiritual awakening, according to Vasanthi, was her increasing ability to control her otherwise highly volatile temper.

> Some of things she [the Mata] does – if I tell you what happened to me – they are such personal experiences that you will think it is nothing. Like in the case of my mother. She was in Kerala. There was nobody to look after her, so we decided to bring her here. For some reason, my mother forgot I was her daughter and began to see my husband as her son. I came to be at the receiving end of her constant cribbing and criticism. I would get angry. I tried to control my temper. For one thing, I have high blood pressure. It only worsens if I shout in anger. For another, it isn't correct on my part to shout at my aged mother. She may say whatever she has to, but I must learn to keep quiet. I believe you can't change another person, you must try to change yourself. I used to try very hard to control myself but it was impossible. But after meeting Amma, she had such a soothing influence on me that now my mother may say whatever she pleases, but I just don't get angry any more. I have changed my attitude towards her. She is just the same, but I don't get upset any more.

Vasanthi noticed similar changes in her son, who too was an ardent devotee of the Mata.

> My son was very materialistic. His one great ambition was to earn enough to take us to a five-star hotel and have us eat whatever we wanted. We are not very rich. We don't have wads of notes to throw around. My husband is a government servant, I am a college lecturer . . . Somehow he had this idea in his mind. Now he says he just wants to earn enough to be able to get the sick animals on the road treated. His attitude towards life has changed completely.

Another devotee spoke of the changes she had noticed not just within her but with respect to an entire group of devotees in her locality.

Over the years the core group has ceased to socialize at all. It has happened automatically. It wasn't even a conscious decision. People normally go out, go for dinner, go to restaurants. We don't do that. All of us have somehow just stopped doing things we would normally do. Like watching television. I read about Amma saying that television isn't a good habit. She calls it tele-*visham* [Malayalam for poison]. Right from that day I never watched TV. It is two or three years now, I have not watched TV. The only thing I do watch is Amma's videos. Or videos on any spiritual subject. TV I have stopped totally. If it is on at home I just walk out. Simply because I know the subtle influence it has. If you are not interested and you watch, the next day you watch again. It is very, very subtle. So I understand what Amma says – what a *visham* it is. A lot of us have given up a lot of things after coming in contact with Amma, since knowing that they are not good for us.

Others spoke about a shift away from non-vegetarian food, alcohol and cigarettes. They described this shift not as the result of any conscious decision but as a natural change that gradually came over them once they began to feel the Mata's influence in their lives. Parents spoke gratefully about the transformation in their children which they themselves had been unable to effect but which Amma's grace had brought about naturally. Kishore, who, as I mentioned earlier, is a father of three, described it thus:

Before the *bhajans* [audio-cassette recordings of *bhajan* renderings by the Mata and her disciples] came to our house, it was pop music only. Nothing except pop music. Now that the *bhajans* have come, every morning we play *bhajans* in our house. Now there is more of *bhajans* and less of pop music. Now there is a balance. One important thing is – these children were growing up. In today's circumstances it is impossible for us to convince them about anything. They have minds of their own and a wide exposure outside the home. Look what Amma did. Without our even knowing it she was moulding them. They now know what exists in the material world but they also know what the Sahasranama is. Amma could convince them where we might have failed . . .

So we find that where we cannot convince the children about certain things, Amma in her own way is convincing them. I am finding a change in my children for the better. We were very

98

worried at one time. Now we find them getting better and better. That is one big contribution of Amma. Our family has now got one axis – Amma – that is very important for us. Earlier we did not have that axis. I was thinking in one direction, my wife in another, the children remained unconvinced about a lot of the things we believed in . . . Everybody had his or her own thoughts and ideas. Now too we have our own ways but there is one axis that brings us together.

One of the three children, a school-going daughter in her early teens, had at first been disinclined to follow the rest of the family in their devotion to the Mata. The father had not attempted any persuasion.

A year back she [the daughter] had, you know, friends in school and all, she struck off on her own, and displayed no interest in Amma. I said to her, you know, *beta* [child], we are not going to force you. We are not even going to ask you to come and pray with us. Forcing is not our way. But I will always say, keep your eyes open. See Amma. If you get convinced, come to Amma, if not, it is up to you. And now I find this same child, who a year back was so defiant, is more flexible now. She herself comes for the family puja, sings *bhajans* sometimes, and now I laugh at her sometimes and say, what happened? How can we change our children, how can we convince them? It is Amma who does everything, it is her grace that changes things.

In all these accounts, what we see is devotees' attempts at negotiating a new selfhood through small, but for them significant, changes in their personalities and lifestyles, which they invariably attribute to the Mata's intervention in their lives. Underlying this process of (perceived) change is of course a shared understanding of modernity and its 'imbalances' as postulated by the Mata. This collective understanding facilitates the negotiation of a new selfhood in three crucial ways. First, it provides devotees with a means of explaining their suffering and sorrow in terms of the imbalances and depletions caused by a skewed engagement with the conditions of modernity. Second, it sets out a *telos*, or a sense of a long-term goal and purpose in devotees' lives. They are now concerned with reviving the 'depleted' aspects of their personalities, and restoring a sense of 'balance' to their modern selves, through attachment to this guru.

Third, devotees are assured of achieving their desired goal without undergoing any radical upheaval in their lives. For the urban professional devotees of Mata Amritanandamayi, many of whom define their self-hood and social status in terms of consumption patterns and educational and career achievements, the Mata's spirituality is particularly attractive because she does not make demands for drastic alterations in their lifestyles and consumption patterns. Instead, as a guru whose mission is to effect a spiritual transformation in her devotees and thereby lessen their worldly suffering, she absolves the latter of all responsibility in this regard. Devotees, in this scheme of things, do not actively bring about their own spiritual growth, even though they may make sincere efforts towards this end. Instead the changes happen as a result of the spiritual awakening that the Mata subtly and gradually effects in their individual personalities. When they notice these changes taking place, devotees know that their guru attachment is proving to be effective.

This tendency not to see any perceived progress towards a spiritual goal as the result of individual effort translates equally into a plea of helplessness where such progress is perceived to be lacking. Individuals are quick to describe themselves as spiritually 'immature' when they do not see the desired changes taking place. This is not so much a self-deprecatory stance as one of implicit faith in the Mata and security in the knowledge that she will bring about the necessary change when she feels the time is right. This complete relinquishing of all personal responsibility and agency, a point I shall return to in the next chapter, releases devotees from the burden of having to effect their own spiritual transformation through a radical change in lifestyle or a conscious effort at curbing their consumerist inclinations. As Swallow (1982: 157) observes in connection with Sai Baba, in the case of Mata Amritanandamayi too, what she offers her devotees is the traditional *bhakti* resolution to their problems: the chance of salvation while continuing to carry out their worldly duties, if they offer her their unstinting devotion.

Interestingly, what starts out for most devotees as an emotional upheaval when they first experience the Mata's embrace, gets transformed, they claim, into a state of peace and calm as they undergo gradual spiritual transformation under the guru's guidance. One devotee, describing the sense of peace he had attained after entering the Mata's fold, said, 'Now I am just like a calm river flowing into the ocean'. Another devotee used a particularly evocative analogy (and one that reflects his keen product awareness as a modern consumer) to describe the transformation he underwent after entering the Mata's fold. He described himself as having 'learnt to absorb things', much like a good motorcar on rough roads.

A good vehicle, you know, is one that does not bounce too much when it is travelling on the road. That is why there is so much difference between an Ambassador car and a Mercedes Benz. You can easily drink a cup of coffee in a Benz but you can't do that in an Ambassador. The Benz's absorbing capacity is much better. In a similar way, with Amma's love guiding you along life's difficult and rough patches, your journey becomes cushioned and you are able to absorb all things.

Conclusion

The last chapter argued that individuals exercise considerable freedom in selecting their guru(s) from a vast and diverse range of available choices. In this chapter I have gone on to demonstrate how, even after entering the fold of a guru like Mata Amritanandamayi, her devotees and disciples continue to exercise freedom in negotiating their guru-attachment in diverse ways. Rather than conform to a narrowly defined set of religious codes, they are free to make selections from within (and beyond) the Mata's repertoire of ritual and spiritual recommendations, thus constructing highly unique and personalized forms of spiritual life in accordance with individual needs, tastes and preferences. The 'Hindu' selfhood of these individuals is clearly flexible and revisable – predicated largely upon the choices they make while negotiating the religious and spiritual aspects of their lives. As devotees of the Mata, they are concerned with revising their selfhood such as to enable a more 'balanced' engagement with modernity as advocated by the Mata. Their religious selfhood, besides, is not seen to be incompatible with modernity. On the contrary, these persons see themselves as self-consciously 'modern'. The Mata, as I argued in Chapter 3, represents, in devotees' perceptions, a 'modern' face of spirituality, and their attachment to the Mata is, in their view, very much in keeping with their modern orien-tations and world-views.

An important aspect of this modern faith is its emphasis on the indi-vidual devotee rather than on the larger group or community of adherents. Indeed any such notion of an 'imagined community' or of 'group identity' is virtually non-existent in the Mata Amritanandamayi Mission. The cornerstone upon which this faith is based is the crucial and intimate bond that devotees seek to establish with the guru (the central theme of the following chapter); ties between devotees tend, in comparison, to pale into insignificance.

6

EXPERIENCING DIVINE LOVE

I have argued in Chapters 4 and 5 above that devotees' attachment to Mata Amritanandamayi is largely a matter of personal freedom and choice. First, they are free to select the Mata, from among a vast array of spiritual leaders, as their chosen guru. Second, they are free to select, from the MAM's religious and spiritual repertoire, those practices and orientations that best suit their temperaments and lifestyles. Third, as I shall demonstrate in this chapter, devotees also exercise considerable freedom in deciding how long they might want to sustain this guru-attachment. Devotees choose to remain attached to the Mata so long as her mode of spirituality 'works' for them. How then is the effectiveness of their guru-attachment gauged? When does devotion to the Mata cease to satisfy, making it necessary to seek other sources of spiritual gratification?

The most crucial factor sustaining their devotion to the Mata is confirmation of her love and protection in their everyday lives. By this I mean not love in an abstract, generalized sense, but love which is personalized, which is intimated through various signs which devotees claim to recognize, and which carries with it the much-needed reassurance that the Mata is protecting and guiding them individually, at every step along their life's journey. It is this one-to-one bond of love and intimacy between guru and each individual devotee that sustains followers' faith in the Mata. When confirmation of her love is not forthcoming, and the guru–devotee bond weakens, devotees may consider the option of seeking out alternative ways of satisfying their needs.

Devotees refer to intimations of the Mata's love and protection as their 'experiences'. 'Experience' is a key word among devotees of the Mata and constitutes the mainstay of their devotion to her. Their faith in the Mata, they often emphatically assert, is based not on 'belief' but on experience. In this chapter I explore this key term, 'experience', examining, most importantly, the performative or illocutionary aspect of certain kinds of experience. The main source of my information about the 'experiences' of the Mata's devotees are their narratives. These narratives may in turn be seen as an indispensable part of the process of experiencing itself. As Turner (1982: 18) rightly points out, an experience is incomplete until 'meaning' is ascribed to the events and parts of the experience through an act of creative retrospection. 'Thus experience is both "living through" and "thinking back". It is also "willing or wishing forward", i.e., establishing goals and models for future experience in which, hopefully, the errors and perils of past experience will be avoided or eliminated' (ibid.). The narratives which I will examine can thus be seen as 'restored' experience, that moment in the experiential process in which meaning emerges through 'reliving' the original experience. The narration of the experience serves as a 'regularizing process' through which the fluidity and indeterminacy of lived experience gets transformed into organized and systematic form, and the narrative becomes 'a piece of communicable wisdom' which assists the narrator and others in better understanding what was experienced in the first instance.

In drawing attention to the 'performative' aspect of experience, therefore, I refer to the process by which experience is brought about and consummated through narrative. In the narration, experience is not only shaped, but also something new may be generated. The narrative transforms the experience itself and in that process, provides unprecedented insights, even generates new symbols and meanings, which may be incorporated into subsequent experiences. Narration in this sense is an illocutionary act, which does not merely *say* something, but which, more importantly *does* something – it is part of the *doing* of an action. It brings about a change of state, does something effective. The narration of experiences on the part of my informants, I argue here, effects a process by which they come to conceptualize and construct a new sense of self *as* devotees of the Mata.

Proxy control

The experience narratives of devotees are based on the metaphor of the embrace, and appear to revive the very sensations that devotees claim they 'experienced' in the moment that the Mata first held them in her arms. Their descriptions of the initial embrace dwell on three central themes which are repeated in most accounts. First, the embrace marks a moment completely removed from the realm of the known and familiar. Devotees suddenly find themselves in a new and strange situation, which induces in them reactions hitherto unknown and alien to them. They find that, for no apparent reason, they have lost control over themselves, and they weep and sob inexplicably in the arms of the Mata. Second, even as they weep, they become aware of immeasurable joy and overwhelming relief in the knowledge that they have reached a safe haven, a sanctuary where they are confident of protection and love. This experience of security and reassurance in the Mata's arms leads to a renewed sense of control and certainty. Finally, the embrace establishes a personal one-to-one bond between the self and the Mata. This is not a state of 'communitas' (Turner 1969: 138) where, in the midst of a thronging crowd, individuals undergo 'a transformative experience that goes to the roots of each person's being and finds in that root something profoundly communal and shared'. Rather than an affirmation of one's status as a social being, where one experiences society as a 'seamless and structureless whole' (ibid.: 127), what devotees experience in the Mata's arms is something wholly personal and individual. For devotees, it marks a unique moment of communion between the Mata and the individual self when, for a brief instant, the devotee remains conscious only of the Mata's protecting presence, and the rest of the world blurs into insignificance. The sensations awakened during the embrace, like the embrace itself, are momentary. No sooner do they appear, than they disappear. Yet, in that brief moment, they expose devotees to something that they perceive as sublime and divine, and completely out of the ordinary.

Subsequent narratives of devotees' 'miracle experiences' dwell on similar themes. These are mostly narratives of episodes in their lives when the Mata 'miraculously' saved them from imminent danger or when her protecting presence helped them tide over situations of crisis. At times of crisis, devotees find themselves in unfamiliar and troubling situations. Even as they struggle to cope, they suddenly become aware of the Mata's enveloping love. This knowledge and the Mata's loving intervention then helps them tide over the crisis. Their knowledge of the Mata's love is reinforced, and their faith in the Mata is thereby renewed. All such 'experience' narratives make a crucial contribution towards creating and sustaining a vibrant collective imagination linking Mata Amritanandamayi's devotees across the world in common adoration of the guru.

Because this 'experiencing' is not a collective, but an extremely personal and individual exercise, devotees are usually keen to share their experiences with others. Most devotees record their experiences in their personal diaries, read them often to refresh their memories, and share these with fellow devotees either when they meet up at the local branch or when they visit the Mata's ashram in Kerala. Several of the books published by the Mission carry personal narratives of such experiences, and its newsletters and journals invariably carry accounts of miracle experiences sent in by devotees scattered across the globe. The narration of these experiences is an important means by which devotees reaffirm their faith in the Mata and establish repeatedly that they are graced by her constant love and presence in their lives. It is also an important means by which newcomers get socialized into the devotionalist patterns within the Mission, and become acquainted with the ways in which they are expected to 'experience' the guru's love and glory.

Below, I reproduce two such experience narratives. The first of these is based on a typescript given to me by the narrator, a Tamilian settled in England. It had previously appeared in a local newsletter, *Friends of Amma*, produced by, and circulated among, Mata Amritanandamayi devotees in the UK.

> As I approached the motorway there were no street lights and the three lanes narrowed to one lane because of the roadworks. Suddenly the car began to slow down, the lights dimmed and the battery warning light came on. I still had 70 miles to go, and because of my back problem I knew I wouldn't be able to push the car to a safe place. A line of cars followed me at 60 mph. The car started missing, and I realized that it would not be visible as the front and rear lights had failed. I yelled in terror: 'Amma, without your help I cannot do anything in this situation!' No sooner had I cried out than a bright blinding flash of light shot up from the dashboard and the head lamps and interior lights came on. The lights were as bright as a new car's. The battery warning light remained on, however, and the alternator was not charging the battery at all. I was filled with a strong self-confidence which I never had before, because I knew Amma was with me. Normally I would have stopped at the next service station and fixed the fault before driving on. This time it did not occur to me to stop, and I drove the 70 miles home without any fear or problems. I was filled with happiness as I pulled up in front of my house at 11 p.m. and turned off the ignition. A second later, I anxiously turned it back on to discover there was no power at all. I believe with all my heart that this was an example of Amma's many miracles and that at desperate times She will be there to help her children.

The second, narrated by a medical doctor at a hospital in Kerala, appeared in the English edition of the *Matruvani* as part of a series entitled 'Amma in My Life'.[1] In this narrative, interestingly, it is the Mata who first warns the narrator of the crisis awaiting him, and subsequently it is through her intervention that he is able to tide over the crisis.

During one of Her *darshans* Amma felt my hands and said, 'Son, you have a physical problem that you need to look into'. As a person who had pride, and to an extent, vanity, about his health, this came as a rude shock to me . . . However, as Amma had warned me, I underwent medical tests, and all of them turned out to be negative. During the next *darshan* I brought [this to] Amma's attention. With no pause or hesitation, Amma told me to seek the aid of a specialist friend of mine. Going through all the tests and my physical, he said that though there was nothing positive, it was worthwhile to undergo a stress test with a tread mill . . . Within two minutes of the test . . . I could see the patterns of strain in my heart beat when it had been subjected to stress . . . I did not get time to think about the gravity of the situation as I was overpowered by reverence and joy. Reverence for Amma the supreme force, who foresaw the problem long before anybody else, and joy for the thought that at last I have a guardian angel who could show me the way and take care of me. [Soon after] I had an angiography that revealed major blocks in my main vessels. [A day was fixed] for the bypass surgery.

. . . prior to [the surgery] . . . Amma called me and gave Her blessings. She asked me whether I was frightened of the ensuing operation. I said 'not much' but confessed that I was terribly frightened of the post operative days. Having had exposure in this field I was aware of all the hardships a patient has to undergo, so many tubes, artificial respiration, injections and above all the severe pain that may last for days. Amma heard in detail all that I described and finally said, 'Don't worry, everything will be fine' . . .

The following morning when I was wheeled to the theatre I felt no tension and my mind was at peace. Though the atmosphere in the operation room was familiar to me, it was the courage Amma had instilled that helped me to be tranquil . . . I had visions of Amma from the time I was sedated. Amma appeared in all her splendour and gaiety . . . There were never-ending visions of Amma, one superimposing on another [sic] . . . This delight was broken when the nurse woke me up asking whether I wished to have a drink. To my astonishment I found that I had surpassed [sic] the exacting and onerous post-operative period. All the tubes had been removed, the support systems were not needed . . . For thirty-six long hours I had had the most divine visions and Amma had seen to it that I was spared the agony of fearful post-operative period . . .

By the time the sweet effect of Amma's vision started waning I was fit to go home. Amma, besides seeing me safely through the journey, had given me a state of ecstasy during those thirty-six hours. A few weeks later when I came to Amritapuri, I had mixed emotions of joy, pride and respect which I wished to express, but when Amma came near me all I could do was kneel before her, grasp her firmly and cry out loud. From that day onwards not a single week has passed without Amma's counsel even for trivial problems of my health.

The metaphor of the embrace with its assurance of protection and security in the Mata's arms, which is so crucial to the Mata–devotee relationship, thus comes to be repeated in devotees' lives whenever they find themselves in trouble and distress. Devotees' narratives of their experiences reveal a tendency on their part to retreat into a state of 'proxy control', a condition which Bandura, as quoted in Madsen and Snow (1991: 14), describes in the following terms:

People are not averse to relinquishing control over events that affect their lives in order to free themselves of the performance demands and hazards that the exercise of control entails. Rather than seeking personal control, they seek security in proxy control – wherein they can exert some influence over those who wield influence and power. Part of the price of proxy control is restriction of one's own efficacy and a vulnerable security that rests on the competencies and favors of others . . . The dependent ones enjoy the protective benefits without the performance demands and attendant stresses.

Madsen and Snow, who use this concept to explicate the phenomenon of charisma, see the acceptance of proxy control as a psychologically self-preserving strategy that goes to the very heart of the charismatic bond. In this process, they explain, those in despair restore their own sense of coping ability by linking themselves to a dominant and seemingly effective figure – a leader who seems to be acting in their behalf, but also seems to be not beyond their sphere of influence, if only because that leader is 'known' to be devoted to their interests and therefore reachable through petition and supplication. Commenting on the emotional aspect of the charismatic bond, Madsen and Snow (ibid.: 15) further note that:

In any event, because it is profoundly relieving, such bonding is accompanied by very strong positive emotion – the crucial feature of charisma. It is important to note that this relief from stress and fear is itself a reinforcer of commitment. Although the initial belief in the leader surely must be inspired by at least some hint of a real ability to deal with the followers' problems, once faith is in place the relief it brings with it makes that faith itself something of great positive value, something to be held onto and conserved.

What is truly paradoxical about the entire process of securing proxy control (as Madsen and Snow point out), is the idea that only by yielding personal control is a sense of control retained, and only by accepting a leader's understanding of events is a sense of personal understanding restored. Yielding control to the Mata clearly provides devotees with a sense of security and protection. Through their belief in the Mata's powers of wish-fulfilment and miracle-working, and their faith in her divine blessings and guidance, devotees are able to negotiate the everyday uncertainties and anxieties of their fast-paced urban lives.

This relinquishing of control to the Mata leads to devotees' growing dependence on her. When in crisis, they seek her help. When confronted with the uncertainty of choice, they seek her advice and counsel. One devotee, for instance, narrated his experience of seeking the Mata's guidance on a problem which vexed him no end. His daughter, a science graduate from the prestigious Indian Institute of Technology in Chennai (Madras), had just secured admission to a PhD programme at a university in the USA. The father was loath to send her away because he feared that she would be unhappy away from the protective environment at home. He was also afraid he would 'lose' her to the alien values and lifestyle of the West. The daughter on the other hand was keen to study abroad and was insistent that she should be allowed to go. The father, torn between his own wishes and those of his daughter, approached the Mata for guidance. The Mata's advice to him was to allow the daughter to pursue her studies abroad. She assured him that this was the best course of action both for him and the daughter. The father complied, his anxieties now alleviated. He knew he was doing the 'right' thing because the Mata had said so. When I met this devotee, his daughter had already been away from home for several years, and he proudly told me of her academic success in the USA. He was now on the lookout for a marriage partner for her and hoped that, with the blessings of the Mata, he would soon be able to find a suitable groom for her. Another devotee described how he was unhappy in his job as a software expert in a computer firm and was keen to start an independent consultancy, but was anxious about the outcome of such a move. He approached the Mata for advice. She replied promptly that the consultancy was a bad idea and that he should put off this move until some years later by which time he would have more experience and skills to support his new venture. The devotee acted accordingly and was now biding his time in the same software company. He knew he would receive some sign from the Mata as and when she felt he was ready to take the plunge.

Reason and experience – an integrated approach

The significance of devotees' 'experiences' must be understood in the context of their familiarity with the realm of scientific rationality, an indispensable aspect of modern life which necessitates a complex cognitive stance vis-à-vis their faith in the Mata's supernatural powers. A strikingly high proportion of the Mata's devotees, as I noted earlier, are academics, scientists, medical doctors, engineers, software personnel and people employed in the finance and business sectors, whose careers are built around knowledge systems governed by the principles of science and logic. These devotees routinely engage with a world of science and rationality which they see as an indispensable part of their lives. They represent what Babb (1987: 177) describes as a 'living and extremely influential subculture' of urban India in which the scientific outlook is 'well understood and held in high esteem'. This outlook challenges the religious ease with which these individuals might assert their faith in the guru's supernatural powers. Their belief in her divine omnipotence requires 'a leap across an incredulity' (ibid.) that is burdensome though desirable for most devotees, and demands of them a justification for their faith.

This 'leap' is facilitated, and their faith justified, by devotees' recourse to the language of 'experience'. Most devotees, despite their command over rational expertise in modern disciplines such as engineering, medicine, accountancy and commerce, and computer programming, share the Mata's view that rationality provides a severely limited means of understanding the world, and must be complemented by the realm of experience. This kind of argument not only makes their position as devotees invulnerable to the onslaughts of sceptics, but also places them in a position of privilege as people who have access to a 'higher' mode of cognition to which lesser beings cannot aspire unless they transcend their faculties of reasoning.

Scholars of Indian society have, in the past, puzzled over the ease with which modern professional Indians shift between two apparently antithetical modes of thinking – those of scientific rationality, and of faith in the supernatural. While some see this as an essential 'hypocrisy' and 'inconsistency' in the 'Indian way of thinking' (Ramanujan, 1989: 44–5), others see this as the peculiarly Indian way of accommodating cultural borrowings from the 'West' within the traditional system. Singer (1972: 320), for instance, observes how, when Indians learn modern science, business or technology, these new ways of thought and behaviour do not replace, but live along with older 'religious' ways – this, for him, represents what he calls 'compartmentalization' by Indians of their different interests. For Ramanujan, the key factor underlying this process of accommodation is 'context sensitivity' where the use of completely contradictory modes of thinking and behaviour by the same individual comes to be justified in terms of the particular contexts in which they are applied. In his perception, the 'Indian way of thinking' is characterized by a remarkable attention to contexts and particularisms, such that there are no universals that govern thought and behaviour at all times and in all contexts. According to Ramanujan: 'The 'modern', the context free, becomes one more context, though it is not easy to contain' (1989: 57).[2]

In striking contrast to the ideas of Singer and Ramanujan, the Mata and her devotees see the relationship between the realms of the mind and the heart, or those of scientific rationality on the one hand and those of faith and experience on the other, not so much in terms of 'context-sensitivities' or a 'compartmentalization' of mutually exclusive opposites, but as a 'balancing' of complementary categories in a comprehensive whole (see Chapter 3 above). A devotee who described himself as a senior scientist at the Bhabha Atomic Research Centre in Mumbai (Bombay), a long-time devotee of the Mata, explained to me how the perception of a conflict between the scientific approach and the attitude of faith, is 'the biggest myth'. Without faith, he said, nothing works, not even science. Every act in our daily lives, he insisted, is an act of faith.

> When you embark on a flight, you don't go to the pilot's cabin and ask to see his licence. How do you know he is a qualified pilot? You simply take your seat in the aircraft without worrying about the pilot's credentials. Is that not an act of faith – your faith in the pilot and his abilities? And when you lie down on an operation table, what does that show? That you have placed your faith in the surgeon who is about to operate upon you? Nothing proceeds without faith, and that goes for science as well. Science is nothing but the pursuit of truth. Without faith, we can't pursue the truth. A scientist must have faith in himself, in his approach, his method.

An ideal scientist, in this devotee's scheme of things, is one who relies equally on his scientific knowledge, based on reasoning, *and* his faith, based on personal experience, in order to understand the 'truth'. This perception, which posits faith and reason not as mutually exclusive categories in competition with each other, but as two parts in a whole, existing in a relationship of mutual complementarity, serves to legitimize the faith of devotees, and allows them to give their devotion to the Mata pride of place beside the scientific rationality that they use in their everyday lives. They do not, however, allow their awareness of the limitations of scientific rationality to diminish their appreciation of its achievements. Instead, devotees often make an effort to lend their faith in the Mata a 'scientific' colouring.[3] One devotee, for instance, referred to the quest for spirituality under the Mata's guidance as *atmic vigyan* ('science' of the soul). Devotees also express a keen regard for what Bharati (1970: 282) describes as 'gadgetry language'. They use simple technological paradigms to explain the various facets of their faith. Thus several devotees use the analogy of a 'cosmic radio receiver' to explain the Mata's abilities. The Mata, they say, is like a high performance radio receiver that can tune in to the supreme consciousness and receive the weakest of radio signals from across the cosmos. Her high receptivity gives her the powers of omniscience, omnipresence and omnipotence. Another commonly used analogy compares her ashram with a laundromat, where devotees and disciples are given a thorough wash and rinse so that they come out spiritually cleansed. The common use of such analogies reveals a tendency on the part of devotees to cast their entire 'spiritual' experience in 'modern' terms that can be understood much like the processes of modern technology.

Experience construction

The realm of 'experience' thus not only fortifies devotees' faith in the Mata, but also legitimizes it in a world that valorizes scientific rationality. What happens, however, when personal experiences proving the Mata's divine love for the devotee are not forthcoming? In the first instance, devotees tend to persist in their devotion to their guru and intensify their efforts to win her grace and protection. They attribute the spiritual drought to inadequacies in their own devotion, or see it as a test which the Mata is putting them through for their own good. What will eventually see them through the period of drought, they believe, is their constancy, patience and unflinching trust in her. Even while stoically tiding over the drought, devotees are constantly on the look-out for instances in their lives which might potentially be interpreted as miraculous 'experiences' of the Mata's love. Towards this end, they often engage in an active process of experience construction in order to establish their state of grace as the Mata's devotees. Devotees' 'miraculous experiences' include such mundane incidents as getting train reservations during rush season or discovering a petrol station close at hand after being stranded with an empty tank in an unfamiliar part of the city, all of which are attributed to the guru's divine intervention in their lives at critical junctures. The 'experiences' of a devotee of Mata Amritanandamayi, recounted in a spiritual journal published by the Mission, are a case in point. This devotee (of Indian origin but permanently resident in the USA) narrates how the Mata arranged for her smooth passage from India to Singapore (and onward to USA) after a brief *darshan* in Bombay.

> After getting Amma's *darshan* [in Bombay] I bade Her farewell with a tearful, heavy heart. Later that day I flew to Madras from where I was to leave for Singapore. The Bombay–Madras flight was delayed and hence I missed my flight to Singapore. I was given a voucher to fly by another airlines on the next day. Early in the morning I reached the counter and waited to get a seat. There were about fifty people at the counter. Due to lack of order in the queue, whoever was rough, rude, unmannerly [sic] and strong always stood at the front of the row. Since I am not good at pushing and shoving, I was left behind . . .
>
> I met another lady who hailed from Quilon. She saw the Amma locket on my neck and we started talking about Her. Soon it was evident that this lady did not have anything nice to say about Amma, so I did not encourage the conversation. I ended up by saying I had faith in Amma. After a few minutes of waiting, this lady got a seat on the flight – I was still left out. Before she left me she told me sarcastically, 'You told me you believe in Amma, why don't you pray to her to help you?' I told her, 'Madam, that is exactly what I plan to do.' I fervently prayed to Mother. 'Mother, the chance of me getting on this flight is very slim, but please help me. You just saw how this lady ridiculed me. Please show her that You care about me'.
>
> Then all of a sudden an idea flashed in my mind. I asked a nearby officer if I could go inside and talk to the Chief Duty Officer. He allowed me to go in and I told my tale of woe to the gentleman. He took pity on me and told his staff to give me a seat. That was the only seat left in the plane and it happened to be first class! So finally I boarded the plane and was now sitting

in front in a first class seat which is quite roomy. The lady I spoke with before passed by my seat through the aisle. She was shocked to see me there. She said, 'Oh, so you also got a seat'. I replied, 'I did what you advised me to do, I called on my Amma and this is what I got.'

Another such story, a similar so-called 'miracle' experience narrated to me by a male devotee of the Mata, describes the sequence of events that led to his obtaining a rare photograph of the guru. This photograph, which shows the Mata smiling radiantly, her chin cupped in her hand, is prominently displayed in the living room of his well-appointed suburban home in Delhi.

> I first saw this bewitching photo of Amma with a *sannyasi* in the Delhi ashram. I told him I wanted it. He said he had only one copy. When I told him how much I loved the photo, he said I should look for it at the ashram in Vallikkaavu [Amritapuri]. 'You will find the photograph there', he said. 'Some English lady has taken this photograph; you find out. Describe it to them . . . ' When I went to Vallikkaavu soon after, I went to each and every person there asking if they knew of this photo. This became a sort of obsession. I went to every single person there. But drew a blank. They then told me to check in the ashram archives. I did. I described the photo to the English lady in charge of the archives. I told her I was searching for this particular photo. She said she couldn't place it but she would show me all the photos in her collection. I pored over them. Found another photo, not quite the one I was searching for, but similar to it. I asked if I may take it and she said yes. It was a very small print. I got it here and had it enlarged . . .
>
> When Amma came here after that in March 1996, I happened to go to the ashram branch. I was just coming out of the ashram office when I saw in the stands a single copy of the very photo I was searching for. I picked it up. Amma knew how I had struggled to get it, how I had gone from pillar to post like a man obsessed . . . Amma knew I had been searching, and she had kept that photograph there for me – nobody else had it. I rushed to it, and grabbed it. I was thrilled. She knew I had been searching so hard.

It appears from these accounts that these devotees have no room in their lives for 'luck' or 'chance'. Every fortuitous event in their lives comes to be interpreted as a miracle worked by the guru and a sign of his/her grace. It is thus up to the devotees to be able to see the guru's divine love behind the most ordinary, the most mundane incidents in their everyday lives, and to see every chance happening as a miracle worked by him/her. Devotees' 'experiences' then are not merely a sign of the guru's love for them. Equally, they are devotees' expressions of their absolute faith in their guru. The onus of making miracles happen rests not on the guru but on each individual devotee. By engaging in a narrative process by which 'experiences' are actively constructed, devotees painstakingly reinforce their faith in the guru and adhere to it.

The question of agency – monkeys or kittens?

I now turn to an examination of how devotees of the Mata perceive themselves and their personal agency, in relation to their guru and the proxy control they attribute to her. A popular analogy in India draws a contrast between two different attitudes that devotees may adopt vis-à-vis the object of their devotion.[4] The first is that of the baby monkey. When in danger, baby monkeys take a fast grip on their mother's abdomen and have themselves conveyed to safety. In contrast to this, the second attitude, that of the kitten, is more passive. In times of danger, kittens sit and wait for their mothers to carry them away by the scruff of their necks without providing active assistance. The contrast between the two clearly lies in the matter of agency. Baby monkeys are portrayed as active agents who seek to control their own destiny by readily seeking assistance when they need it. Kittens on the contrary are portrayed as passive and lacking all agency. Rather than make any attempt to gain control, they leave all control and agency to a protecting figure who, they hope, will assume charge over their lives.

Are devotees of the Mata kittens or baby monkeys in the way they relate to their guru? In attempting to answer this question we find ourselves confronted with a peculiar paradox. On the one hand, the Mata's devotees pride themselves on their autonomy as independent and active agents, free to assert their religious preferences, and to author their religious lives in ways they consider personally appropriate. On the other hand, we also find them anxious to deny all personal agency, submitting all control (in their narratives) to the Mata, whom they make out to be a kind of divine stage manager (Exon 1997) who calls the shots, down to the last personal detail in their everyday lives. How does one account for this apparent contradiction in devotees' perception of selfhood? The answer to this question lies in devotees' conceptualization of their spiritual lives as constituting a journey, where they perceive a disjuncture between their real selves, as they exist in the present, and their ideal selves, as they *ought to be* if they are to achieve their spiritual goal. What we see here is not a static, but a dynamic and processual sense of self, based on the expectation of change in one's personality, and the hope of realizing new potentialities as one is led along the spiritual path.

One perceptible transformation in the selfhood of devotees, after they embark on the spiritual journey prescribed by the Mata, is their newly acquired sense of purpose and meaning. Following their encounter with the Mata, devotees appear to be driven by a sense of striving for some ultimate good, which now provides them with the meaningfulness they claim they previously lacked. Having embarked on a spiritual quest, their everyday experiences acquire a new significance and become redefined as 'adding up to' or 'leading on to' something bigger than, and beyond, the mundane and ordinary. In describing their initial encounter with the Mata, and the changes in their lives following from this, devotees' narratives reveal a coherence, a clear sequence and flow, and an unmistakable sense of direction and purpose. The first meeting, subsequent meetings, changes in devotees' behaviour patterns and belief systems, their engagement with the Mata, at first tentative and then increasingly certain, their understanding of themselves as recipients of the Mata's love, all acquire a narrative unity and *telos* which devotees describe as conspicuously absent in their lives prior to their encounter with the Mata.

Besides acquiring a sense of direction and meaning, devotees also reveal a marked tendency towards self-reflexivity, where they constantly scrutinize their own actions in order to detect changes in themselves and seek 'higher' meanings for the events in their lives. The desired changes in their selfhood, as I noted in Chapter 5, range from an increasing disinterest in material acquisitions, to a growing preoccupation with spiritual matters, and a noticeable decline in egoism. As devotees understand it, their journey must lead on towards higher levels of spiritual maturity. Spiritual maturity (Chapters 3 and 5 above) is defined in terms of a heightened emotionalism, a primed heart increasingly receptive to the Mata's loving ministrations, a dilution of one's ego-centredness, and a growing humility. Shedding tears, adoring their chosen deity through worship, and serving the Mata 'selflessly', are all seen as important means to this end. Taken to its logical conclusion, this journey must lead away from sorrow to eternal happiness. It must lead to a state where the devotee becomes a pure and yielding receptacle of the Mata's love, where all doubts, misgivings and apprehensions about the Mata must be washed away and in their place must grow humility, tranquility and an abiding trust in the Mata's grace. The devotee must cease to value his/her sense of individuality and autonomy, and must submit completely to the Mata's will.

Most devotees acknowledge that the spiritual goal represents a far cry from their present reality. Not only this, but they also see this goal as unattainable through their individual striving, and choose to see the Mata as solely responsible for bringing it about. Their ideal spiritual selfhood, which devalues individual distinctiveness, independence and autonomous agency, remains just that, an ideal, which, devotees admit, is unattainable through their personal striving. In admitting to the unattainability of their ideal spiritual self, devotees in effect simultaneously affirm their real selves *as* autonomous individual agents. It is this *real* selfhood that the Mata readily acknowledges, and it is by propagating a spirituality that respects her devotees' individuality and autonomy, that this modern guru manages to secure the loyalty and devotion of hundreds of thousands of middle-class urbanites in India and abroad.

There is thus a clear disjuncture between devotees' sense of their *real* selfhood as baby monkeys (worldly individuals with a distinctive identity and autonomous agency who actively seek the Mata's protection) and their *ideal* kitten-like selves (as other-worldly spiritual aspirants, who, by shedding their individuality, hope to surrender completely to the Mata's love). This disjuncture accounts for the apparent contradiction in their perceptions of agency and selfhood. Their denial of individual agency and autonomy in their experience narratives appears then to be a way by which devotees seek to collapse the gap between the real and the ideal, and bring one step closer (at least in their imagination) their admittedly impossible spiritual goal of complete and selfless surrender to their chosen guru.

Moving on

However hard devotees may work at constructing 'experiences' of the Mata's love, long and apparently interminable phases of drought do tend to wear down the devotees' faith in the guru, especially if the devotee happens to be in urgent need of miraculous solutions to pressing problems. A guru-attachment devoid of miraculous experiences or of demonstrable signs of the guru's love, tends to become dull and uninspiring. Faith in the guru requires a constant cranking up through experiences ever more wonderful and miraculous. In the absence of such cranking up, devotees begin to lose faith in the guru and may drift away to other gurus who show greater promise of delivering the desired results.[5]

Of the many devotees of the Mata I met in the course of my fieldwork in 1997–8 some had ceased to be devotees by the time I revisited the field in 2001. The reasons for their disenchantment with the Mata were many and varied. Some had simply found other gurus who offered more effective solutions to their problems, others had tired of their devotion after long spells of drought when no 'experiences' were in evidence, yet others were disillusioned by some aspect of the Mata's organization and wished no longer to be part of it. Among those who had thus moved on to other gurus, some spoke harsh words about the Mata and her devotees. While still her devotees, they had revelled in a narrative that glorified the Mata; they now appeared to hold both her and her devotees in contempt.

One such individual, who insisted that his reasons for leaving the MAM be kept 'off the record', and for whom devotion to this guru had clearly stopped delivering the desired results, now described faith in her guruship as 'blind faith' which lacked a 'scientific attitude towards religion'. He criticized the Mata's devotees for seeking only material gain through their attachment to the Mata, and for never questioning their own beliefs, and therefore for failing to grow and develop spiritually. He even went so far as to describe them as spiritual 'ignoramuses'! The Mata, by encouraging this miracle-preoccupation, he claimed, actively contributed towards stunting her devotees' spiritual growth. All this was a far cry from the eulogistic tones in which he had described the Mata during my previous interview with him, more than a year before. At that time, he had said:

Amma is everything. If we look through coloured glass, we see everything in that colour. When we look at her as a guru, she appears as a guru. When we see her as Amma, she appears as Amma. So she is everything. But then she is none of this. Only god can assume all forms. So Amma is none of these things, but she is everything. Only such an entity can be all things at once.

On this latter occasion, however, this devotee had changed his mind completely about the merits of the Mata as a guru. He saw her as little more than a 'miracle monger'. His own spiritual quest, he explained, had come to focus increasingly on an exploration of his true inner being – on the 'science of the inner self of humankind'. He had now found a new guru who was able to help him on this quest. This new guru, recommended to him by friends, was well-versed in the Hindu scriptures. With the aid of this guru, he was now acquainting himself with ancient Hindu texts and striving to rediscover what he described as the 'true' essence of spirituality.

Conclusion

Several important points follow from the discussion in this chapter and the last. It is clear that the mainstay of devotees' faith in Mata Amritanandamayi and her Mission is neither obligatory loyalty to the spiritual organization, nor close adherence to a common set of beliefs and practices, nor a shared sense of community with fellow devotees.[6] Devotees may have multiple guru attachments simultaneously. They are not bound in any way to the chosen guru organization but may enter and leave at will. Devotees form a loose network of participants in the guru faith, often with no clear sense of a boundary differentiating insiders from outsiders. Rather than dissolve into a community of like-minded adherents, they are free to negotiate their guru faith as they choose.[7] Each individual makes selections from the available options, and constructs a personal and individualized faith in accordance with his or her needs and preferences.

The appeal of popular gurus like the Mata lies in their ability to facilitate, rather than restrict, this process of individual creativity and innovation. The result is not the individual's submission to external authorization or to a set of supposedly 'traditional' Hindu values and norms. Instead what we see here is an intensely interiorized and private form of faith which defines religion as an inner horizon predicated upon the personal choice and self fulfilment of each individual.[8] This faith is buttressed and bolstered by the highly intimate and personal bond that is forged between the Mata and her devotees. The vast popularity of Mata Amritanandamayi appears to vindicate Pocock's (1973: 100) insightful comment on the modern devotionalist sect in India. '[I]t is precisely the extent to which the central importance of this guru-relationship is lost, or minimized by an over-emphasis upon solidarity, organization and uniformity,' he argues, 'that the sect appears to lose its hold over the population of the modern Indian city'. Conversely, then, it is precisely the extent to which the guru sustains an intimate and personal relationship with her followers, and allows room for diversity and difference within her fold, that she manages to attract, and secure a hold over, her urban Indian middle-class devotees.

7

EAST MEETS WEST?

As the preceding chapters show, core elements of devotionalism within the Mata Amritanandamayi Mission include first, a shared understanding of modernity and modern selfhood; second, a common project of transforming modern selves so as to redress their 'imbalances'; and third, a common adoration of the Mata. These elements play a crucial role in nurturing and sustaining the collective imagination of the Mata's following. This collective imagination links together Indian devotees of the Mata across India and abroad, and also connects them with the Mata's non-Indian, mostly Western, followers. Within this collective imagination, however, there are arenas of contestation between (Indian) devotees of differing ideologies and persuasions who perceive differently their location in a globalized world. Some define 'Indian' and 'Hindu' selfhood in opposition to its 'Western' counterpart; others follow a more inclusive and universal approach, perceiving no opposition between an 'Indian self' and a 'Western other' within the Mata's fold. This contestation introduces interesting nuances of meaning in devotees' understanding of modernity and modern selfhood.

My concern here is with the 'global orientatedness' of the Mata and her devotees, which Coleman (2000: 49–71) describes as transformations in self-awareness resulting from globalization, which lead to new imaginings of a global community, reconfigurations of one's sense of space and place, as well as new ways of experiencing, and orientating oneself to, the world. In examining the global orientatedness of the Mata and her followers, it is useful to refer to Beyer's (1990) analysis of the impact of globalization on religion and religious organizations. He delineates two possible options (or orientations) facing a religious group or organization that is increasingly and ever more intensively conscious of global interconnectedness. He refers to these as the 'liberal' and 'conservative' options. In the former case, the notion of boundaries separating different communities ceases to exist. The dichotomy between the self and the other loses its relevance, and pluralism comes to be acknowledged and accepted as an inevitable aspect of modern life. The community that is targeted is defined vaguely and generally as the world community, encompassing a variety of cultures, religious orientations and individual lifestyles. Issues pertaining to the realm of the sacred and the transcendental, to salvation and the after-life tend to get confined to the private sphere, and the public face of the religious group or organization is turned largely towards such secular concerns as economic welfare, world peace, health and education.

In contrast with this, Beyer describes the 'conservative' option as characterized by not only the reassertion of traditional views of transcendence but also the political mobilization of the religious community as a clearly bounded group defined in opposition to an enemy. In this case the world is seen as dichotomized into us and them, the religiously pure and impure. Such a reassertion, 'far from being a mere yearning for imagined bygone days', Beyer (ibid.: 391) notes, 'is a logical outcome of a globalization which has generated and continues to generate fundamental conflicts among different regions of the world'. Which of these two options characterizes the global orientation of the Mata's Indian devotees? The answer to this question differs considerably depending on which section of her following we choose to examine. It must be evident from earlier chapters that participants in the MAM by no means constitute a homogeneous community sharing the same attitudes, preferences and beliefs. The wide diversity that marks their religious preferences and practices also characterizes their orientations and attitudes towards a globalized world.

The Mata's own message to the 'world', as I shall argue below, appears universalistic and inclusivistic in its tone. Her Indian devotees, however, interpret this universalism in different ways. Their orientations range from an increased reflexivity, and relativization of their faith, to a defensive approach to their own particular world-view and religious belief. The Mata and her message are therefore best understood as constituting an arena of contested meanings,[1] and this contestation is played out at her Amritapuri ashram in Kerala, where people of different cultural and religious backgrounds as well as ideological orientations come together in common devotion to the Mata.

Media representations – a global leader with a universal appeal

The voluminous publicity material about the Mata that the MAM churns out every year actively plays up the 'global' reach and 'universal' appeal of this guru. She is described in the literature as 'Divine Mother and most revered Satguru to millions all over the world,' who is 'conquering the hearts of people everywhere'.[2] The MAM's vast publicity and propaganda machinery serves to link devotees in India with its worldwide spiritual network. Its official websites provide a detailed listing of MAM centres abroad. The MAM's monthly publication, the *Matruvani*, as well as its web pages, provide an itinerary of the Mata's 'world' tours. They carry reports and photographs of her activities in various countries. These reports highlight foreign devotees' eagerness to be reunited with their 'mother', their enthusiastic participation at the public programmes conducted by the Mata, the teeming numbers, the air of happiness and gaiety at these events, and devotees' sense of loss when the Mata finally bids them farewell and moves on to the next city on her travel schedule. The thrust in these reports is the irresistible appeal of the Mata and her vast ability to draw crowds and heal and cheer with her inspiring presence. Typical reports on the Mata's tours abroad read as follow:

Amma's visit to France, 1997: . . . A few hours of rest and Amma was off again to Paris, where once again the crowds were gigantic. Just as in California, devotees from all over the European continent had come to Paris, to attend Amma's programs . . . Though it was very cold, with occasional drizzle (it even snowed for a short time), nothing could deter Amma's eager children from making their way to the programme venues . . . Amma's presence filled everyone with energy and enthusiasm.[3]

Amma's US Tour, 1998: . . . Los Angeles, home to the American cinema industry, set the stage for the next part of Mother's US tour. Amidst all the superficial pomp and splendour of this fast-track city, large crowds, including many movie and TV stars, filled the hallroom of the Furama Hotel, to listen to the Mother's inspiring satsangs and bhajans, teaching them to go beyond attachment to the external world and look for real peace and happiness within . . . Throughout this year's tour, Mother was interviewed by many regional as well as national TV channels and newspapers like *New York Times*, *The Washington Post*, *Chicago Tribune*, *San Fransisco Chronicle* . . . published big, inspiring articles about Amma's visit. Amma's fame has spread all over the US.[4]

The Mission's promotional literature thus invites Indian devotees to celebrate the Mata's popularity abroad. It treats the Mata's foreign acclaim as something for her Indian children to take pride in. An even greater cause for celebration, it would appear from the tone of the MAM reportage, is the Mata's attendance at 'prestigious' international faith conferences where she is often honoured with prizes awarded by international charitable and other organizations. Important among these to date have been her attendance at the Parliament of World Religions at Chicago in 1993, at the Interfaith Celebration in New York in 1995 which coincided with the fiftieth anniversary of the United Nations, at the Millennium World Peace Summit of Religious and Spiritual Leaders at New York in 2000, and, most recently, in 2002, at the World Conference of Women Religious and Spiritual Leaders in Geneva where she was presented with the 'Gandhi-King' award for non-violence.[5] All these honours and awards are a matter of great pride to her devotees and are widely publicized through the Mission's propaganda network.[6] The typical tone for much of this publicity is one of awe and admiration for the Mata. Consider, for instance, the opening lines of the 'Preface' to a volume entitled *Unity is Peace*, which carries the text of the Mata's speech delivered at the UN Interfaith conference in 1995.[7]

> Can you imagine an ordinary village girl from a remote fishing village in southern India, who never completed her formal education, who is utterly humble and earthly in appearance, clad in simple white clothes . . . delivering a speech at the Interfaith Celebration which was held in New York . . . and there capturing the attention and the appreciation of the most learned people? Living in an age in which the existence of God and the relevance of spirituality is being seriously questioned and even criticized, what explanations can the so-called intellectuals and sceptics give to such an irresistible personality as Amma, the Divine Mata Amritanandamayi Devi?

Likewise, the 'Introduction' to the volume begins with a dramatic flourish.

> A wave of whispers, 'Who is She? . . . ' 'Who is that? . . . ' 'Who . . . ?' 'Who . . . ?' filled the Synod Hall at the Cathedral of Saint John the Divine in New York as numerous cameras flashed and necks craned to watch as our beloved Amma entered to take Her seat. The occasion was the recent gathering of religious leaders in celebration of the 50th Anniversary of the United Nations on 21 October. It was no reflection on the speaker at the podium when heads turned away from him 180 degrees towards the Shining Light who has stolen all our attention and our hearts.

All these representations depict the Mata as a force transcending distinctions of nationality, class, religion, race, physical appearance and colour. Her 'divine' presence is portrayed as overwhelmingly attractive to all, and this universal appeal in turn is presented as proof of her divinity. The Mata's own message delivered to the 'global community' would appear to be one that celebrates universalism and the oneness of all humanity. She appears to speak the 'universal' language of love as epitomized in her motherly embrace. Her message, of promoting love and compassion, of conquering one's ego and selfishness, may be seen to have a universal relevance and to relate equally to people of different cultures, religions and ideological beliefs. I noted in Chapter 1 that the Mata prefers to refer to her teachings as representative of Sanatana Dharma or an eternal truth. She sees this truth not as 'Hindu' in its origins and scope but as a principle common to all the religions in the world. She argues for an essential unity underlying their diverse beliefs and practices.

> Children, there is no harm in having many religions and faiths but it is harmful to think that they are different and that one faith is higher and another lower. Do not see the differences, see the unity in them and the great ideals which they teach. What all religions show is to develop compassion, love, faith, forbearance, endurance, renunciation, etc. That is what is important. Religion means expansiveness, the ability to accommodate anything and everything. Religion is the merging of minds where all differences disappear.[8]

It is this global or universal vision which runs through the text of the speech that the Mata delivered at the Interfaith conference in New York. This speech, entitled 'Unity is Peace', and based on Hindu non-dualist philosophies, emphasizes inner self-realization as leading to a consciousness of unity in everything. The Mata, describing her vision for the new millennium, says:

> Let our effort to discover our own essential nature – that indwelling Universal Power – be a characteristic feature of the new millennium we are about to enter. Let this be recognized as one of the important goals of the next century. We have nothing to lose by trusting the infinite power of the Self, except the bondage of our own ignorance. The chain of limitations that binds us must break in order to open our hearts, to know each other, and to understand the pain and suffering of others by putting ourselves in their place . . .

The entire world will become our family once we realize our oneness with that Universal Power. Once this knowledge dawns on us, we can no longer work for just a few people, or for a single community, or for one particular nation. Once we realize this truth, the entire universe becomes our own abode. All of creation becomes our own. We behold that everything is pervaded with God-consciousness, with the Supreme Divine Power. Everything is seen as different names and forms of that Divine Power. This universe becomes our own body; the different nations and its people become parts of our universal body. People who experience this are beyond any division . . .

Together we are a power, an undefeatable power. When we work together, hand in hand, with love, it is not just one life force but the life energy of countless people, of the groups, that flows in harmony, unimpeded. From that constant stream of unity, real progress will take place, and we will see the birth of peace.

In all of this, the fact of the Mata's Hindu and Indian origins appears completely irrelevant. Instead she appears as a universal mother, who is anxious to ease the woes of her children worldwide. In this scheme of things, the entire world is the Mata's 'playground', as one devotee described it. Her life on the earth, intended to complete the 'divine' mission of alleviating human suffering, cannot proceed unless she has access to ever larger sections of the globe. Thus, every new devotee, every new geographical area which she visits and in which she gains recognition, is a triumph of the avatar, and takes her one step closer to fulfilling her earthly mission.[9]

Multiple 'global' orientations

Not all the devotees of the Mata, however, share this universalist vision. Indeed the Mata accommodates a multiplicity of ideologies and orientations within her fold, ranging from the most liberal to the most conservative and chauvinistic. At the liberal extreme, devotees and disciples prefer not to see the faith she propagates as Hindu or Indian. They see it instead as a universal truth applicable to all, and relevant for all time. At the conservative extreme on the other hand, individuals interpret her message in narrowly nationalistic and chauvinistic terms. For these persons, the Mata is first and foremost a Hindu and Indian leader, and her popularity in the rest of the world represents India's spiritual 'triumph' over the 'materialistic' West.

Persons of the latter persuasion include, I discovered, some of the Mata's most senior Indian ascetic disciples. A few of these, I found in the course of interviews, had had connections with Hindu nationalist organizations like the Rashtriya Swayamsevak Sangh in the past, and had been influenced by their militant nationalistic ideology.[10] When these individuals entered the MAM, they had clearly brought with them some of the influences acquired through this previous association. One of the senior *sannyasis* of the MAM whom I interviewed, for instance, not only saw the MAM as 'Hindu', but also emphatically asserted his belief in the superiority of Hinduism over all other religions.

> When we talk of basic truths we see all the world as comprising Amma's children. We see no distinction between people in terms of religion or race or nationality. The whole world is god's creation. In truth, in order to see things in this perspective, Bharatam (India) alone has succeeded in keeping an open mind. All others have sought to indoctrinate, proselytize. None of the other religions is tolerant of, or respectful towards, its sister faiths, whereas the Hindu faith includes all these others. Therefore for those who understand Hinduism's expansiveness, there is no problem. If you can't appreciate this expansiveness, you will be critical of other faiths. That kind of perception doesn't help us. The essence of every religion is contained in the Hindu faith. The others don't say anything that we don't say. If all these essences are contained in the Hindu faith, we must then consider Hinduism as the mother of all religions. In which case there is no religion distinct from ours. In that sense we can't describe ourselves as adhering to any one faith. You might say we are part of the Bharatiya *samskara* (Indian cultural tradition) – something that has existed for all time.

This view comes remarkably close to the ideology of Hindu nationalists in India, for whom the term 'Hindu' embraces all the people who believe in, respect, or follow, the 'eternal' values of life – ethical and spiritual – that have evolved in Bharat (India). Hinduism, portrayed as a civilization or a culture rather than a religion, is defined such as to transcend internal differences of a doctrinal, organizational or regional nature. Hinduism further is made out to be a 'tolerant' religion, much as the individual quoted above makes it out to be. This tolerance, as van der Veer (1994a) argues, is a poor translation for what is in fact a form of Hindu inclusivism and hierarchical relativism. While acknowledging that there are many paths towards realizing god, this ideology maintains that first, all paths are included within the all-embracing Hindu fold, and second, that precisely because of its inclusiveness, Hinduism is somehow superior to all others – the 'mother' of all religions!

In sharp contrast to such right-wing interpretations of the Mata and her mission, are others which refuse to see the Mata's philosophy as anything but the most liberal, humanitarian and universalistic. Individuals of this persuasion prefer not to perceive the MAM as a 'Hindu' organization. Thus one devotee, an Indian woman settled in England, said:

> You can't call this [the MAM] Hindu because it's never – sort of – there is no reference to its being Hindu. It's more – the emphasis is always on the oneness of humanity. So the Indianism doesn't come in there. Which is why, I think, a lot of Westerners find it easy to come to Amma. There's nothing to say this is one particular type of organization or religion. The universality of Amma's teachings is coming across to people more than ever before. More and more, why Amma is becoming popular in the West is because of this universality, the oneness of humanity, that clearly comes out in her teachings. When she or the swamiji [her disciple] talks, there are references to Christ, which you don't find in many other religions. That makes them [the Western devotees] understand that this is not exclusively Indian. Christians, Catholics all come in thousands to this saint. Madonna, Amma are all the same. There is no distinguishing Amma as Indian – nothing of that sort comes into any of this. It's mainly the fanatics who worry about whether this is Hindu or not.

Similar views were expressed by a young *brahmachari* at one of the ashram branches in Kerala, who preferred to stress an underlying unity between religions and religious experiences worldwide, and preferred not to define the Mata and her message in 'Hindu' and 'Indian' terms.

> The word *santanam* itself indicates that it is eternal. It is not contained in temples, in rituals, or in forms of worship . . . These come and go. Modes of worship change . . . Yet they all fall under the same category – Sanatana Dharma. Dharma means the eternal experience. That is how I would define it. Once you realize god, the experience cannot be different for one who has attained that realization now and one who attained it 2,000 years ago. What Ramakrishna experienced is the same as what Amma is experiencing now. It is the same as what Christ experienced

and what Krishna experienced. So when you reach that level of experience, you become one with the eternal. Whatever god-realized persons say on the basis of that experience is the same truth . . . because truth is only one. Whoever has had the experience – whether it is Muhammed or Krishna or Christ or Kabir or Ramakrishna or Amma – they have all experienced the same thing. And to experience this is to become one with the eternal.

Many of the devotees I met in Delhi and Kerala were emphatic in their condemnation of Hindu nationalist ideologies and politics, preferring to see the faith propagated by the Mata as quite the opposite of what Hindu nationalists uphold. Kishore, for instance, who had strong views on the matter, appeared to echo the sentiments of several others I had interviewed when he said:

I definitely believe in one thing. If a Hindu believes that his own gods, his own temples, his own way of worship is the only correct one, if he becomes a fanatic, I think he is killing himself. He is becoming a stumbling block in his own progress . . . When he says his own way of life is the only correct one, there the degradation starts.

The Amritapuri ashram – a multi-cultural context

I have argued thus far that the Mata's universalistic message is interpreted differently by devotees and disciples of different persuasions. While for some, she is a universal mother whose message transcends religious and national boundaries, for others she is first and foremost a Hindu and Indian leader, and her popularity bears testimony to Hinduism's superiority over all other religions. These different views have an important bearing on how Indian devotees perceive, and relate to, the Mata's devotees and disciples from the West. It is in the Mata's remote ashram at Amritapuri in rural Kerala that devotees and disciples of different cultures and nationalities come together to live in close proximity with each other over extended periods of time. Though Indian devotees expect to see a sizeable non-Indian presence when they visit Amritapuri, most find it an altogether novel and unfamiliar experience to have to share living space with foreigners. In the following sections I examine the attitudes of Indian devotees towards Westerners in the ashram context.

Visitors from afar usually fly into one of the two airports located at equal distances from Amritapuri, Kochi (Cochin) to the north and

Thiruvananthapuram (Trivandrum) to the south. From these airports Amritapuri is a two-and-a-half-hour drive by car along Kerala's bumpy and congested roads. Those who prefer a train ride can travel as far as Kayamkulam which has the nearest train station, at a distance of 12 kilometres from Amritapuri. Bus routes take visitors as far as Oachira, eight kilometres from the ashram. Amritapuri is situated in a narrow strip of land just off the western coast of Kerala. It is separated from the mainland by a shallow stretch of sea navigable by punt. Visitors negotiate the journey from the bus or train station to the boat jetty by taxi or rickshaw. From there punters ferry them across to the ashram for a nominal fare.

Halfway through the boat ride, the ashram suddenly looms into view as a pink multi-storeyed tower rising high above the dense canopy of coconut palms on the opposite shore. My first impression of the ashram was of a rather cramped and crowded little compound dominated by two large buildings, both painted pink and looking startlingly incongruous in the lush green setting. The taller of the two buildings, I soon discovered, houses several hundreds of one-room flats for use by visitors and ashram inmates. These are the ashram's Amrita Apartments, where I lived for several weeks, paying a nominal fee of a hundred rupees (a little more than a pound) per day for a tiny bare room with an attached toilet and shower. The other building houses the ashram's main temple shrine, prayer hall, the Mata's residential quarters and also those of some of her senior ascetic disciples, dormitories for visitors as well as long-term residents, and many of the ashram's offices. Besides these two main buildings, the ashram also contained several smaller structures, some of them crudely built and makeshift, scattered across its tiny compound. Among these were its main dining hall; small huts where the *brahmacharis* and *brahmacharinis* lived; shops that sold items ranging from prayer mats, pillows, toothpaste and washing powder to Kellogg's breakfast cereal and Kit Kat bars; a cow shed; other sheds where volunteers manufactured various Amrita herbal products including soaps, incense and tea; the ashram's kitchens and canteens; an Ayurveda clinic; and the MAM's printing and publishing unit. To the west of the ashram compound stretches the endless expanse of the Arabian Sea; to the east, beyond the backwaters, lies mainland Kerala. To the north and south are some relatively plush private dwellings of various local residents including the Mata's parents, as well as the poorer huts of local fisherfolk.

New arrivals to the ashram go first to a prominently sign-posted 'Enquiry Desk' close to the ashram entrance. From there they are directed to their respective reception areas – a 'Foreign Office' for non-Indians and an 'Accommodation Office' for Indians. At the respective offices, volunteer helpers receive the visitors, enter their particulars in the ashram's registers, receive payment for their accommodation arrange- ments, hand them the key to their flat or direct them to their dormitories as the case may be, and acquaint them with the dos and don'ts of ashram life. One of the first stops for visitors after they have located their rooms and unpacked their belongings is the Seva Desk, again separate for Westerners and Indians. At the Seva Desk the visitors are required to volunteer their seva or service. Once they have made their selection from the range of services the ashram requires from its visitors for its maintenance and upkeep, they are expected to set aside a few hours every day to discharge their chosen *seva* responsibilities.

The rules of the ashram prohibit the consumption of meat, alcohol, drugs and cigarettes within its premises. Visitors are required to remain celibate for the duration of their stay. They are requested to dress simply, exposing as little bare skin as possible. They are also requested to speak softly and to refrain from all public demonstrations of affection, especi- ally with people of the opposite sex. Residents usually greet each other with the chant 'Om Namah Shivaya' (salutations to Shiva). Despite the stress on low levels of noise, I was struck by the constant din inside the ashram compound during my stay there. Much of the din came from the generators which chugged away during extended power cuts, generating electricity for the ashram. Visitors, especially Indians, tended to be very noisy and talked and called loudly to each other. Many of these were day-trippers from neighbouring towns and cities in Kerala, whose loud merriment and boisterous chatter lent an air of festivity to the ashram. The *bhajan* singing too, amplified through loud speakers and lasting through the night at periodic events when the Mata appeared in her Devi *bhava*, added significantly to the ashram's already high decibel levels.

Visitors are required to abide by the ashram's daily routine. During my stay at Amritapuri, the day's schedule looked something like this: 5 a.m., chanting of the Lalitha Sahasranama; 9 to 10 a.m., breakfast; 10 to 11 a.m., occasional classes on spirituality; 11 onwards, the Mata's *darshan*; 1 p.m., lunch; 6.30 to 8 p.m., *bhajans*; 8 p.m., dinner. This routine allowed visitors plenty of time, between scheduled events, to discharge their *seva* responsibilities. These could range from cleaning the ashram, managing its stores, clearing out garbage, and cooking for the ashram community in its dark and damp kitchens, to sorting the ashram's incoming mail, and managing its fax, phone and e-mail facilities. One area of activity that engaged scores of volunteers was the ashram's press and publications division which required services as diverse as editing and proof-reading the articles that were to appear in the MAM's journals and books, providing art design and illustrations, and printing, binding and despatching the publications to the MAM's branches and centres in India and abroad.

The relatively unhurried daily schedule also allowed time for visitors to engage in what I discovered was one of their favourite activities. This was *satsang* and usually meant that devotees got together in small groups and chatted with each other, mostly exchanging narratives of their miracle experiences. Most devotees welcomed my request to interview them, seizing this opportunity to recount endless stories about the Mata's grace and glory, and thus engage in what they saw as ever more spiritually meritorious activity.

My stay in the ashram extended between August and October of 1997. At the time there were about 800 permanent residents in the ashram. These included, besides the Mata's 600 or more ascetic disciples, about 200 householders, most of them elderly couples or widows and widowers. Some had donated all their property to the MAM, and now lived simple and frugal lives in the ashram, contributing to its *seva* effort and relying on whatever support the MAM provided. Others were self-financing people who had invested in a flat in the Amrita Apartments and stayed on hoping to spend all or part of their remaining years in the 'spiritually cleansing' environment of the ashram. At the time of my stay, there were about 100 Westerners living in the ashram as permanent residents. Besides this, there was a constant floating population of Indians and Westerners who would come and stay for anything from a few days to a few months.[11] The ashram often found itself badly cramped for space, and its permanent residents recounted to me several instances in the previous few years when they had to 'camp out' in the ashram's balconies, corridors and halls in order to make room for the rush of visitors. The rush is particularly acute during the 'Western season' between December and February each year, when the Mata's American and European devotees flock to the ashram in their hundreds.

One of the most striking aspects of ashram life is the demarcation between its Western and Indian areas of operation. Besides the separate Foreign Office to which Westerners are ushered when they first come to the ashram, and the separate Seva Desk, there is a separate Western canteen, a Western shop, separate dormitories for Western occupants and even separate (and faster-moving!) queues for Westerners when they await their turn for the Mata's *darshan*. During my stay in the ashram I noticed little or no interaction between the Mata's Western devotees and her Indian ones. In fact, much of the interaction between ashram residents (permanent or otherwise) seemed to take place within small social groups. Non-Indians tended to interact mostly with people of their own nationality, while Indians interacted with fellow Indians from common regional and linguistic backgrounds.

Despite this, or because of it, Indians, as I discovered in the course of interviews, had definite views about Westerners, and about the relationship between India and the West as it was played out in the context of spiritual seeking in the Mata's fold. By and large, they conceptualized this relationship in terms of that between (Indian) hosts and (Western) guests. The host–guest rhetoric, however, encompassed a wide variety of mutual perceptions and feelings, ranging from the more sympathetic to the most patronizing and even severely critical.

Indian selves and Western others

Many Indians saw the Mata's Western devotees as their materially rich and spiritually poor cousins from halfway across the globe who were in greater need than themselves of the Mata's spiritual ministrations. The Indians, as the benefactors of the West, played up their beneficence by 'accommodating' (or claiming to accommodate) Western ways in the ashram. They were happy to allow their 'Western guests' to run separate canteens, shops and kitchens, live in separate dormitories and wait in separate queues for the Mata's *darshan*. None of the Indians I spoke to complained about this practice of segregation; instead it was the odd Westerner who objected to it and questioned its propriety. Indian devotees and disciples spoke generously about how ashram rules had been relaxed to accommodate the Westerners. Dress codes, for instance, they said, were more rigorous in earlier days. Whereas now men and women moving about in T-shirts and jeans was a common enough sight, only five years previously, I was told, such a thing was unthinkable. This was seen as a vital concession to Western preferences. Rules regarding food too had been relaxed. Earlier rice gruel was about the only thing that was served in the ashram. Now there was a whole range of snacks and delicacies available. Cakes, crisps, chocolates and ice cream were all available at a tiny cafe run by some German residents. The ashram's residents told me that the consumption of eggs, considered non-vegetarian by most Indians, and therefore not conducive to a spiritual life of abstinence, was strictly prohibited in the premises until 1997. Then one day in that year, they said, the Mata announced that egg preparations would be allowed in the ashram in order to satisfy the Westerners' need for protein supplements to their vegetarian diet.[12]

All these, in the view of some Indian devotees, were signs of the Mata's (and their own) generosity in accommodating her spiritually weaker children from abroad. This notion of Western spiritual inadequacy perhaps follows logically from the Mata's basic contention that modernity, with its emphasis on the material rather than the spiritual, leads individuals to lose touch with their spiritual selves. The West, with a head start in the 'modernization' process, would thus be in far greater need of spiritual revival than the East. Many of the Mata's Indian devotees, in speaking about the West, tended to portray the West as a sorry victim of modern 'imbalances', and to see the Mata as the saviour who could release the victim from its sorry plight by restoring a sense of balance to the modern world. The Vice President of the MAM Trust, commenting on the West in this vein, said, for instance:

> Material comfort is not everything. You go to the West. You expect people should be happy since materially they are so much better off than we are. But you should see people there crying in Amma's arms. They aren't happy. Why? A man in his forties would have dated thirty or forty different women. He would have drawn close to many, then broken away. Each break-up would have inflicted a deep wound in his heart. After that, he might marry somebody. There is often no harmony between the spouses so the marriage breaks up. He is separated from his children. Another wound. His life by the time he is forty or so is a saga of wound after wound. He can't reveal this wound to anybody. He hides his sorrows beneath a surfeit of material comfort. When he comes before Amma, all the pain comes rushing forth – all that he has bottled up through his life and been unable to share with another, even though others too, like him, are suffering. With Amma he sees his own sorrow reflected in her and he is able to unburden himself . . . That often results in a transformation. Amma says, the true *samskaram* [refinement or sophistication] – that you cannot get from material comfort. That you get from spirituality alone. She says it is not your body that needs air conditioning, it is your mind.

Similar perceptions of the West as a bundle of problems stemming from its preoccupation with the material and transient are reflected in the following comments from an essay with a revealingly alarmist title, 'Be careful my darling son . . . ' which appeared in the *Matruvani*.[13] Here the West is represented as a place where youth lead such 'complicated' lives that they are unable to differentiate between right and wrong, and where, as a result, they are led astray by such 'vices' as drug addiction.

As in India, Amma has been capturing the hearts of more and more Western youngsters, setting the perfect example of patience, dedication and love for them to follow. However, unlike in India, in the West, children are forced to deal with peer pressure, drugs, intoxicants, and a more complicated world at a much younger age. And in such a world, Amma provides the best loving support and care that children need. These children have the innocent faith that in all their problems and difficulties, Amma will be there for them to turn to for comfort.

Corresponding to this notion of the West being spiritually impoverished is of course the idea that India has a spiritual advantage over the modern world. This essentializing discourse provides devotees a vantage point to situate themselves and the Mata vis-à-vis the rest of the world. The senior scientist at the Bhabha Atomic Research Centre in Mumbai, whom I quoted in the last chapter, explained it thus:

All this modern world – with our great scientific achievements – landing on the moon, on Mars – what does it all amount to finally? Everyone is turning around and coming back to spirituality. The most modern nations like the United States and the European countries, they are all coming back to India to know something more than what they have already achieved. That shows that there is something more that we possess in this country. Which has been given to us by our ancients. Our country is really great and has produced great men who have gone to other great countries in the world and given them a certain direction, shown them a certain path, to achieve something – the spiritual . . . [14]

He further explained that the main problem with the West was its inability to 'accept the authority of god'.

Our lives are programmed like a computer. Whatever is bound to happen will happen. If we accept the authority of god, all problems will vanish. In India, everything is accepted as the will of god. We have no problems, we don't feel the need to run to a psychiatrist every time we suffer a misfortune. People are able to accept. Unlike in the West, where they feel the need for more and more psychiatrists. People in the West are suffering from mental distortion because they are unable to accept the will of god. The best psychiatric treatment our *maharishis* [sages] gave us is to teach us to accept the will of god . . . Which is why we rarely need psychiatrists while they, the Westerners, regularly need psychiatrists. And psychiatrists in turn need other psychiatrists for their own cure! Which is better? Our belief or theirs?[15]

Not all Indian devotees were thus critical of their Western counterparts. Many expressed profound admiration for what they saw as the 'sincerity' and 'dedication' with which Western devotees of the Mata pursue the spiritual path. This admiration was only enhanced by the conviction that for many of the Westerners who visit the ashram or enter it as permanent residents, their hardship and struggle in the ashram's inhospitable and alien environment must pose a sharp contrast to the comfortable lives they probably led back at home. Some Indian visitors to the ashram spoke of what they saw as the inefficiency and slackness in several aspects of the ashram's management and day-to-day operations. They expressed sympathy for their Western counterparts who, they said, often try very hard to 'adjust' to the ashram's ways. Some Westerners, they said, take it upon themselves to try and change things. The separate facilities for Westerners were, they argued, a commendable attempt on the part of the more enterprising of the Mata's Western devotees to set up a smoother and more efficient system alongside the slow-moving Indian one.[16]

In the view of many of the devotees I interviewed, moreover, the notion of India's spiritual superiority over the supposedly problem-ridden materialistic West is no longer tenable given India's own preoccupation with consumerism, modernity and materialism. As one of the ashram's senior *sannyasis* put it:

> We follow the West blindly . . . Material comfort alone cannot be the goal of our lives. Life doesn't mean merely physical existence, there is a larger consciousness operating that gives us strength and shows us the way. We must pay attention to that consciousness and cultivate it, refine it . . . Today we will do anything for the sake of physical and material comfort, no matter how gross, how crude. There is no fear, no accountability, instead there is complete freedom to do what you like, live how you will . . . Boredom, that is our biggest problem. Nobody stays in the same house for more than two years, nobody uses the same car for more than two years, or even lives with the same partner for more than two years. Children get bored with their parents, they stay separate after a bit. The emphasis is entirely on one's physical existence, one's higher existence is ignored altogether.

Not surprisingly, the 'spiritual East versus materialistic West' logic often tends to be reproduced by Western devotees of the Mata. Many tend to exoticize India as a land of spirituality and represent their attachment to the Mata in terms of a profound rejection of the Western world's so-called 'materialism'. Others, however, reverse the spirituality/materialism dichotomy, asserting what they see as the spiritual foundations of the West. These persons often express dismay that Indians should think of them in unflattering and stereotypical terms. An American female devotee of the Mata, who appeared keen to set the record straight, spoke at length, in the course of an interview, about her sense of hurt that America's spiritual strengths often went unrecognized in India.

> We [Americans] have so much depth, humour, aliveness . . . so much vital energy. And there's lots of spirituality in the US . . . I come here and every one thinks that we are heathen, materialistic, have sex five times a day and with different people. That's not true, no. In the US people lead normal lives, they take care of their family. Here they believe people in the US don't take care of their parents, if their car gets a dent they get rid of their car, they waste food . . . Things that aren't true. Cars get recycled. If there is a high rate of divorce in the US, there is also a large number of people who stay married till they die. There are so many other things in the US – the energy, the education, helping people socially, helping the poor. There are many good things happening but the people here choose to ignore them.

In a further reversal of the 'spiritual East' and 'materialistic West' stereotype, an American *sannyasi*-disciple of the Mata, the founder and now head of the thriving MAM centre in San Ramon, claimed that Indian devotees who seek the Mata out often do so primarily for the fulfilment of their immediate material wants and desires. Western devotees, by contrast, he claimed, are mainly concerned not so much with wish-fulfilment as with inner spiritual growth and seek out gurus like the Mata in the hope of developing inwardly and spiritually. In this person's scheme of things it is Indian materialism and selfishness that comes to be contrasted with Western spirituality.

Clearly then the collective imagination of the Mata's devotees and disciples, even though it has the potential to override social and cultural particularism, at the same time serves to reconstruct or invent it through the promotion of discourses of uniqueness and difference – a process which Robertson (1995) aptly describes as 'strategic essentialism'. This strategic essentialism in the Mata Amritanandamayi Mission bears out

Appadurai's (1996: 4) point that the work of the imagination is neither purely emancipatory nor entirely disciplined, but is a space of contestation in which individuals and groups seek to annex the global into their own (local) practices of the modern.

Conclusion

To sum up the discussion in this chapter, then, I have argued here that Indian perceptions of the Mata as a 'world' leader and her 'global' message are best seen as arenas of contested meaning. Different individuals within the Mata's fold perceive her differently depending on how they interpret her (and their own) location in a global context. Their global orientation in turn has important implications for the ways in which they construct modernity, as well as the ways in which they construct their own selfhood as modern persons. For some, the Mata is a universal guru who alleviates the sufferings of humanity at large. These persons perceive themselves first and foremost as suffering individuals, much like thousands of fellow sufferers scattered across the globe, all of whom are equally in need of the guru's divine ministrations. A fundamental unity, marked by suffering, characterizes humanity as a whole, and this suffering is the consequence of imbalances in the modern world to which the Mata provides a 'divine' antidote.

For others, the Mata is most crucially an Indian, and Hindu, guru. Modernity and its imbalances are problems associated largely with the West, and the Mata is India's solution to these problems. In this scheme of things, there is a dichotomy between the 'Indian self' and the 'Western other', which translates into a fundamental opposition between spirituality and materialism, and between the East's supposed potential for 'balanced' modernities, as opposed to the so-called tendency towards 'imbalance' in the modernized West. India's spiritual self, in providing solutions to the problem-ridden modern, materialistic West, claims for itself an inherent superiority which the Western other supposedly cannot match. This strategic essentialism is the logical fall-out of globalization processes, and provides (some) Indian followers of the Mata a vantage point from which to orientate themselves in relation to the rest of the world.

These different global orientations, and the resulting contestations of meaning, are played out in the context of the Mata's Amritapuri ashram in Kerala where we see the Mata's transnational spiritual empire in microcosm. Mutual perceptions of Indian and non-Indian devotees in the ashram context are centred on a host–guest paradigm where Indian devotees play host to their guests from abroad. This host–guest paradigm in fact covers not one but a range of Indian orientations to Westerners ranging from the most appreciative to the supercilious and disapproving. Despite the host–guest rhetoric, however, there is little or no actual interaction between Indian and Western devotees at Amritapuri. This lack of intermixing between Indians and Westerners is indicative not of an East–West divide per se, but of an entire range of divisions (of nationality, locality and language) that run through the ashram context. Devotees, both Indians and Westerners, mostly tend to socialize in small groups, mostly with others from similar local, regional and linguistic backgrounds. There is, in terms of day-to-day socializing within the ashram complex, evidence neither of a cohesive Indian 'community', nor of a unified Western 'group', any more than there is evidence of anything akin to collective solidarity or group identity for the Mata's followers as a whole.

8

CONCLUSION

A simplistic view of Mata Amritanandamayi's popularity in urban India might see her as providing her middle-class followers some kind of refuge from the stresses and strains of a modern world. This kind of perspective would reinforce the view that the so-called 'traditional' Hindu selfhood of these persons is incompatible with the imperatives of 'modernity'. It would further reinforce the oft-repeated idea of an absolute opposition between Hindu and Western selves, the former representing a traditional and uniquely religious orientation, the latter a modern and rational one.

My attempt in this book has been to point out the inadequacies of such an approach. I have attempted to show, first, that the selfhood of the Mata's devotees must be understood not in terms of passive essences ('traditional', 'religious') but in terms of the active processes by which they come to construct it. Modernity too, I have argued, is best seen not in terms of essences but again in terms of the processes by which these individuals construct and conceptualize it. It is through such constructions that the Mata's devotees negotiate the fast pace of change in contemporary India's urban milieu. This negotiation in its turn entails an active process of selecting, rejecting, picking and mixing from a diverse range of ideas, beliefs and practices that these persons encounter in their everyday lives. Among the many and varied choices and selections they make are those in the religious domain, not least in the matter of guru-attachment.

I have explored, in this book, the ways in which individuals choose between different gurus and their wares available in the varied and often competitive world of Indian spirituality. I have examined the different yardsticks that these persons use in making their selections, and the different ways in which they often combine the teachings and prescriptions of the chosen guru(s), with other available religious options, in concocting their personal religious lives. From the perspective of her middle-class devotees, Mata Amritanandamayi is but one in a range of gurus and other

spiritual attractions abounding in contemporary India's densely popu-
lated religious landscape with its global networks and transnational
connections. Those who select the Mata as their chosen guru do so for
particular reasons. Once they enter the Mata's fold, they are exposed to
a particular view of the modern world, and of themselves as actors in
it. The Mata explains suffering as a consequence of imbalances in
the modern world, and prescribes certain spiritual practices which, she
claims, serve as an antidote both to suffering in the short term, and to
modernity's imbalances in the long term. From the Mata's repertoire of
spiritual teachings and ritual prescriptions, devotees make particular
selections that best suit their inclinations and preferences. Devotees value
the Mata's instrumental–rational approach, where every prescribed ritual
and other observance has its particular set of promised rewards. Devotees
also value their independence and individuality as autonomous agents
who are free to lead their religious lives as they see fit. Most of these
persons are concerned with 'meaning' in their spiritual lives, and reject a
traditionalist view that sees religion and religious authority as something
which they must take for granted and to which they must submit
unquestioningly.

Modernity, as it is constructed within the Mata's fold, appears
as a bundle of elements, desirable and otherwise. Among these are
consumerism, revolutionized technology, scientific advancements,
rationality, acquisitiveness and egotism. The Mata encourages devotees
to engage with modernity in a judicious and discerning way, and not
get so excessively preoccupied with some of its elements that they
lose a sense of perspective or 'balance' in their lives. It is this loss of
perspective, and the resulting imbalances which, in her reckoning,
contribute to the suffering of the modern world. In striving to alleviate
modern humanity's suffering and sorrow, she seeks to restore the realm
of the heart in a world of 'dry minds', and to reinfuse the world with
love. Towards this end, she prescribes the cultivation of spirituality,
emotionalism and humility among her devotees.

The ways in which devotees seek to construct their selfhood once they
enter the Mata's fold, is of course inextricably connected with this
particular understanding of the modern world. By examining at close
quarters the religious choices and decisions that her urban middle-class
followers make in the context of their attachment to the Mata, I have
explored here the means by which these individuals come to construct
their religious lives as modern Hindus located in a post-colonial world
of revolutionized communications, high consumerism and individual
choice. After entering her fold, they embark on what they see as a spiritual
journey that must lead to ever greater levels of spiritual and emotional

awakening, and that must result in an increasingly balanced life which enables them to negotiate the modern world in ever more fulfilling ways. As devotees of a modern guru who addresses a global audience, their orientations towards the global arena vary. Perceptions of their own and the Mata's location in a globalized context reveal both liberal and universalistic, as well as conservative and particularistic, attitudes and world-views.

From an etic perspective, it is evident that devotees' selfhood is neither a given, nor composed of a fixed set of 'essences', but is something to be negotiated constantly. Their choice of guru, their acceptance of particular elements in the guru's spiritual prescriptions and rejection of others, their decision to sustain their loyalty to the chosen guru over any length of time, are all important elements in this process of negotiating a particular selfhood. This selfhood is revisable, so that devotees are free to abandon one guru in favour of another, and to negotiate a new selfhood based on the new guru's spiritual prescriptions. This is a self that sees personality as a project, and perceives life in modern times as a set of possibilities and potentialities in which there is need for conscious self-fashioning in every sphere, including that of religion and spirituality. The Mata's appeal, then, lies in her acknowledgement of her devotees' need for autonomy and self-authorship. By emphasizing the personal, rather than the social, functions of faith, and by defining religious identity as an inner horizon predicated upon the personal fulfilment of adherents rather than on external authorization, she succeeds in propagating a novel and innovative form of spirituality which answers her devotees' need for personal freedom and choice.

It follows from this that modernity, as the Mata and her devotees conceptualize it, while it may well destroy the certitude of custom and tradition, does not necessarily lead to a greater 'brittleness' or 'fragility' in modern selfhood. Devotees' modern selves are not more fragile, but certainly become more flexible, changeable and revisable as a result of the greater self-reflexivity of the individual. Their religious identity is also made relative by the emergence and awareness of new options, possibilities and choices, and it too requires more frequent negotiations and affirmations.

My study clearly does not bear out the contention[1] that 'modernity' has ruptured the Hindu sense of self. In contrast to oft-repeated assertions regarding the 'distinctiveness' of Hindu selfhood, and its 'incompatibility' with modernity, my study points, in the case of Mata Amritanandamayi's urban educated devotees, to important shifts in their conceptions of selfhood, resulting from their construction of modernity. These shifts represent not a sense of defeat and alienation but instead indicate the means whereby individuals cope with, accommodate and negotiate change. In sharp contrast to claims that 'there is no scope for compromise' between the 'old' and the 'new' (Nandy 1990: 97), my study shows how the spiritual enterprise of Mata Amritanandamayi proves to be an instance of 'Hindu' faith and practice adapting to change in contemporary India. What we see in the case of the Mata's devotees is not a self that is 'fragmented' and 'ruptured' as a result of its encounter with social change, but one that is empowered to meet its diverse strains and pressures, by securing an anchor in the accommodating love of this popular guru. By placing their faith in Mata Amritanandayi, then, the urban middle-class devotees of this modern guru seek not to retreat from modernity but to engage with it, by striving, within the Mission's accommodating environment, to negotiate their selfhood in novel, innovative, and personally fulfilling ways.

Religion in modern India

Nandy's (ibid.) analysis, as I noted in Chapter 1, is merely one in a series of recent scholarly writings on India's supposedly 'fragmented' post-colonial selfhood. These writings have been highly influential in attempting, as Nandy does, to explain, through their analyses of the 'Hindu' self, one of the most significant developments in India's recent history – the upsurge of Hindu nationalism in India since the early 1980s, and the religious violence that has followed in its wake.[2] Many of these scholars argue, like Nandy, that present-day Hindus suffer from a sense of alienation and defeat as a result of the legacy of India's colonial experience and their own exposure to post-colonial modernity.[3] Organizing themselves as a militant Hindu force and directing their hatred towards the 'enemy', the Muslim, has enabled Hindus (these writers argue) to recover their self-confidence, recuperate their 'masculinity', and assert their selfhood as Hindus and Indians.

In this context, it would certainly be worthwhile to compare and contrast notions of the ideal self, as it is conceived by devotees of Mata Amritanandamayi, with those attributed to supporters of the Hindutva cause.[4] While an extended analysis along these lines is beyond the scope of this book, I would like to outline some of the important areas of contrast that do emerge from this study. One such pertains to the key motifs around which selfhood is constructed in each case. In the case of the Hindutva proponents and supporters, a central motif has long been Ram, the epic hero of the Ramayana, believed to be an avatar of Vishnu, who is widely depicted in the propaganda of the 'Sangh Parivar' Hindu supremacists in his aspect as a warrior king, wielding bow and arrow, representing martial valour, and suggesting a state of readiness for confrontation and battle.[5] This representation provides a striking contrast to the central MAM motif, the Mata herself, again an avatar, but one representing compassion and maternal love, and promising to enfold the devotee in her loving and all-encompassing embrace. Related to this is a second point of contrast, this time in the way the 'enemy' is defined. For Hindutva ideologues, the enemy is the Muslim, who, as the demonized other, is the object of their intense communal hatred.[6] In the case of the Mata's devotees, there is no external enemy. Instead the enemy is located within oneself, in the form of accumulated *prarabdhas* and *vasanas*, which must be eliminated if the individual is to progress towards his or her spiritual goal. Third and most important, the construction of selfhood in the Hindutva scheme of things is envisaged as a process of recuperating masculinity, the overcoming of a perceived emasculation of the Hindu self – a common, deep-running theme in Hindu nationalist discourses and organizations.[7] In sharp contrast to this, the devotees of the Mata envisage the construction of their own selfhood in very different terms. Theirs is certainly not a quest for re-masculinization. If anything, it is an effort at 'effeminization' (though none of my informants perceive their selfhood thus in polarized gender terms) wherein they seek to revive their emotional selves, and enhance their receptivity to the Mata's love and compassion.

While supporting the militant campaign for a Hindu nation may be one of the ways in which some sections of India's Hindus ('middle classes' and others) have, in recent times, responded to their encounter with modernity, it is certainly not the only way in which modern Indians have sought to cope with change. This book, by providing a detailed ethnography of perceptions of selfhood among Mata Amritanandamayi's devotees, has sought to challenge some of the prevalent stereotypes regarding the 'Hindu' self. Rather than dwell on oft-repeated themes which centre around India's overwhelming sense of defeat, a 'ruptured' sense of Indian (and 'Hindu') selfhood, and an inability to cope with modernity's demands and pressures, this study has attempted to reveal a more complex picture of contemporary Indian realities. The personalized and individualized form of faith I have explored in the case of the Mata Amritanandamayi Mission, the wide-ranging choices made by followers, and the variety of modes of self-fashioning in the religious sphere, all clearly indicate possibilities and potentials for new and alternative configurations of Hinduism that run contrary to what many scholars studying Hinduism in contemporary India see as the inevitable 'incompatibility' between Hinduism and the imperatives of modernity in a fast-paced and rapidly changing world.

APPENDIX

Interviewee profile

Followers of Mata Amritanandamayi

Total number of followers interviewed:	75
Number of Indian followers:	50
Number of non-Indian followers:	25

Composition of Indian followers (50 in total)

Lay Indian devotees: 35   (19 males, 16 females)

Ascetic Indian disciples: 15   (10 males, 5 females)
(Of the 15, 6 were probationers, 4 were *brahmachari/nis*, 5 were *sannyasi/nis*)
The *sannyasis* interviewed included the President and General Secretary of the Mata Amritanandamayi Mission Trust

Composition of non-Indian followers (25 in total)

The interviewees' nationalities were American, British, Australian, French, Italian, Swiss, Dutch, Sri Lankan and Lebanese.

Lay foreign devotees: 20   (10 male, 10 female)

Ascetic foreign disciples: 5   (3 male, 2 female)
(Of the 5, 3 were probationers and 2 were *sannyasi/nis*)
One of the *sannyasis* interviewed was the head of the MAM centre in San Ramon, California

Other interviewees (23 in total)

The Mata herself, the Mata's father and one of her sisters

The Mata's biographer

The State President, and two organizing secretaries of the Vishwa Hindu Parishad in Kerala

Three interviewees belonging to an international guru-busting organization called the 'Indian Rationalists Association'

Eight students studying at various institutes of higher studies run by the MAM

Five persons who had been to *darshans* of the Mata in Delhi and Kerala but remained non-devotees after the experience

GLOSSARY

aarati ritual offering of light to the deity

adrishta invisible

atman the individual soul

bhajan devotional song of prayer, often rendered collectively by a group of devotees

bhakti devotion

bhava mood or aspect

brahmachari/ brahmacharini spiritual aspirant who has been initiated into a life of asceticism and rigorous spiritual discipline

brahmacharya a stage of life marked by scholarship, celibacy and spiritual striving

brahman the divine absolute, as transcendent, formless and disembodied; also referred to as the 'supreme consciousness' or 'divine essence'

chakra centre of psycho-spiritual consciousness

daridra poor

darshan visual feasting on the deity's and/or guru's form, believed to bring good fortune, grace and spiritual merit to the devotee

dhyana meditation as spiritual practice

diksha initiation

drishta visible

grahadosha planetary affliction

gyana knowledge

japa chanting (of a mantra, of god's name, etc.)

jiva individual life form

maharishi sage

mahotsavam annual temple festival

manas the mind: the seat of one's emotions and intellect

manasa of the mind, mental

math monastic order

moksha liberation from the cycle of birth and death

mooladhara located at the base or root

naamavali devotional composition comprising a string of names, usually of a god or goddess

narayana god; more specifically Vishnu

nirguna formless, disembodied

pandal colourful tent-like shelter often erected at public ceremonies like marriages and religious festivals

pracharana the act of publicizing, broadcasting

prana pratishtha the act of infusing divine energy into the image or idol, thus sanctifying it

prarabdha burden accumulated from negative karmas in past lives

prasad sanctified substance, usually food, flowers, sandalwood paste or ashes, believed to be imbued with divine grace through contact with the image of the deity

pratishtha sanctified image or idol in a temple

purna complete, whole

pushpam flower

sadguru guru

sadhak spiritual practitioner

sadhana spiritual practice

saguna that which has attributes or qualities

sahasranama one thousand names

sahasrara located in the head or crown

samagri paraphernalia

samiti committee

samooha congregational

sampradaya teaching or hermeneutic tradition, denomination

samsara the realm of the worldly

sankalpa a resolve; in the Mata's case, her 'divine' resolve that transforms a wish into reality

sannyasa renunciation (hence *sannyasi/ni* – renouncer)

sanskriti culture or refinement

satsang the company of the good; in the MAM, *satsang* refers to devotee gatherings where participants engage in spiritual activity

seva selfless service

sevak one who renders service

shakti/ parashakti female divine energy

shanti peace

shishya disciple

siddhi divine power acquired through spiritual practice

vasana   tendency or habit accumulated from previous births, leading to worldly attachment

vibhuti   ashes, considered sacred and pure in Hindu mythology

vidyalaya   school

visham   poison

yagna   congregational ritual of sacrifice; in the MAM's usage *yagna* refers to any collective effort

NOTES

Introduction

1 The Mata also has a sizeable following in Brazil, Mauritius and Reunion.

2 See Rosaldo 1993: 127–46.

3 *Amrita*, in Sanskrit, means 'immortal'. According to popular understanding, the English translation for Mata Amritanandamayi is 'mother of immortal bliss'. She is often referred to as Amma or Ammachi by her devotees. Both terms mean 'mother' in Malayalam, the Mata's native language.

4 The biography identifies her as belonging to the Araya (fishing) caste, a group classed in both pre- and post-Independence ethnographies (including census reports and other official accounts) as 'economically backward'. The state of Kerala classes this group as one of the 'Other Backward Castes' for purposes of 'reservation' benefits in educational institutions and certain categories of employment. My enquiries in the village revealed that the Mata's parents had marketed fish for a living. They had had no formal education themselves but sent most of their eight children to school. The Mata, according to her biography, has been formally educated up to the fourth standard of the local primary school.

5 See McDaniel's (1989) discussion of alternative paths to spiritual enlightenment demonstrated by seekers in various Hindu traditions. McDaniel distinguishes between the 'path of progression' within a lineage order and the 'path of breakthrough' followed by ecstatics and mystics. The Mata's spiritual attainment fits well within McDaniel's description of the latter path.

6 *Darshan* literally means 'sighting', and refers here to occasions when devotees get to see their guru or god and visually feast on the latter's form – an important element in Hindu devotionalism.

7 *Awaken Children* 1989 (1: 338), Mata Amritanandamayi Mission Trust, Kollam, Kerala.

8 These refer to three different strands of devotionalism centred on the worship of Shiva, Vishnu and Shakti (female divine energy) respectively. On the historical origins of these traditions, see Flood 1996, chapters 5 to 8.

9 See Carey 1987 for a detailed ethnographic description of initiation into monkhood in the Ramakrishna Mission. On rituals of initiation in other renunciatory orders, see R.B. Williams 2001; van der Veer 1988.

10 At the time of my fieldwork in Amritapuri in 1997–8, there were about 700

148

ascetic disciples in all in the MAM. Of these the majority were probationers awaiting *brahmacharya diksha*. Less than a hundred were *brahmachari(ni)s* and about fifteen to twenty were *sannyasi(ni)s*. The majority of the disciples were Indian. About one-third the total number were female. Among the *sannyasis* about five were foreigners, two (both non-Indian) were female.

11 The Ramakrishna Math and Mission is a devotional and social service oriented organization founded in the early twentieth century in memory of Ramakrishna, the well-known nineteenth-century mystic in Bengal in eastern India. It is pertinent to note here that this organization is a key precursor to the MAM not only in terms of its devotionalist tradition and social service orientation, but also with respect to its particular appeal to a predominantly middle-class following. On the Ramakrishna Math and Mission see Gupta 1974; Beckerlegge 1990, 1998, 2000a, 2000b; Sen 2000; Sinclair-Brull 1997; Sarkar 1992; Gambhirananda 1957.

12 A typical ashram branch in India comprises a modern building that houses a prayer hall used for the collective ritual and prayer sessions organized by the officiating disciple(s), office rooms for carrying out the ashram's administrative tasks, and living quarters for the resident disciple and for the Mata when she comes on her annual visit.

13 The Mata does have a small non-Hindu (Christian and Muslim) following within India as also a small number of low-income devotees from urban and rural backgrounds, mostly the beneficiaries of her charitable ventures. Both in terms of numbers, as well as the extent of their involvement in the Mission's activities, these individuals constitute only a tiny fraction of her total Indian following, the bulk of which comprises hundreds of thousands of urban affluent middle-class persons.

14 See C.A. Bayly 1983 and Joshi 2001 for historical accounts of the origins of India's middle classes in the colonial era.

15 See Gordon 1978; Ray 1979; Markovits 1985.

16 See Misra 1961; Frankel 1988; Khanna 1987; Lakha 1999; Ninan 1990; Appadurai and Breckenridge 1995.

17 See S. Bayly 1999, especially chapters 8 and 9, on the complex issue of caste identities in modern India.

18 Kaul 1993.

19 See Appadurai and Breckenridge 1995; Ninan 1990; Robison and Goodman 1996; Mazzarella 2003.

20 Swallow (1982) argues that Sathya Sai Baba's devotees, mainly of high-caste background, feel threatened by a social environment they can no longer control as they once did. In the new towns and the newer suburban sectors of old towns, areas where Sathya Sai Baba's following is most evident, Swallow argues, it is often extremely difficult to maintain the traditional Hindu cycle of religious observances, or to maintain a network of dependent ritual service caste families. Meritocracy has, in principle, replaced caste ideologies, and old service castes are forced to compete with newcomers. Traditional patterns of authority are threatened. Gender roles are shifting and women demand more freedom than they were granted in the past. All of this, according to Swallow, results in these urban dwellers having to constantly make accommodations in every aspect of their social and religious life. Many persons see the present situation as one in which order has disappeared. In such a 'disordered' world, Sathya Sai Baba holds out the promise

of restoring order, and demonstrates that the Hindu religious tradition is still a living force.

21 Kakar (1984) sees India's 'transitional sector', the newly urbanized emerging middle classes, as a 'natural reservoir of cults'. These people, he argues, are neither the 'traditional majority' nor the miniscule minority of the highly modernized and Westernized. For them membership in a guru's following provides a much-needed social anchor, and a new group identity that can replace village or caste community (ibid.: 214). The 'cult' or guru organization thus stands in between the individual and the impersonal institutions of an urban society.

22 A significant exception to this mode of analysis is presented in a recent study of Sathya Sai Baba by Urban (2003) where the author represents Sai Baba as an embodiment of the cultural contradictions of late capitalism, and therefore as very much an icon of global modernity and mass consumerism. Urban's study, while providing important insights into the Sathya Sai Mission in what he sees as a late capitalist context, does not, however, explore in any depth the agency of the followers of Sathya Sai Baba or indeed the specific spiritual and other choices they make in their everyday lives.

23 For instance Chryssides 1999; Coney 1998.

24 For a discussion on Weber's thesis on Hinduism, see Munshi 1988; Kantowsky 1986; Gellner 1982.

25 Among the few scholars who have challenged this view are Béteille 1991b; Mines 1994, 1998, 1999; Mines and Gaurishankar 1990.

26 The over-simplified and essentializing assertions of these writers have been challenged by Khilnani 1997; Baber 1996; Vanaik 1997; C.A. Bayly 1985, 1998; Upadhyaya 1992; Basu and Subrahmanyam (eds) 1996.

27 A contrasting view is presented by van der Veer who sees Hindu nationalism not as a backlash against Western modernizing influences, but instead as a uniquely Indian (Hindu) form or expression of 'modernity' (see van der Veer 1994a and 1994b, 2001 and van der Veer and Lehmann (eds) 1999). While treating nationalism as an indispensable constituent of 'modernity', van der Veer nevertheless challenges the notion that secular forms of nationalism alone qualify as 'modern'. Exploring the crucial link between religion and forms of national identity and nation-building not just in the Indian case but also in Western, and especially British, historical contexts, van der Veer argues for a revision of conventional understandings of the relationship between modernity, secularity and nationhood. He emphasizes the need to acknowledge the place of religious ideology and symbolism in the formation of 'modern' nation-states across the colonial divide.

28 See Frykenberg 1989; Thapar 1989; cf. Smith 1998.

29 cf. Sanderson 1985; Bharati 1985; Khare 1993: 191–212; Morris 1994: 71–95.

30 See Arnason 1996; Gaonkar 1999; Knobl 2000; Friese and Wagner 2000; Linkenbach 2000; Eisenstadt 2000; Wittorck 2000; Tambiah 2000; Knauft 2002.

31 See for instance Berman 1982; Miller 1994; Comaroff and Comaroff 1993; Appadurai 1996; Knauft 2002.

32 See the Appendix for details about interviewee profile and composition.

33 See Mankekar 2000 and Narayan 1989, 1993 for insightful discussions of

the complex relationship between 'native anthropologists' and 'informants' in contemporary urban Indian middle-class contexts.

34 Extract from a letter dated 5th July 1997 from the Joint Secretary of the Mata Amritanandamayi Mission. Note the nationalistic tones in the letter, which, as I explain in Chapter 7, are in no way representative of the general orientation in the MAM.

2 Encountering the Mata

1 These items, produced at the Mission headquarters, are named after the Mata. *Amrita* in Sanskrit means 'immortal'.

2 The majority of the politicians sharing the stage with the Mata were from the BJP. This is one of the many occasions where I noticed the Mata welcoming public endorsement by the BJP, the political party leading the Indian government at the time of writing this book, and a leading proponent of Hindu nationalism. There were, however, other occasions in the course of my fieldwork when I noticed the Mata make platform appearances alongside members of anti-BJP political parties such as the Congress. What is significant for the Mata and her devotees, it would appear, is not the political ideology of the politicians concerned, but the authority they represent by virtue of their location in India's highest echelons of power.

3 These are traditional Indian percussion (tabla) and keyboard (harmonium) instruments, used as accompaniment both in classical music and dance performances as well as in folk performances and in conventional *bhajan* singing.

4 See Juergensmeyer 1991: 88–109 on the importance, in the Radhasoami faith, of melody and sound, along with light, in facilitating the soul's journey to salvation. See also the contrasting views of Milton Singer 1968 and Fuller 1992 on whether Radha-Krishna *bhajans* of Madras (now Chennai), in the south Indian state of Tamil Nadu, dramatize ideals of social equality (Singer) or serve as expressions of existing inequalities in society (Fuller). In the case of the *bhajan* session I attended, the most crucial element was not so much a sense of the collective assertion of either egalitarian or hierarchical principles (indeed most of the members of the audience did not even appear to know each other), as the importance of music, rhythm and melody in building up the audience's emotions and leading them to a state of high excitement in anticipation of the events to follow.

5 *Darshan* is an important concept in Hindu devotionalism and refers to a visual feasting on the deity's and/or guru's form by the devotee. The sight or vision of the deity is believed to bring good fortune, grace and spiritual merit to the devotee. See Eck 1981; Babb 1987: 79; Kakar 1984: 128–40; Juergensmeyer 1991: 83–4. In the Mata's case, *darshan* involves not just beholding the Mata but also being held in her embrace.

6 *Prasad* is the material symbol of the deity's power and grace. It is any sanctified substance, usually food, or ashes, or sandalwood paste, or flowers, which, during rituals of worship, comes in contact with the image of the deity being worshipped and is believed, as a result, to become imbued with divine power and grace (see Fuller 1992: 74–5). In this case, the boiled sweet is *prasad* by virtue of the Mata's touch.

7 See, for instance, Babb's (1987: 173) comments on how Sathya Sai Baba

keeps a 'somewhat wary distance from his female followers', and how 'this is only prudent, given endemic suspicions about relations between male and female followers'. See also R.B. Williams' (2001) comments on the strict rules of celibacy observed by the leader of the Swami Narayan sect, which kept him from touching, looking at, or talking with women.

8 Again, Babb (ibid.: 184) notes how devotees of the popular Indian guru Sathya Sai Baba 'clamour to touch his feet' where no other form of touching is permitted. He describes this in terms of 'hierarchical intimacy' between guru and devotees. On the hierarchical symbolism of bodily gestures in India, see Fuller 1992: 3–4. For Sathya Sai Baba's followers, the most 'desirable of boons' is a personal interview with this guru. This never lasts more than a few minutes, and very few devotees are granted this special favour. In contrast, every devotee queueing up for the Mata's embrace gets an opportunity to ask her brief questions. Devotees often compare the respective styles of the two gurus, asserting their appreciation for the intimacy and equal treatment of all, that characterizes the Mata's mode of interacting with her devotees.

9 The guru as mother is a familiar theme in Hindu devotionalism. Through much of India's history there have been Hindu female gurus, who have been revered as mother figures. Their representations as mother figures, however, reflects the problematic nature of female asceticism in Hindu religious traditions. As Narayan 1989: 66 notes, this problem arises from the cultural expectation that women be defined relationally to men, as wives, daughters and mothers. Women who cut off all social ties to embark on a solitary ascetic life are an anomaly in this scheme. When a woman is recognized as a guru, her devaluation as a single woman is countered by idealizing her as a mother. As holy mothers, female ascetics and gurus are likely to gain a large following. On female asceticism in India, see Ramanujan 1986; Denton 1991; Ojha 1981; Khandelwal 1997; King 1984; Sinclair-Brull 1997.

10 This emphasis on 'experience' on the part of Mata Amritanandamayi's devotees bears comparison with the centrality of individual, personal 'experience' in popular charismatic and evangelical movements in north American, west European and also Latin American and African societies. See Cartledge 1998; Percy 1998.

11 Emotionalism is a common feature of Hindu devotional practice and is seen as facilitating absolute identity and communion between the devotee and the object of devotion. See Lynch 1988, 1990; Toomey 1990; Bennett 1990; van der Veer 1988. Guru–devotee transactions are often highly emotional experiences, as noted in Babb 1987; Kakar 1984; and Juergensmeyer 1991.

12 This is comparable to the 'conversion' and 'threshold crossing' described by Babb (1987: 182) for devotees of Sathya Sai Baba. This, for devotees, is the moment of 'intellectual surrender' and evidence of their 'personal experience' of something inexplicable and out of the ordinary.

13 Questions regarding whether emotions are passively experienced or actively constructed through the actors' cultural subjectivities have been much debated in anthropological works on the subject. See Shweder and Levine 1984; Lutz and Abu-Lughod 1990; Lutz and White 1986; Lynch 1990. In particular see Lynch (ibid.: 'Introduction'), who along with other contributors to his volume (Marglin, Bennett and Toomey) stresses the importance

of catalysts or stimulants in evoking particular sentiments in Hindu devotionalist contexts.

14 *Mata Amritanandamayi: A Biography* [henceforth simply *Biography*] by Swami Amritaswarupananda, Mata Amritanandamayi Mission Trust, Kollam, Kerala, India, 1996. For those with access to the Internet, information about the Mata, though not in the kind of detail provided in the biography, is available at the Mission's websites at www.ammachi.org and www.amritapuri.org.

15 Dark complexions are negatively valued in India, and, as Harlan and Courtright (1995: 9) rightly point out, they are generally considered less desirable than light ones, especially in the context of marriage negotiations which take into account the complexion of the bride. The biography describes the Mata's skin-colour as 'blue-black' and indicates that this is a sign of her proximity to Krishna and Kali, the dark-skinned god and goddess respectively, often described as being of a dark bluish complexion.

16 Descriptions in the Mata's biography echo themes common to hagiographies of *bhakti* saints (and also Muslim *pirs*: cf. S. Bayly 1989) many of which read like eulogistic accounts of the extraordinary characteristics displayed by these 'divine' figures. See, for instance, McDaniel's (1989) accounts of the hagiographies of *bhakti* saints in Bengal, Swallow's (1982) account of Sathya Sai Baba's biographical narrative, and Babb's (1987) reference to the biographies of three gurus, including Sathya Sai Baba.

17 Krishna is widely worshipped in Kerala, and there are many temples in the state dedicated to him. Three such temples are located in Kerala's Kollam district where the Mata's village is located. The best-known Krishna temple, and the most popular pilgrimage centre in the state, is located at Guruvayur, in central Kerala.

18 The mythology surrounding Krishna traces his life through several stages. Prominent images of Krishna in the *bhakti* tradition are those as a young playful child, a mischievous adolescent, and a divine lover. See Kinsley 1979; Vaudeville 1996; Case 2000; Hawley 1981. The Mata's early Krishna manifestations appear to be representations of the deity as a mischievous adolescent.

19 A popular Hindu devotional text which narrates the story of Krishna's life.

20 *Biography*: 73–4.

21 Goddess worship is widely prevalent throughout Kerala and assumes many forms. These include the worship of blood and power divinities, the divine female warriors described by S. Bayly (1989: 27–31), who fight to keep at bay demonic forces threatening to harm the universe. They also include devotion to the more benign and gentle forms of the goddess, such as that of Saraswati, revered as the goddess of learning, or of Lakshmi, the consort of Vishnu and goddess of wealth. The Devi for whose vision Sudhamani, according to her biography, longed, does not appear to be any particular goddess, but female divinity in an abstract sense.

22 *Biography*: 125.

23 Ibid.: 127.

24 The biography also makes repeated references to various 'sceptics' and 'rationalists' in the area who apparently made several attempts to expose the Mata as a fraud. The Mata, according to this account, thwarted each such attempt, often winning over the sceptics to her fold in the process. One

individual who was a constant thorn in the Mata's flesh was her brother Subhagan, who not only disbelieved his sister's claims to divinity, but also physically abused her for not relenting and owning up to what he alleged was a racket. Subhagan died early under mysterious circumstances. The biography explains his death as a suicide but claims also that the Mata willed his demise because he was proving to be a nuisance to her and her devotees and disciples. During fieldwork in Kerala I came across a book in Malayalam entitled *Amrtianandamayi: A Divine Mother?* by a so-called 'rationalist', Sreeni Pattathanam (published in 1990 by the 'Indian Atheist Publishers' in Delhi) which treats Subhagan's death as a murder allegedly committed by his father. This book, though it does not provide any direct evidence to support its allegations, questions the veracity of the Mata's claims and attempts to debunk her and her Mission.

25 In keeping with ascetic conventions, Sudhamani never married. The biography claims, however, that soon after she realized her identity with the goddess, Sudhamani stopped having her monthly periods. This claim appears to be an effort to negate her female sexuality, which otherwise would pose a problem for a female guru interacting unrestrainedly with members of the opposite sex.

26 Photographs (invariably ones in black and white) of the Mata in Krishna *bhava* show a younger and slimmer Mata, a mischievous smile on her face, wearing on her head a bejewelled crown decorated with a peacock feather, ornaments in her ears, a garland of flowers around her neck, and a silk drape around her shoulders. According to disciples, she wore yellow, the colour associated with Krishna, during these *darshans*.

27 These early *darshans* took place in an old temple near the Mata's family home, in a dimly lit and often crowded and confined space. Then, as now, the Mata received devotees in her arms, and offered solutions to their problems, often carrying on through the night till the last of the visitors had left.

28 Her biography makes no mention of these shifts in her self-representations, but her earliest devotees recollected these changes in the course of interviews. One disciple, an American and now the head of the Mission's centre in San Ramon, California, described the trident-wielding dance as revealing the Mata's *rudra* (fierce) aspect. She is now in her *shanta* (peaceful) *bhava*, he explained.

29 *Matruvani* 1989, 2(5/6): 47–51.

30 See Hardy (1994: 298–304) on textual representations of the avatar concept and of Vishnu's ten incarnations.

31 According to some devotees of Mata Amritanandamayi, it is they, rather than the Mata herself, who make the claim that she is an avatar. This assertion is important, given the value placed on self-effacement in Hindu guru traditions. The ideal-typical renouncer-guru does not flaunt his or her own abilities or assert his/her enlightened status; it is for others to discern the extent of the guru's spiritual achievements. In the case of the Mata, it is true that she often makes self-denigrating statements about herself, denying that she is an avatar or a goddess. She does, however, claim to 'reveal' her divine status to devotees during her Devi *bhavas*. This self-profession of divinity is reinforced when devotees perform the *arati* (ritual of worship) before the Mata, a ritual otherwise addressed only to the idols of gods and goddesses in Hindu temples and household shrines. The *bhavas*, the Mata's interpretation

of their meaning, and the ritual performed during the *bhavas*, all appear to confirm the Mata's 'avatar' status and her ready acknowledgement of the same.

32 On Sathya Sai Baba, see Swallow 1982; D. Taylor 1987; Babb 1987, 1991; Exon 1997; Urban 2003; White 1972. Gombrich and Obeyesekere (1988: 53–5) discuss Sai Baba's urban middle-class following in Sri Lanka, where he is incorporated into Buddhist faith as an incarnation of Buddha. Howe (2002) likewise discusses the emergence of a Sathya Sai Baba following in the complex and fast-changing religious landscape of Bali in Indonesia.

33 See Chryssides 1999: 179–93.

34 See Dumont 1970; Burghart 1978, 1983a, 1983b; van der Veer 1987a, 1988; Heesterman 1985; Parry 1994.

35 The phenomenon of the avatar with a mission to accomplish is clearly a culmination of earlier trends, evident in the Swaminarayan order in the late nineteenth century, and the Ramakrishna Mission in the early twentieth century, towards redefining the ascetic as one who serves society and works towards its welfare and reform. See R.B. Williams 2001; G.M. Williams 1991; Gupta 1974; Beckerlegge 1998, 2000a and b.

36 Note the insightful account provided by Babb and Wadley 1995 on the impact of printed images and popular oleographs on religious experience in India. The standardization of devotional experience, brought about by the print and electronic media, is particularly relevant in the case of a popular figure like the Mata, whose icons and representations are shared by devotees across the country and abroad. The complete range of modern iconography, however, is yet to be explored, particularly with respect to iconographic representations on huge roadside hoardings, newsmagazine covers and trinkets bearing miniature pictures of gods and gurus. See Beckerlegge, Preston and Waghorne in Beckerlegge 2001; see also Pinney 2003.

37 *Bhava* here must not be confused with the devotee's *bhava*, described in ethnographies of Hindu devotionalist traditions (for instance Toomey 1990: 29–30; van der Veer 1988: 159–72). The latter refers to the devotee's emotional attitude towards the guru or the deity, whereas the former refers to the 'divine mood' or 'aspect' not of the devotee but of the guru or god.

38 *Biography*: 186–7.

39 For an ethnographic account of creating the sacred image and consecrating it, also see Courtright (1985: 172–84), who vividly describes the infusion of divinity into the clay image of the elephant god Ganesh at the annual festival of Ganesh Chaturthi in Maharashtra. Here too, the impermanence of divinity is a key theme.

40 Hardy's (1994) comments are pertinent here. He notes how the avatar's 'objective' interference in the world and the cosmos does not exhaust the purpose of the incarnation. 'Behind the many and variegated events narrated about avatars is revealed a permanent love – divine love for earthly mortals. When individual human beings come into personal contact with the avataras they directly encounter this love' (ibid.: 302–3). It is this 'encounter' and the immediacy of the contact that is centrally important to the Mata's devotees.

41 In drawing attention to the contrast between the intimacy and immediacy of the Mata's love, and the impersonal nature of expert institutions and specialist services in the modern world, I want to emphasize that neither the Mata nor her devotees see the ministrations of a guru as a substitute for the

services provided by expert institutions. Instead they see the two things as complementing each other. Individuals might turn to the Mata hoping for the cure of a disease, for instance, while simultaneously availing of the services of modern medical establishments. Likewise they may seek her help to resolve a family dispute, even as they simultaneously seek out the services of legal experts.

42 See Fuller 1992: 178.

3 An avatar with a mission

1 For discussions of Hindu conceptions of karma, see Keyes and Daniel 1983; Sharma 1973; O'Flaherty 1980.

2 Several devotees of the Mata understand her teachings to be based on the Advaita, or non-dualistic, school of Hindu philosophy. The most famous propounder of Advaita is Shankara, an eighth/ninth century Indian mystic, philosopher and theologian. According to Shankara's theology, in order to secure liberation from the world of suffering, *samsara*, what is required is an altered state of consciousness which is able to discriminate between that which is the true self and that which is not. Through discrimination and the guidance of a guru, spiritual aspirants must disengage themselves from the illusory world and realize the fundamental identity or non-dualism (*advaita*) between *atman* (the individual self) and *brahman* (the eternal and all-pervasive divine essence or supreme absolute). Such realization leads to liberation (*moksha*). On Shankara's Advaita, see Potter 1981; Isayeva 1993.

3 *AC* I, 1989: 162–3.

4 At the time of my fieldwork, there were Brahmasthanam temples in several MAM centres – at Kodungallur, Kozhikode and Thiruvananthapuram (formerly Trivandrum) in Kerala; Chennai (Madras) and Madurai in Tamil Nadu; Pune and Mumbai (Bombay) in Maharashtra; and in Delhi. New Brahmasthanams were under construction in Talassery, Mananthavadi and Palakkad (Kerala) and in Coimbatore (Tamil Nadu) within India, and two outside, in Mauritius and Reunion Island.

5 These references to '*chakras*' or centres of psycho-spiritual consciousness represent a notion of the 'subtle body', as in tantra and hatha-yoga traditions, with its nerves and centres fuelled by a pervasive subtle energy that courses through the human and divine, the body and the cosmos (see Kakar 1984: 194–210). Also see Coney 1998 for an account of the treatment of *chakras* and energy centres in Mata Nirmala Devi's recommended system of Sahaja Yoga.

6 This temple, both in architecture and in thematic representation, appears as a simplified and abbreviated version of the more complex temple structures which are characteristic of the southern part of Kerala (see Pillai 1985; Stein 1978; Bernier 1982). The temple has a main outer entrance, a small doorway with a roof over it, space around the temple for circumambulation by devotees, and a flight of steps on each side leading up to the square platform of the sanctum sanctorum mounted with a pyramidical tiled rooftop. The sanctum sanctorum contains the four images carved on a block of stone. There are four doors leading to the sanctum, one on each side of the square structure, and only one of the four images on the stone block is visible through each door. Worship in the temple, I was told, follows the prescribed

rules in the Agamas and Tantras (Fuller 1984 and 1992: 66) a body of Sanskrit texts treated as authoritative prescriptions on ritual in south Indian temples. The temple priest, a disciple appointed by the Mata and trained in ritual practice at her ashram, performs daily pujas in the conventional style of south Indian temple worship.

7 See, for instance, van der Veer 1987a, 1988; Burghart 1983a and 1983b; Daniel 1984; A. Gold 1988; D. Gold 1987; Madan 1982, 1983, 1987b.

8 *AC* IV, 1992: 148.

9 *AC* V, 1993: 216–18.

10 *AC* IV, 1992: 248–50.

11 AC V, 1993: 71–2.

12 AC V, 1993: 72.

13 AC V, 1993: 73–4.

14 Tambiah's (1990) discussion of the 'multiple orderings of reality' comes closest to understanding this complementarity between apparently conflicting realms. His categories of 'participation' and 'causality' correspond to the Mata's categories of faith and rationality. 'If participation emphasizes sensory and affective communication and the language of emotions', Tambiah argues, 'causality stresses the rationality of instrumental action and the language of cognition. But these are ideal type exaggerations, and neither can exclude the devices of the other' (ibid.: 108). Tambiah stresses the *complementarity* of cognitive and affective interests, both of which are *simultaneously* available to human beings as modes of ordering the world. In this sense, he concludes, 'we are [wo]men for all seasons, and engage in many ways of worldmaking. And although societies and cultures do differ in the variety of discourses they permit and encourage, certainly no society hitherto known is an impoverished practitioner of only a single orientation' (ibid.: 108–9).

15 This echoes the views of Vivekananda on the need to synthesize 'science and Sanskrit'. See Baumfield 1998.

16 See Fuller 1992: 241–5 and Pugh 1983 on planetary affliction or *grahadosha* as a common explanation for misfortune in India, and the measures taken to counter the affliction. Astrology is a vastly popular aspect of contemporary Hinduism, as borne out by the numerous websites on the Internet (see, for instance www.cyberastro.com) which offer astrological predictions of one's future on the basis of the date and time of one's birth, and offer advice on appropriate action based on these readings. The Mata's website at www.ammachi.org (as accessed on 12 December 2002) advertises the services of an in-house astrologer, a devotee of the Mata who is in residence at the Amritapuri ashram, and who travels with the Mata on her world tours, offering his services to devotees. This astrologer reads devotees' horoscopes for a fee of $50 per half-hour's consultation. The proffered services include the analysis of one's 'natal chart' and of 'current life trends', the analysis of 'relationship compatibility' and 'astrolocation analysis' for finding out the best place for an individual to live. After identifying 'areas of difficulty' in a client's birthchart, the astrologer recommends appropriate remedial action in the form of pujas which are organized by the MAM, again for the payment of a fee. 'Astrology', according to the website, 'can optimize our potential so our lives develop according to our true destiny.'

17 The Lalita Sahasranama, central to the ritual prescriptions of the Mata, is an

invocatory poem to Devi contained in the *Devi Bhagavatha Purana*, an ancient text on the great goddess dating back to the eleventh and twelfth centuries. On this text, see Erndl 1993: 22; Kinsley 1986: 132–50; Dahejia 1999: 23, 99.

18 The ritual symbolism of puja is described in Babb (1975), Courtright (1985) and Fuller (1992). Discussions of Jain puja, which share similarities with puja in Hindu contexts, are available in Humphrey and Laidlaw (1994) and Laidlaw (1995).

19 For accounts of gurus initiating lay devotees into their *sampradayas*, see van der Veer 1988; R.B. Williams 2001; Juergensmeyer 1991. In many cases (unlike in the MAM), initiation does not only entail the transmission of the order's secret mantra to the lay initiate, but also requires the latter to take vows binding him/her to a life of discipline.

20 I was never told the mantras themselves since these were secret and known only to individual devotees who had taken the *diksha*.

21 *AC* IX, 1998: 85–90.

22 Interestingly, much like the composition of names of the goddess, there is within the MAM a similar composition of names describing the Mata. This is the Mata's Ashtotarashata Namavali – the 108 names of the Mata. It was composed in Sanskrit in the early 1980s by a Brahman poet highly acclaimed in Kerala for his literary prowess. This poet, the late Ottoor Unni Namboodiripad, became, towards the end of his life, an ardent devotee of Mata Amritanandamayi. For some of the Mata's devotees in Kerala, it is highly significant that despite her 'low-caste' status, the Mata should have been thus honoured by a widely acclaimed Brahman poet. For them, Ottoor's Sanskrit composition in praise of the Mata confers upon her the ultimate stamp of legitimacy as an authentically 'divine' personage.

23 In particular, see Bennett's (1990) account of ritual within temples of the Pushti Marg. Bennett notes how ritual, through its acts, thoughts and procedures, serves as a meaningful and efficacious vehicle for expressing, and thereby shaping, enhancing and transforming inner devotional experience.

24 Different devotionalist orders emphasize and foreground different emotional attitudes that the devotee may adopt towards the deity. The worshipper may be to the worshipped as a loving mother to her child, as a lover to the beloved, or as a servant to his/her master. See Bennett 1990; Toomey 1990; Marglin 1990; Lynch 1988; van der Veer 1988. The attitude of worshipper to worshipped as child to parent is noted by Babb (1987) for three relatively recent guru-centred devotionalist traditions in India, and by Sarkar (1992) for the devotional attitude emphasized in Ramakrishna's teachings.

25 'Heart' here is translated from the the term '*manas*', originally Sanskrit, and commonly used in more than one Indian language including Malayalam. Though *manas* does not refer to the heart as a physical organ, it does convey some of the abstract meaning associated with the faculties of the heart. It is understood to indicate the seat of one's emotions. See Lynch 1990: 18–19.

26 On the sacrality of the Ganges in Hindu thought and belief, its purificatory and curative powers, and the mythology surrounding its supposedly divine nature and heavenly origins, see Eck 1982; Kinsley 1986.

27 *AC* V, 1993: 20–1.

28 Paradoxically in their case, they are required to stay away from the Brahmasthanam once every month on account of the pollution taboo.

29 See Ortner's (1996) discussion on the distinction between prestige and power in the analysis of gender inequalities.

4 Choosing to surrender

1 Bruce (1998: 224) notes the multiplicity of religious and spiritual alternatives in the affluent societies of western Europe and north America, where the spurt of new religious organizations since the 1960s has opened up a wealth of choices for potential adherents, leading to a 'potent mix of pluralization and heightened competition' (Hefner 1998: 88). Whereas this profusion of spiritual alternatives in the Western world has attracted much attention from sociologists and anthropologists, the same phenomenon in an Indian context has received little or no attention in the existing literature. India's communications revolution and the impact of mass media, particularly since the mid-1980s, has contributed in no small measure to enhancing public awareness about available religious and spiritual options.

2 This is an aspect of guru devotion again largely neglected in existing studies of guru organizations and their adherents. Most studies of guru devotionalism in India tend to deal almost exclusively with the internal dynamics of the particular guru faith or organization chosen for study. See, for instance, Kakar 1984; Swallow 1982; Juergensmeyer 1991; Babb 1987; R.B. Williams 2001; Carter 1987, 1990; Knott 1986. Followers tend to be seen as 'members' of the group, and often there is the (problematic) assumption of a clear demarcation of status between 'insiders' and 'outsiders'.

3 See, for instance, Narayan's (1989: 132–59) insightful observations on stories of 'false gurus and gullible disciples' narrated, interestingly, by one who is himself a guru. Two of the most controversial guru figures in India in recent times have been Chandraswami and the late 'Bhagwan' Rajneesh. Chandraswami's myriad political connections and intrigues as well as money-making rackets made him a much-maligned figure in the popular press in the 1980s. Rajneesh, throughout his career until 1990 as an international guru with a large American following, invited media attention for his sensational teachings, the most widely known of which was his advocacy of sex as a path to enlightenment. See Mitchener 1992: 16, 116–13; Carter 1987, 1990; Mehta 1993. Both gurus faced allegations of corruption in the course of their careers as gurus, and fell into disrepute among sections of the Indian public. Sathya Sai Baba too has for some time been under a cloud of controversy, with ex-devotees making allegations of murder, sexual abuse and financial racketeering within his organization. (See for instance Menon and Malik 2000; Thapa 2000.)

4 Various communist-backed 'rationalist associations' in Kerala and elsewhere have repeatedly attacked the Mata as a fraudulent guru and sexually perverse individual who uses her spirituality as a cover-up for nefarious activities. The sexuality of gurus and questions regarding their moral conduct have long constituted a highly contested and publicly debated issue in India. See for instance Pocock (1973: 118–19) on the scandal surrounding a Vaishnavite order, the Pushti Marg, in Gujarat in the nineteenth century. A newspaper of the time, the *Satya Prakash*, accused the sect's leading figures, known as Maharajas, of adultery with the wives and daughters of their devotees. Pocock notes how even in the 1970s, the members of the Pushti

Marg remained over-sensitive about the events that had occured over a century ago. See also Jeffrey Kripal's (1995) book on the sexual dimensions of the life and teachings of the nineteenth-century Bengali mystic, Ramakrishna. A recent article by Swami Atmajananda (1997) challenges Kripal's contentions and defends Ramakrishna against allegations of sex-scandals and cover-ups.

5 In accordance with my informants' requests for anonymity, I have used pseudonyms in place of their real names throughout this book.

6 The Divine Life Society, founded by Swami Sivananda in 1936, is notably different from the Mata Amritanandamayi Mission in its emphasis on Hindu philosophical speculation and scholarship, rather than devotion, as the mainstay of spiritual progress. For Kishore, this stress on intellectualism presents itself as an unbridgeable gap between the lay devotee and the learned monks of the organization. On the Divine Life Society and its founder, see Miller 1991. This spiritual organization also commands a substantial following both in India and abroad, and has centres in most of India's big cities and towns.

7 See G.M. Williams 1991; Beckerlegge 1990, 1998, 2000a and 2000b; Sinclair-Brull 1997; Sen 2000; Gupta 1974; Radice 1998; Sarkar 1992; Gambhirananda 1957.

8 Sarkar 1992 notes the colloquialisms in Ramakrishna's conversations with devotees, his use of a language that was 'attractively earthy and unsophisticated, and perfectly understandable', which he argues, held a unique appeal for the Bengali *bhadralok* of the nineteenth century, who constituted the bulk of his followers. These individuals, according to Sarkar, saw Ramakrishna's parables and analogies as a welcome change from the formal logic, precise argumentation and discipline of time to which their clerical jobs in mercantile and government offices exposed them. These urban groups, plagued by a sense of alienation from their roots, found in Ramakrishna a guru with whom they could relate 'without undue discomfort' (ibid.: 1544).

9 Swami Chinmayananda started off as a disciple of Swami Shivananda, the founder of the Divine Life Society. He founded the Chinmaya Mission whose main activity was to educate school students and teachers about early Hinduism's Vedantic philosophical tradition. He also established an ashram, the Sandipany Academy, in Mumbai to provide training to Hindu preachers. One of his lifelong concerns was to win modern educated middle classes in India back to the Hindu fold. To this end he organized conferences on the Vedanta and delivered sermons in English, winning a sizeable following from among India's urban middle classes. See Jaffrelot 1996: 194–5; Mitchener 1992: 45–52.

10 Parry 1985 and Heesterman 1978 note the paradox in popular Hindu belief that the ancient Sanskrit texts, such as the Vedas, which are commonly cited as the ultimate authority on matters of moral and religious duty, in fact do not contain any pronouncements on these matters. Because of this paradox, the transcendent vision of a human authority – a sage or a guru – becomes the moral and religious authority for laypersons to rely on. The guru's followers judge his/her credentials on the basis of the guru's knowledge of scriptural revelations, which in fact have no bearing on his/her pronouncements. The way thus seems open for the guru to say what he or she likes. See also Halbfass 1991.

11 Parry's (1985) observations on popular Hindu perceptions of the ancient Sanskrit texts are relevant here. He notes how, though few people have any knowledge of the contents of the scriptures, and even fewer of their meaning, that which they believe to be textual is, at least in principle, beyond debate. The textual tradition, he notes, is accorded an 'ideological immunity to sceptical scrutiny' (ibid.: 205). This valorization of the Sanskrit scriptures is based on the belief that they contain the original revelations by the gods, and are therefore the repositories of all authentic knowledge.

12 This reflects Fuller's (1992: 61–2) observation about how some religious virtuosi persistently argue that material images are needed only by the simple-minded and spiritually immature, who cannot turn their minds to the godhead without visible representations on which to focus. The Mata, in the passage quoted above, represents her Devi *bhava darshans* as a concession to the needs of the simple-minded and ignorant, who need to see her dressed as a goddess in order to be convinced of her divinity.

13 *Biography*: 188–9

14 Though devotees often cite instances when the Mata spoke in different languages to different people, in fact she is fluent only in Malayalam, and can barely manage two or three words in English and Hindi. Throughout my fieldwork, I heard miracle stories of the Mata's ability to speak different languages including Croatian and Japanese, but these were invariably stories based on hearsay, and none of my informants themselves had had any experience of the Mata's supposed lingual dexterity.

15 The story of the leper is particularly poignant given the social stigma attaching to leprosy in the Indian context. See de Bruin 1996.

16 These statements are important in the context of the caste concerns that operate in most middle-class 'Hindu' households in contemporary India. It is precisely in such matters as engaging a domestic help or seeking eligible marriage partners for their sons and daughters, that modern middle-class Indians, who might otherwise appear caste-free in their thought and behaviour, do tend to reveal their caste-consciousness. See S. Bayly 1999: 312–16; Frøystad 2003. Cf. Béteille (1991a) who argues that, among many of those who see themselves as middle-class Indians, caste considerations appear to be increasingly marginalized in favour of a more egalitarian, and achievement- rather than ascription-based orientation.

17 This reflects what S. Bayly 1999: 306–7 describes as a 'particular conception of caste identity that has come to the fore, especially among people who see themselves as informed and modern-minded' where caste has come to operate in the manner of an 'imagined community' fostering bonds of idealized allegiance much like those associated with the nation or the ethnic religious community. This, as Bayly (ibid.) points out, makes contemporary caste interactions appear very different from the 'networks of interdependence or structural opposition described in the classic ethnographies of the post-Independence era'.

18 In fact the issue of caste in modern India is more complex than these statements suggest. See Bayly (ibid.) on the diverse elements of caste consciousness in modern India. Though my informants appeared to idealize a casteless society, and valorize what they see as the Mata's indifference to, and transcendence of, caste considerations, neither they nor the Mata openly challenge prevailing caste inequalities. To that extent their attitude may be

seen as one of passive accommodation, rather than resistance, to the realities of caste in India.

19 Gurus who have earned a reputation abroad command greater prestige among followers in India. Bharati (1970) makes some insightful comments on this phenomenon, using the analogy of the Italian pizza, and what he calls the 'pizza effect'. The pizza, he explains, originally a simple hot-baked Italian bread without trimmings, came to acquire the status of a highly elaborate and popular dish in the US after the First World War. The US version of the pizza, with its many sizes and flavours, made its way back to Italy with visiting kinsfolk from America. The result was that the pizza now acquired a new status and meaning in its homeland. In a similar way, the success overseas of many of India's spiritual products often gives them a stamp of legitimacy and accords them greater prestige in the eyes of Indians.

20 Among the more famous of Kerala's spiritual leaders in the early twentieth century was Sri Narayana Guru who played an important role in social reform and caste uplift in the region. His appeal, however, did not extend to non-Malayalis, and was therefore mostly confined within a small geographical area. See Menon 1994: 67; Jeffrey 1974. Swami Chinmayananda, also originally from Kerala, chose to set up his headquarters in Mumbai. His following, though extending well outside the Malayali fold, remained limited in comparison with that of the Mata, mainly because his appeal was based not on the kind of popular *bhakti* which the Mata propagates, but on his intellectual erudition as a Sanskrit pandit and a commentator on Hindu scriptures. See Mitchener 1992: 45–52; Jaffrelot 1996: 194–5.

5 Spiritual pathways

1 *AC* IV 1992: 174

2 ibid.: 219

3 *AC* I 1989: 35

4 ibid.: 116

5 *AC* VI 1994: 185

6 This ethic of social service propagated by the Mata has clear parallels in that propounded by Swami Vivekananda in the early part of the twentieth century which informed the activities of the renouncers of the Ramakrishna Mission. Here worship was identified with service to the poor. In Vivekananda's reformulation of religious symbols, god reappeared in the world in the form of Daridra-Narayana – the poor (*daridra*) as god (*narayana*). To help the poor became an article of Hindu faith. (See Beckerlegge 1998, 2000a and 2000b; Gupta 1974.) The ethic informing Mata Amritanandamayi's social service projects, however, differs from this in one vital respect. The Mata's social service is directed not at the poor alone but also at the materially well-off sections of society. Those not wanting in material comfort are seen as spiritually deprived and therefore equally in need of the Mata's 'services' as their poorer brethren who need material uplift.

7 In the case of very young entrants, the ashram authorities usually encourage them to complete their studies, and often finance their school or college education up to whatever level the aspirant wishes. Most complete at least their first degree – in subjects ranging from English literature, Sanskrit and

philosophy, to commerce, computer science and engineering. Some go on to study further and obtain degrees at the Masters level. The ashram invariably has a use for whatever knowledge and skills the disciples acquire, and they are encouraged to utilize these skills in their service efforts.

8 My informants at the Mission's various educational establishments were never very clear about what they meant by 'value-based' education, even though this was set out as the defining objective of each institution. Some, in response to my questions, pointed to the strict regulations which students are expected to observe in these institutions. These regulations forbid smoking, consumption of non-vegetarian food, alcohol and drugs within the educational complex, and require that students should dress simply and 'modestly', and treat their elders with respect. For these informants, value-based education is about scholarship under conditions of strict discipline, obedience to the authorities, and little or no self-indulgence. Others pointed to the beneficial effect students must derive from proximity to the Mata's ascetic disciples who occupy important positions in these institutions. In their view, value-based education has to do with learning from the examples set by these ascetics in matters of austere living and selfless service. Apart from laying down a code of conduct for students, these institutions appeared to do little by way of actively 'inculcating' values, focusing instead on improving student performance at public examinations and thus enhancing their reputation as high achievers in the educational arena.

9 On the interplay between the spiritual and renunciatory components in the Hindu householder's life, see Madan 1982, 1983, 1987b; Daniel 1984; A. Gold 1988; Parry 1994. In particular, see Laidlaw 1995 for an insightful discussion of Jain householders and the problematic relationship between the realms of material acquisition and the spiritual ideal of renunciation in Jain philosophy. Many of the dilemmas identified by Laidlaw for the Jain householder confront the Mata's devotees as well, but are resolved differently in each case. Also see Banks 1992; Carrithers and Humphrey 1991.

10 *AC* I, 1989: 338–9.

11 See Clothey 1978 and Erndl 1993 respectively on the mythologies surrounding Murugan and Vaishno Devi.

12 Menstruating women, in many traditional Hindu ritualistic contexts, are considered impure and defiling and are therefore debarred from entering the 'sacred' and 'pure' realm of ritual observance.

13 Parry (1985) notes this concern, in the reproduction of the contents of ancient Sanskrit texts, with the precise reproduction of sound rather than with the retention of the meaning it conveys. 'The words in themselves are believed to have power once they are vocalised. For this power to become manifest they must be pronounced with precision and exactly the right inflections' (ibid.: 209).

14 See Fuller 1992: 241 who notes how, according to popular myth, the popular monkey god Hanuman, because of his immense physical strength, has been 'the only god to have ever worsted Saturn'.Those who believe themselves to be Saturn's victims worship Hanuman to seek his aid in quelling Saturn's influence on their lives.

15 These *seva* activities belong to a common repertoire of social service engagements undertaken by a wide range of organizations in India including

old religious movements like the Arya Samaj (D. Gold 1991), newer right-wing groups like the Rashtriya Swayamsevak Sangh (ibid.) as well as devotionalist orders like the Radhasoamis (Juergensmeyer 1991) and the Ramakrishna Mission (Gupta 1974; Beckerlegge 1998, 2000a and 2000b). Most religious organizations in India now engage in some charitable and social service activity, mainly because the Indian government requires non-profit religious institutions to divest themselves of their income periodically if they are to retain their tax-exempt status. Spending on medical, educational and other charitable projects is a convenient means of achieving this, and has the added benefit of garnering favourable publicity for the religious organization.

6 Experiencing divine love

1 *Matruvani* December 1998, 10 (4): 17–20.
2 On the larger debate in the social sciences between rationality and relativism, of central importance since the 1970s, see for instance Wilson 1970; Bourdieu 1977: 110–12; Evans-Pritchard 1976; Favret-Saada 1980; Hollis and Lukes 1982; Tambiah 1990; Luhrmann 1989; E. Gellner 1992a and 1992b.
3 This reflects Parry's (1985: 206–7) observation that in traditional Indian thought there is no conceptual divide between 'religious' and 'scientific' knowledge. In the context of his fieldwork in the city of Banaras, a key Hindu pilgrimage site, he notes how ritual officiants there see some justification or other, in terms of modern science, for every ritual detail described in the Sanskrit texts to which they refer. In the case of my informants, this same 'scientific' justification extends to all aspects of their faith in the Mata. Also see Kakar (1984: 214–15) who notes how his informants, urban educated devotees of the popular Indian guru Mata Nirmala Devi, use 'scientific language' in order to pay 'homage to the technological world' in which they live. This perception of harmony between modern science and religious faith is equally common to new religious movements elsewhere in the world. See Mendelsohn 1993.
4 See, for instance, Pocock 1973: 140; Exon 1997.
5 Coney's (1998) observations regarding the experience of persons disengaging themselves from a religious organization to which they were previously attached are significant here. The ease or otherwise with which devotees can break away from a guru's fold would depend, Coney argues, on the extent of their 'socialization' within the organization. In the case of an organization like the MAM, lay devotees can disengage themselves from the Mata's fold with relative ease because of the high value attached by the organization to notions of personal freedom and choice in the matter of religious preference.
6 None of this is to say that the Mata does not command the kind of deep-rooted and exclusive loyalty that is conventionally associated with guru faiths. She often does, but this rootedness and exclusiveness is entirely a matter of personal choice on the part of the devotee. The organization itself does not impose restrictions on its followers or demand their long-term loyalty in any way.
7 Where the spiritual practices and beliefs of different devotees coincide, this

is more a case of elective affinity between spiritual orientations, rather than the result of any external pressure to conform to prescribed standards and conventions.

8 This is not to imply that the religious lives of devotees is entirely an internal thing, negotiated by each individual internally and privately. Though Mata Amritanandamayi's devotees reveal a high degree of individual choice in negotiating their religious lives, this choice is not entirely internal but is negotiated through the individual's contact with the Mata's personality, her teachings, and her prescriptions for a rewarding spiritual life. It is by engaging with this 'public space of discourse' (Taylor 1985, 1989), and negotiating with it individually and severally, that devotees come to construct their religious lives in unique and distinctive ways. It is significant that their chosen guru is one who, in her turn, respects her devotees' personal freedom as individuals, and allows them to continue, even after entering her fold, to think and act as autonomous, self-directing, independent agents.

7 East meets West?

1 See Eade and Sallnow 2000; Coleman and Elsner 1995: 'Epilogue'.
2 This is from an undated promotional pamphlet published by the MAM, entitled *Divine Mother Mata Amritanandamayi Devi and Her Mission*, which was widely in circulation among devotees of the Mata during my fieldwork in India in 1997–8.
3 *Matruvani*, January 1997, 8 (5).
4 *Matruvani*, October 1998, 10 (2).
5 Her websites provide detailed information about the Mata's attendance at each of these conferences as well as the full text of her speeches at each forum.
6 From the point of view of her Indian devotees, the Mata's attendance at these 'world' conferences has resonances with Vivekananda's mission in USA and Europe in the late nineteenth century, the first of its kind to be undertaken by an Indian renouncer abroad. His mission was aimed at raising funds abroad in order to provide for the poor in India. The highpoint of his mission was an invitation to speak at the Parliament of World Religions in Chicago in 1893. At this conference of religious leaders and representatives from across the globe, Vivekananda, representing his version of Hinduism (primarily an exposition of Vedantic metaphysics), is believed to have captured the Western imagination in an unprecedented way, and generated a popular Western interest in the religion of the 'East'. (See Beckerlegge 2000a; Sen 2000; Burke 1958; Das Gupta 1994; Datta 1993; Gambhirananda 1983; Sil 1997; Chowdhury-Sengupta 1998; Killingley 1998.) Many Indians see this as a landmark development in Hinduism's recent history and one of India's earliest 'triumphs' at an international forum – an example seen to be followed by contemporary gurus like the Mata.
7 This conference, held on 2 October 1995, was, according to the MAM publication, *Unity is Peace*, sponsored by the Temple of Understanding and the Council of Religious and Interfaith Organizations. It was intended to provide a forum for religious leaders, diplomats, NGOs and educators to present their vision for the next century. There were 32 speakers in all, including religious leaders from diverse faiths and also some heads of state

and scholars of religion. A conference statement was presented to the United Nations while its 50th Anniversary Summit was still in session.

8 *AC* 1, 1989: 340.

9 How far the Mata's mission abroad can be perceived as the result of purely universalistic and non-denominational aspirations is a debatable question. Both her own self-representations abroad, and also the accounts of her foreign trips as they appear in the MAM's promotional literature, seem to self-consciously steer clear of all cultural and nationalist propagandism. Yet it is not impossible to read cultural propaganda with nationalistic overtones into her forays abroad. Commentaries on Vivekananda's spiritual message contain similar debates on his motivations and orientations (see Radice 1998). Was he a Hindu 'revivalist', a 'fundamentalist' or 'communalist'? Indeed there are no definitive answers to these questions, yet the debates themselves are interesting, and reveal how these figures lend themselves to varying interpretations of what they stood/stand for, a universalistic truth or the particularism of narrowly-defined conceptions of religion and culture.

10 Hindutva, the ideology of Hindu nationalists, manifests itself in India today as an organized and militant form of religious supremacism whose proponents call for the setting up of a Hindu Raj – a state in which civic rights, nationhood and national culture would be defined by Hinduism. The politicized, activist religious nationalism of the present has considerable precedent in various movements of organized Hinduism which arose in British India in the first two decades of the nineteenth century. Today proponents of Hindutva, comprising mainly the Rashtriya Swayamsevak Sangh (RSS), the Vishwa Hindu Parishad (VHP) and the Bharatiya Janata Party (BJP) constitute the main organs of the Sangh Parivar, a so-called 'family' of social and political organizations that work to propagate Hindutva. See Gold 1991; Embree 1994; van der Veer 1987b, 1994a and 1994b, 1996; Jaffrelot 1996; Ludden 1996; Hansen 1996, 1999; Hansen and Jaffrelot 1998; Zavos 2000.

11 The popular travel guide series, *Lonely Planet*, contains, in its volume on India, a reference to the Amritapuri ashram as a place of tourist interest. Many of the Westerners I met at the ashram claimed to have first learnt about it from the travel guide.

12 See Juergensmeyer 1991: 129 on the controversy in the Radhasoami order over egg-consumption. Questions regarding whether egg is 'non-vegetarian' and whether it leads to bad karma as the consumption of non-vegetarian food is believed to do, are often highly vexed issues particularly among Western devotees of Indian gurus.

13 'Memoirs from Amma's World Tours', *Matruvani*, April 1998, 9 (8): 35–6.

14 These diatribes against the 'evils' of the material West are interesting expressions, on the part of some sections of India's affluent middle classes, of what Urban (2003) refers to as the 'cultural contradictions of late capitalism'. On the one hand, these persons express a keen appreciation of the material benefits and consumer freedom brought to India by global trade. On the other, they are anxious to define a uniquely Indian and Hindu identity, which they seek to defend from the encroachments of Western capitalism.

15 Devotees like this one are mostly silent about the well-known fact that it is largely the material beneficence of the very same Western children that

sustains the ashram. Donations from wealthy devotees, including Indians, but mostly Americans and to some extent Europeans, are the financial mainstay for the MAM's ambitious institution-building ventures in the educational and medical fields. And it is this that makes the Mata's spiritual enterprise highly suspect in the eyes of sceptics who see the Mission as yet another money-making racket in India's rapidly expanding spiritual market, which, according to some, is India's biggest, though officially unrecorded, foreign exchange earner!

16 This 'slackness' and 'inefficiency' is something I myself encountered during my stay in the ashram. The smallest things, from sending a fax to arranging for an interview with a senior disciple, was often riddled with problems owing largely to the slow-moving bureaucratic arrangements within the ashram hierarchy. While this is something most Indians encounter routinely in other spheres of their life, it often takes Western devotees by surprise. Most devotees cannot fathom why the Mata should allow such inefficiency in her ashram. Some conclude that this is perhaps the Mata's way of teaching them an all-important lesson in cultivating patience, and that perhaps it is the devotee who needs to change and not the ashram management.

8 Conclusion

1 See, for instance, Nandy (1985, 1990).

2 See Madan 1987a, 1997; Chatterjee 1986, 1993, 1997; Baxi and Parekh 1995. The over-simplified and essentializing assertions of these writers have been challenged by Khilnani 1997; Baber 1996; Vanaik 1997; C.A. Bayly 1998; Upadhyaya 1992; Basu and Subrahmanyam 1996.

3 Particularly significant from the point of view of this thesis is the dubious and simplistic nature of the assertions made by some of the writers on Hindu nationalism about India's middle classes and their complicity in the politicization of religion in contemporary India. According to commentators like Freitag 1996: 26; Shah 1991: 2921; Chibber and Mishra 1993: 665–72; Parikh 1993: 684, the expansion of the middle classes following India's liberalization efforts of the 1980s and 1990s, has been a crucial factor contributing to the emergence of India's main Hindu right-wing political group, the Bharatiya Janata Party, as a major force in national-level politics. This, it is argued, has been the result of discontent and frustration arising from the encounter of these middle classes with modern ways of life in urban India.

4 On the various aspects of Hindu nationalism in contemporary India, see for instance van der Veer 1994a and 1994b; Tonnesson and Antlov 1996; Ludden 1996; Jaffrelot 1996, 1998; Hansen and Jaffrelot 1998; Basu and Subrahmanyam 1996; Sarkar 1993; Hellman 1994.

5 See Davis 1996; van der Veer 1987b.

6 See Davis 1996: 49–51; Sarkar 1993: 165–6; Jaffrelot 1996, 1998; van der Veer 1987b.

7 See Hansen 1996; van der Veer 1996; Alter 1994a and 1994b.

REFERENCES

Publications of the Mata Amritanandamayi Mission

Swami Amritaswarupananda (1996) *Mata Amritanandamayi: A Biography*, 7th edn, Kollam, Kerala: Mata Amritanandamayi Mission Trust.

The *Awaken Children* Series (*AC*) *Awaken Children: Dialogues with Sri Sri Mata Amritanandamayi*
* Volumes I and II (1989 and 1990 respectively) Kollam, Kerala: Mata Amritanandamayi Mission Trust.
* Volumes III to VIII (1991 to 1996 respectively) San Ramon, California: Mata Amritanandamayi Center.

Websites

www.ammachi.org
www.amritapuri.org
www.cyberastro.com

Other references

Alter, J. (1994a) 'Celibacy, Sexuality and the Transformation of Gender into Nationalism in North India', *Journal of Asian Studies*, 53 (1): 45–66.
—— (1994b) 'Somatic Nationalism: Indian Wrestling and Militant Hinduism', *Modern Asian Studies*, 28 (3): 557–88.
Appadurai, Arjun and Breckenridge, Carol A. (1995) 'Public Modernity in India' in Carol A. Breckenridge (ed.) *Consuming Modernity: Public Culture in a South Asian World*, Minneapolis and London: University of Minnesota Press.
Appadurai, Arjun (1996) *Modernity at Large: Cultural Dimensions of Globalization*, Minneapolis: University of Minnesota Press.
Arnason, J.P. (1996) *Nation and Modernity*, Reykjavik Lectures, Reykjavik: NSU Press.
Atmajananda, Swami (1997) 'Scandals, Cover-Ups, and Other Imagined Occurrences in the Life of Ramakrishna: An Examination of Jeffrey Kripal's "Kali's Child"', *International Journal of Hindu Studies*, 1 (2): 401–20.

Babb, Lawrence A. (1972) 'The Satnamis: Political Involvement of a Religious Movement' in J. Michael Mahar (ed.) *The Untouchables in Contemporary India*, Tucson: University of Arizona Press.

—— (1975) *The Divine Hierarchy: Popular Hinduism in Central India*, New York: Columbia University Press.

—— (1987) *Redemptive Encounters: Three Modern Styles in the Hindu Tradition*, Delhi: Oxford University Press.

—— (1991) 'Sathya Sai Baba's Miracles' in T.N. Madan (ed.) *Religion in India*, Delhi: Oxford University Press.

Babb, Lawrence and Wadley, Susan S. (eds) (1995) *Media and the Transformation of Religion in South Asia*, Philadelphia: University of Pennsylvania Press.

Baber, Zaheer (1996) 'After Ayodhya', *Dialectical Anthropology*, 21 (3/4): 317–43.

Banks, Marcus (1992) *Organizing Jainism in India and England*, Oxford: Clarendon Press.

Basu, Kaushik and Subrahmanyam, Sanjay (eds) (1996) *Unravelling the Nation: Sectarian Conflict and India's Secular Identity*, Delhi: Penguin.

Baumfield, Vivienne (1998) 'Science and Sanskrit: Vivekananda's Views on Education' in William Radice (ed.) *Swami Vivekananda and the Modernisation of Hinduism*, Delhi: Oxford University Press.

Baxi, Upendra and Parekh, Bhikhu (1995) *Crisis and Change in Contemporary India*, New Delhi and London: Sage.

Bayly, C.A. (1983) *Rulers, Townsmen and Bazaars: North Indian Society in the Age of British Expansion 1770–1870*, Cambridge: Cambridge University Press.

—— (1985) 'The Pre-History of "Communalism": Religious Conflict in India 1700–1860', *Modern Asian Studies*, 19 (2): 177–203.

—— (1998) *Origins of Nationality in South Asia: Patriotism and Ethical Government in the Making of Modern India*, Delhi and Oxford: Oxford University Press.

Bayly, Susan (1989) *Saints, Goddesses and Kings: Muslims and Christians in South Indian Society 1700–1900*, Cambridge: Cambridge University Press.

—— (1999) *Caste, Society and Politics in India from the Eighteenth Century to the Modern Age*, The New Cambridge History of India Series IV (3), Cambridge: Cambridge University Press.

Beckerlegge, Gwilym (1990) 'Human Rights in the Ramakrishna Math and Mission: For Liberation and the Good of the World', *Religion*, 20: 119–37.

—— (1998) 'Swami Vivekananda and *Seva*: Taking "Social Service" Seriously' in William Radice (ed.) *Swami Vivekananda and the Modernisation of Hinduism*, Delhi: Oxford University Press.

—— (2000a) *The Ramakrishna Mission: the Making of a Modern Hindu Movement*, Delhi: Oxford University Press.

—— (2000b) 'Swami Akhandananda's *Sevavrata* (Vow of Service) and the Earliest Expressions of Service to Humanity in the Ramakrishna Math and

Mission' in Antony Copley (ed.) *Gurus and Their Followers: New Religious Reform Movements in Colonial India*, Oxford: Oxford University Press.

—— (ed.) (2001) *From Sacred Text to Internet*, Volume 1 of *Religion Today: Tradition, Modernity and Change*, Aldershot: Open University/Ashgate.

Berman, Marshall (1982) *All That Is Solid Melts into Air: The Experience of Modernity*, New York: Penguin.

Bennett, Lynn (1983) *Dangerous Wives and Sacred Sisters: Social and Symbolic Roles of High-Caste Women in Nepal*, New York: Columbia University Press.

Bennett, Peter (1990) 'In Nanda Baba's House: The Devotional Experience in Pushtimarg Temples' in Owen M. Lynch (ed.) *Divine Passions: The Social Construction of Emotion in India*, Berkeley: University of California Press.

Berman, Marshall (1982) *All That Is Solid Melts into Air: The Experience of Modernity*, New York: Penguin.

Bernier, Ronald M. (1982) *Temple Arts of Kerala: A South Indian Tradition*, Delhi: S. Chand.

Béteille, André (1991a) 'The Reproduction of Inequality: Occupation, Caste and Family', *Contributions to Indian Sociology* (n.s.), 25 (1): 3–28.

—— (1991b) 'Individual and Person as Subjects for Sociology' in his *Society and Politics in India: Essays in a Comparative Perspective*, London: Athlone.

Beyer, P. (1990) 'Privatization and the Public Influence of Religion in Global Society', in M. Featherstone (ed.) *Global Culture*, London: Sage.

Bharati, Agehananda (1970) 'The Hindu Renaissance and its Apologetic Patterns', *Journal of Asian Studies*, 29: 267–87.

—— (1985) 'The Self in Hindu thought and Action' in A.J. Marsella, George DeVos and Francis L.K. Hsu (eds) *Culture and Self: Asian and Western Perspectives*, New York and London: Tavistock.

Bourdieu, Pierre (1977) *Outline of a Theory of Practice* (trans. R. Nice), Cambridge: Cambridge University Press.

Brown, C. Mackenzie (1990) *The Triumph of the Goddess: The Canonical Models and Theological Visions of the Devi-Bhagavata Purana*, Albany: State University of New York Press.

Bruce, Steve (1998) 'The Charismatic Movement and the Secularization Thesis', *Religion*, 28 (3): 223–32.

Burghart, Richard (1978) 'The Founding of the Ramanandi Sect', *Ethnohistory*, 25: 121–39.

Burghart, Richard (1983a) 'Renunciation in the Religious Traditions of South Asia', *Man* (n.s.) 18: 635–53.

—— (1983b) 'Wandering Ascetics of the Ramanandi Sect', *History of Religions*, 22: 361–80.

Burke, M.L. (1958) *Swami Vivekananda in America: New Discoveries*, Calcutta: Advaita Ashrama.

Carey, Sean (1987) 'Initiation into Monkhood in the Ramakrishna Mission' in Richard Burghart (ed.) *Hinduism in Great Britain: The Perpetuation of Religion in an Alien Cultural Milieu*, London: Tavistock.

Carrithers, Michael and Humphrey, Caroline (eds) (1991) *The Assembly of Listeners: Jains in Society*, Cambridge: Cambridge University Press.

Carrithers, Michael, Collins, Steven and Lukes, Steven (eds) (1985) *The Category of the Person: Anthropology, Philosophy, History*, Cambridge: Cambridge University Press.

Carter, Lewis F. (1987) 'The "New Renunciates" of the Bhagwan Shree Rajneesh: Observations and Identification of Problems of Interpreting New Religious Movements', *Journal for the Scientific Study of Religion*, 26 (2): 148–72.

—— (1990) *Charisma and Control in Rajneeshpuram: The Role of Shared Values in the Creation of a Community*, Cambridge: Cambridge University Press.

Cartledge, Mark J. (1998) 'The Future of Glossolalia: Fundamentalist or Experientialist?', *Religion*, 23 (3): 233–44.

Case, Margaret H. (2000) *Seeing Krishna: The Religious World of a Brahman Family in Vrindaban*, Delhi: Oxford University Press.

Chatterjee, Partha (1986) *Nationalist Thought and the Colonial World: A Derivative Discourse?*, London: Zed.

—— (1993) *The Nation and its Fragments: Colonial and Postcolonial Histories*, Princeton, NJ: Princeton University Press.

—— (1997) *A Possible India: Essays in Political Criticism*, Delhi: Oxford University Press.

Chibber, Pradeep and Mishra, Subhash (1993) 'Hindus and the Babri Masjid: The Sectional Basis of Communal Attitudes', *Asian Survey*, 33: 665–72.

Chowdhury-Sengupta, Indira (1998) 'Reconstructing Hinduism on a World Platform' in William Radice (ed.) *Swami Vivekananda and the Modernisation of Hinduism*, Delhi: Oxford University Press.

Chryssides, George D. (1999) *Exploring New Religions*, London: Cassell.

Clothey, Fred W. (1978) *The Many Faces of Murukan: The History and Meaning of a South Indian God*, The Hague: Mouton.

Coburn, Thomas B. (1991) *Encountering the Goddess: A Translation of the Devi- Mahatmya and a Study of Interpretation*, Albany: State University of New York Press.

Coleman, Simon (2000) *The Globalization of Charismatic Christianity*, Cambridge: Cambridge University Press.

Coleman, Simon and Elsner, John (1995) *Pilgrimage: Past and Present in the World Religions*, Cambridge, MA: Harvard University Press.

Comaroff, John L. and Comaroff, Jean (1993) (eds) *Modernity and Its Malcontents: Ritual and Power in Postconial Africa*, Chicago: University of Chicago Press.

Coney, Judith (1998) *Sahaja Yoga*, London: Routledge.

Courtright, Paul B. (1985) *Ganesa: Lord of Obstacles, Lord of Beginnings*, New York: Oxford University Press.

Dahejia, Vidya (1999) *Devi the Great Goddess: Female Divinity in South Asian Art*, Washington DC: Arthur Sackler Gallery, Smithsonian Institute.

Daniel, Valentine (1984) *Fluid Signs: Being a Person the Tamil Way*, Berkeley: University of California Press.

Das Gupta, R.K. (ed.) (1994) *Swami Vivekananda: Hundred Years Since Chicago – A Commemorative Volume*, Calcutta: Ramakrishna Math and Mission.

Datta, B.N. (1993) *Swami Vivekananda: Prophet-Patriot*, Calcutta: Navbharat Publishers.

Davis, Richard H. (1996) 'The Iconography of Rama's Chariot' in David Ludden (ed.) *Contesting the Nation: Religion, Community and the Politics of Democracy in India*, Philadelphia: University of Pennsylvania Press.

de Bruin, Hanne M. (1996) *Leprosy in South India: Stigma and Strategies of Coping*, Pondicherry: French Institute.

Denton, L.T. (1991) 'Varieties of Hindu Female Asceticism' in Julia Leslie (ed.) *Roles and Rituals for Hindu Women*, London: Pinter.

Dumont, Louis (1965a) 'The Modern Conception of the Individual: Notes on Its Genesis', *Contributions to Indian Sociology*, VIII: 13–61.

—— (1965b) 'The Functional Equivalents of the Individual in Caste Society', *Contributions to Indian Sociology*, VIII: 85–99.

—— (1970) 'World Renunciation in Indian Religions' in Louis Dumont (ed.) *Religion, Politics and History in India: Collected Papers in Indian Sociology*, Paris: Mouton.

—— (1980) *Homo Hierarchicus: The Caste System and Its Implications*, Chicago: University of Chicago Press.

Eade, John and Sallnow, M.J. (eds) (2000) *Contesting the Sacred: the Anthropology of Christian Pilgrimage*, Urbana and Chicago: University of Illinois Press.

Eck, Diana L. (1981) *Darsan: Seeing the Divine Image in India*, Chambersburg: Anima.

—— (1982) 'Ganga: The Goddess in Hindu Sacred Geography' in J.S. Hawley and D.M. Wulff (eds) *The Divine Consort: Radha and the Goddesses of India*, Berkeley, California: Berkeley Religious Studies Series.

Eisenstadt, S.N. (2000) 'Multiple Modernities', *Daedalus*, 129 (1): 1–30.

Embree, Ainslee T. (1994) 'The Function of the Rashtriya Swayamsevak Sangh: to Define the Hindu Nation' in M.E. Marty and R.S. Appleby (eds) *Accounting for Fundamentalisms*, Chicago and London: University of Chicago Press.

Erndl, Kathleen (1993) *Victory to the Mother: The Hindu Goddess of Northwest India in Myth, Ritual and Symbol*, New York: Oxford University Press.

Evans-Pritchard, E.E. (1976) *Witchcraft, Oracles and Magic among the Azande*, Oxford: Clarendon Press.

Exon, Bob (1997) 'Autonomous Agents and Divine Stage Managers: Models of (Self-)determination amongst Western Devotees of Two Modern Hindu Religious Movements', *Scottish Journal of Religious Studies*, 18 (2): 163–79.

Favret-Saada, Jeanne (1980) *Deadly Words: Witchcraft in the Bocage*, Cambridge: Cambridge University Press.

Flood, Gavin (1996) *An Introduction to Hinduism*, Cambridge: Cambridge University Press.

Frankel, Francine R. (1988) 'Middle Classes and Castes' in Atul Kohli (ed.) *India's Democracy: An Analysis of Changing State–Society Relations*, Princeton, NJ: Princeton University Press.

Freitag, Sandria B. (1989) *Collective Action and Community: Public Arenas and the Emergence of Communalism in North India*, Berkeley and Oxford: University of California Press.

—— (1996) 'Contesting in Public' in David Ludden (ed.) *Making India Hindu: Religion, Community and the Politics of Democracy in India*, Delhi: Oxford University Press.

Friese, H. and Wagner, P. (2000) 'When "the Light of the Great Cultural Problems Moves On": On the Possibility of a Cultural Theory of Modernity', *Thesis Eleven*, 61: 25–40.

Frøystad, Kathinka (2003) 'Master–Servant Relations and the Domestic Reproduction of Caste in Northern India', *Ethnos*, 68 (1): 73–94.

Frykenberg, Robert E. (1989) 'The Emergence of Modern "Hinduism" as a Concept and as an Institution: A Reappraisal with Special Reference to South India' in Gunther D. Sontheimer and Hermann Kulke (eds) *Hinduism Reconsidered*, New Delhi: Manohar.

Fuller, C.J. (1984) *Servants of the Goddess: The Priests of a South Indian Temple*, Cambridge: Cambridge University Press.

—— (1992) *The Camphor Flame: Popular Hinduism and Society in India*, Princeton, NJ: Princeton University Press.

Gambhirananda, Swami (1957) *History of the Ramakrishna Math and Mission*, Calcutta: Advaita Ashrama.

Gaonkar, Dilip P. (1999) 'On Alternative Modernities', *Public Culture*, 11(1): 1–18.

Gatwood, Lynn (1985) *Devi and the Spouse Goddess: Women, Sexuality and Marriage in India*, Riverdale, MD: Riverdale.

Gellner, David (1982) 'Max Weber, Capitalism and the Religion of India', *Sociology*, 16(4): 526–43.

Gellner, Ernest (1992a) *Reason and Culture: The Historic Role of Rationality and Rationalism*, Oxford: Blackwell.

—— (1992b) *Postmodernism, Reason and Religion*, London: Routledge.

Giddens, Anthony (1990) *The Consequences of Modernity*, Cambridge: Polity.

Gold, Anne Grodzins (1988) *Fruitful Journeys: The Ways of the Rajasthani Pilgrims*, Berkeley: University of California Press.

Gold, Daniel (1987) *Lord as Guru: Hindu Sects in the North Indian Tradition*, New York: Oxford University Press.

—— (1991) 'Organized Hinduisms: From Vedic Truth to Hindu Nation' in M.E. Marty and R.S. Appleby (eds) *Fundamentalisms Observed*, Chicago: University of Chicago Press.

Gombrich, Richard and Obeyesekere, Gananath (1988) *Buddhism Transformed: Religious Change in Sri Lanka*, Princeton, NJ: Princeton University Press.

Gordon, A.D.D. (1978) *Businessmen and Politics: Rising Nationalism and a Modernizing Economy in Bombay 1918–33*, New Delhi: Manohar.

Gupta, K.P. (1974) 'Religious Evolution and Social Change in India: A Study of the Ramakrishna Mission Movement', *Contributions to Indian Sociology* (n.s.), 8: 25–50.

Halbfass, W. (1991) 'The Idea of the Veda and the Identity of Hinduism' in his *Tradition and Reflection: Explorations in Hindu Thought*, Albany: SUNY.

Hansen, Thomas Blom (1996) 'Recuperating Masculinity: Hindu Nationalism, Violence and the Exorcism of the Muslim "Other"', *Critique of Anthropology*, 16 (2): 137–72.

—— (1999) *The Saffron Wave: Democracy and Hindu Nationalism in Modern India*, Princeton, NJ: Princeton University Press.

Hansen, T.B. and Jaffrelot, C. (1998) *The BJP and the Compulsions of Politics in India*, Delhi and Oxford: Oxford University Press.

Harlan, L. and Courtright, P.B. (1995) *From the Margins of Hindu Marriage: Essays on Gender, Religion, and Culture*, New York and Oxford: Oxford University Press.

Hardy, F. (1994) *The Religious Culture of India: Power, Love and Wisdom*, Cambridge: Cambridge University Press.

Hawley, John S. (1981) *At Play with Krishna: Pilgrimage Dramas from Brindavan*, Princeton, NJ: Princeton University Press.

Hawley, John S. and Wulff, Donna M. (eds) (1982) *The Divine Consort: Radha and the Goddesses of India*, Berkeley: Berkeley Religious Studies Series.

Heesterman, J.C. (1978) 'Veda and Dharma' in W.D. O'Flaherty and J.D.M. Derrett (eds) *The Concept of Duty in South Asia*, Delhi: Vikas.

—— (1985) *The Inner Conflict of Tradition: Essays in Indian Ritual, Kingship, and Society*, Chicago and London: University of Chicago Press.

Hefner, Robert W. (1998) 'Multiple Modernities: Christianity, Islam and Hinduism in a Globalizing Age', *Annual Review of Anthropology*, 27: 83–104.

Hellman, Eva (1994) 'Dynamic Hinduism', *Seminar*, 417: 49–58.

Hollis, Martin and Lukes, Steven (eds) (1982) *Rationality and Relativism*, Oxford: Blackwell.

Howe, Leo (2002) *Hinduism and Hierarchy in Bali*, Oxford: James Currey.

Humphrey, Caroline and Laidlaw, James (1994) *The Archetypal Actions of Ritual*, Oxford: Clarendon Press.

Isayeva, Natalia (1993) *Shankara and Indian Philosophy*, Albany: State University of New York Press.

Jaffrelot, Christophe (1996) *The Hindu Nationalist Movement in India*, Delhi: Viking.

—— (1998) 'The Politics of Processions and Hindu–Muslim Riots' in A. Basu and A. Kohli (eds) *Community Conflicts and the State in India*, Delhi: Oxford University Press.

Jeffrey, Robin (1974) 'The Social Origins of a Caste Association: 1875–1905: The Founding of the SNDP Yogam', *South Asia*, 4: 39–59.

—— et al. (eds) (1990) *India: Rebellion to Republic – Selected Writings 1857–1990*, Delhi: Sterling.

Joshi, Sanjay (2001) *Fractured Modernity: Making of a Middle Class in Colonial North India*, Oxford: Oxford University Press.

Juergensmeyer, Mark (1991) *Radhasoami Reality: The Logic of a Modern Faith*, Princeton, NJ: Princeton University Press.

Kakar, Sudhir (1984) *Shamans, Mystics and Doctors: A Psychological Inquiry into India and its Healing Traditions*, London: Unwin.

Kantowsky, Detlef (ed.) (1986) *Recent Research on Max Weber's Studies of Hinduism*, Munchen: Weltforum Verlag.

Kaul, Rekha (1993) *Caste, Class and Education: Politics of the Capitation Fee Phenomenon in Karnataka*, Delhi and London: Sage.

Keyes, Charles F. and Daniel, Valentine (eds) (1983) *Karma: An Anthropological Inquiry*, Berkeley: University of California Press.

Khandelwal, Meena (1997) 'Ungendered Atma, Masculine Virility and Feminine Compassion: Ambiguities in Renunciant Discourses on Gender', *Contributions to Indian Sociology* (n.s.), 31 (1): 79–107.

Khanna, Sushil (1987) 'The New Business Class, Ideology and the State: The Making of a "New Consensus"', *South Asia* (n.s.), 10 (2): 47–60.

Khare, R.S. (1993) 'The Seen and the Unseen: Hindu Distinctions, Experiences and Cultural Reasoning', *Contributions to Indian Sociology* (n.s.), 27 (2): 191–212.

Khilnani, Sunil (1997) *The Idea of India*, London: Hamish Hamilton.

Killingley, Dermot (1998) 'Vivekananda's Message from the East' in William Radice (ed.) *Swami Vivekananda and the Modernisation of Hinduism*, Delhi: Oxford University Press.

King, Ursula (1984) 'The Effect of Social Change on Religious Self-Understanding: Women Ascetics in Modern Hinduism' in Kenneth Ballhatchet and David Taylor (eds) *Changing South Asia: Religion and Society*, London: SOAS.

Kinsley, David R. (1979) *The Divine Player*, Delhi: Motilal Banarsidass.

—— (1986) *Hindu Goddesses: Visions of the Divine Feminine in the Hindu Religious Tradition*, Berkeley: University of California Press.

Knauft, Bruce M. (ed.) (2002) *Critically Modern: Alternatives, Alterities, Anthropologies*, Bloomington and Indianapolis: Indiana University Press.

Knobl, W. (2000) 'In Praise of Philosophy: Johann P. Arnason's Long but Successful Journey Towards a Theory of Modernity', *Thesis Eleven*, 61: 1–24.

Knott, Kim (1986) *My Sweet Lord*, Wellingborough: Aquarian Press.

Kripal, Jefferey (1995) *Kali's Child: The Mystical and Erotic in the Life and Teachings of Ramakrishna*, Chicago: University of Chicago Press.

Laidlaw, James (1995) *Riches and Renunciation: Religion, Economy and Society among the Jains*, Oxford: Clarendon Press.

Lakha, Salim (1999) 'The State, Globalisation and Middle-Class Identity' in Michael Pinches (ed.) *Culture and Privilege in Capitalist Asia*, London and New York: Routledge.

Leslie, Julia (ed.) (1991) *Roles and Rituals for Hindu Women*, London: Pinter.

Linkenbach, Antje (2000) 'Anthropology of Modernity: Projects and Contexts', *Thesis Eleven*, 61: 41–63.

Ludden, David (ed.) (1996) *Contesting the Nation: Religion, Community and the*

Politics of Democracy in India, Philadelphia: University of Pennsylvania Press.

Luhrmann, T.M. (1989) *Persuasions of the Witch's Craft: Ritual Magic and Witchcraft in Present-Day England*, Oxford: Blackwell.

Lutz, C.A. and Abu-Lughod, Lila (eds) (1990) *Language and the Politics of Emotion*, Cambridge: Cambridge University Press.

Lutz, C.A. and White, G.M. (1986) 'The Anthropology of Emotions', *Annual Review of Anthropology*, 15: 405–36.

Lynch, Owen M. (1988) 'Pilgrimage with Krishna: Sovereign of the Emotions', *Contributions to Indian Sociology* (n.s.), 22: 171–94.

—— (1990) 'Introduction' in Owen M. Lynch (ed.) *Divine Passions: The Social Construction of Emotion in India*, Berkeley: University of California Press.

McDaniel, June (1989) *Madness of the Saints: Ecstatic Religion in Bengal*, Chicago: University of Chicago Press.

Madan, T.N. (1982) *Way of Life: King, Householder, Renouncer: Essays in Honour of Louis Dumont*, New Delhi: Vikas.

—— (1983) 'Ideology of the Householder among the Kashmiri Pandits' in A. Östör, L. Fruzzett and S. Barnett (eds) *Concepts of Person: Kinship, Caste and Marriage in India*, Delhi: Oxford University Press.

—— (1987a) 'Secularism in its Place', *Journal of Asian Studies*, 46 (4): 747–59.

—— (1987b) *Non-Renunciation: Themes and Interpretations of Hindu Culture*, Delhi: Oxford University Press.

—— (1997) *Modern Myths, Locked Minds: Secularism and Fundamentalism in India*, Delhi: Oxford University Press.

Madsen, Douglas and Peter G. Snow (1991) *The Charismatic Bond: Political Behaviour in Times of Crisis*, Cambridge, MA: Harvard University Press.

Mankekar, Purnima (2000) *Screening Culture, Viewing Politics: Television, Womanhood and Nation in Modern India*, Delhi: Oxford University Press.

Marglin, F.A. (1990) 'Refining the Body: Transformative Emotion in Ritual Dance' in Owen M. Lynch (ed.) *Divine Passions: The Social Construction of Emotion in India*, Berkeley: University of California Press.

Markovits, Claude (1985) *Indian Business and Nationalist Politics 1931–39: The Indigenous Capitalist Class and the Rise of the Congress Party*, Cambridge: Cambridge University Press.

Mayer, Adrian C. (1981) 'Public Service and Individual Merit in a Town of Central India' in A.C. Mayer (ed.) *Culture and Morality: Essays in Honour of Christoph von Furer-Haimendorf*, Delhi: Oxford University Press.

Mazzarella, William (2003) '"Very Bombay": Contending with the Global in an Indian Advertising Agency', *Cultural Anthropology*, 18 (1): 33–71.

Mehta, Uday (1993) *Modern Godmen in India: A Sociological Appraisal*, Bombay: Popular Prakashan.

Mendelsohn, E. (1993) 'Religious Fundamentalism and the Sciences: Harmony between Modern Science and Religion', in M.E. Marty and R.S. Appleby (eds) *Fundamentalism and Society*, Chicago and London: University of Chicago Press.

Menon, A.K. and Malik, A. (2000) 'Test of Faith', *India Today*, XXV, 49.

Menon, Dilip (1994) *Caste, Nationalism and Communism in South India*, Cambridge: Cambridge University Press.

Miller, Daniel (1994) *Modernity: An Ethnographic Approach: Dualism and Mass Consumption in Trinidad*, Oxford: Berg.

Miller, David M. (1991) 'The Divine Life Society Movement' in Robert Baird (ed.) *Religion in Modern India*, Delhi: Manohar.

Mines, Mattison (1994) *Public Faces, Private Voices: Community and Individuality in South India*, Berkeley: University of California Press.

—— (1998) 'Hindus at the Edge: Self-Awareness Among Adult Children of Interfaith Marriages in Chennai, South India', *International Journal of Hindu Studies*, 2 (2): 223–48.

—— (1999) 'Heterodox Lives: Agonistic Individuality and Agency in South Indian History' in R. Guha and J. Parry (eds) *Institutions and Inequalities: Essays in Honour of André Béteille*, Delhi: Oxford University Press.

Mines, Mattison and Gaurishankar, Vijayalakshmi (1990) 'Leadership and Individuality in South Asia: The Case of the South Indian Big-Man', *The Journal of Asian Studies*, 49 (4): 761–86.

Misra, B.B. (1961) *The Indian Middle Classes: Their Growth in Modern Times*, London: Oxford University Press.

Mitchener, John (1992) *Guru: The Search for Enlightenment*, Delhi: Viking.

Morris, Brian (1994) 'The Hindu Conception of the Self' in his *Anthropology of the Self: The Individual in Cultural Perspective*, London: Pluto.

Munshi, Surendra (1988) 'Max Weber on India: An Introductory Critique', *Contributions to Indian Sociology* (ns.), 22: 1–34.

Nandy, Ashis (1985) 'An Anti-Secularist Manifesto', *Seminar*, 314: 14–24.

—— (1990) 'The Politics of Secularism and the Recovery of Religious Tolerance' in Veena Das (ed.) *Mirrors of Violence: Communities, Riots and Survivors in South Asia*, Delhi and Oxford: Oxford University Press; reprinted in Nandy, Ashis (2002) *Time Warps: Silent and Evasive Pasts in Indian Politics and Religion*, London: Hurst.

—— (1995) *Creating a Nationality: The Ramjanmabhumi Movement and Fear of the Self*, Delhi and Oxford: Oxford University Press.

Narayan, Kirin (1989) *Storytellers, Saints and Scoundrels*, Philadelphia: Philadelphia University Press.

—— (1993) 'How Native Is a Native Anthropologist?', *American Anthropologist*, 95: 671–86.

Ninan, T.N. (1990) 'Rise of the Middle Class' in Robin Jeffrey *et al.* (eds) *India: Rebellion to Republic: Selected Writings 1857–1990*, Delhi: Sterling.

O'Flaherty, Wendy D. (ed.) (1980) *Karma and Rebirth in Classical Indian Traditions*, Berkeley: University of California Press.

Ojha, Catherine (1981) 'Feminine Asceticism in Hinduism: Its Tradition and Present Condition', *Man in India*, 61 (3): 254–85.

Ortner, Sherry B. (1996) *Making Gender: The Politics and Erotics of Culture*, Boston: Beacon Press.

Parikh, Manju (1993) 'The Debacle at Ayodhya: Why Militant Hinduism met with a Weak Response', *Asian Survey*, 33: 673–64.

Parry, Jonathan (1985) 'The Brahmanic Tradition and the Technology of the Intellect' in Joanna Overing (ed.) *Reason and Morality*, London: Tavistock.
—— (1994) *Death in Banaras*, Cambridge: Cambridge University Press.
Percy, Martyn (1998) 'The Morphology of Pilgrimage in the "Toronto Blessing"', *Religion*, 28 (3): 281–8.
Pillai, V.R. Parameswaran (1985) *Temple Culture of South India*, Delhi: Inter-India.
Pinch, William (1996) *Peasants and Monks in British India*, Berkeley: University of Chicago Press.
Pinches, Michael (ed.) (1999) *Culture and Privilege in Capitalist Asia*, London and New York: Routledge.
Pinney, Chris (2003) *Photos of the Gods: The Printed Image in India*, London: Reaktion Books.
Pocock, David F. (1973) *Mind, Body and Wealth: A Study of Belief and Practice in an Indian Village*, Oxford: Blackwell.
Potter, Karl H. (ed.) (1981) *Encyclopedia of Indian Philosophies Vol 3: Advaita Vedanta up to Samkara and his Pupils*, Delhi: Motilal Banarsidass.
Preston, James J. (1980) *Cult of the Goddess: Social and Religious Change in a Hindu Temple*, New Delhi: Vikas.
—— (ed.) (1982) *Mother Worship: Themes and Variations*, Chapel Hill: University of North Carolina Press.
—— (1985) 'Creation of the Sacred Image: Apotheosis and Destruction in Hinduism' in J.P. Waghorne and N. Cutler (eds) *Gods of Flesh, Gods of Stone: The Embodiment of Divinity in India*, Chambersburg: Anima.
Pugh, Judy F. (1983) 'Astrology and Fate: The Hindu and Muslim Experiences' in Charles F. Keyes and E. Valentine Daniel (eds) *Karma: An Anthropological Inquiry*, Berkeley: University of California Press.
Radice, William (ed.) (1998) *Swami Vivekananda and the Modernisation of Hinduism*, Delhi: Oxford University Press.
Ramanujan, A.K. (1986) 'On Women Saints' in J.S. Hawley and D.M. Wulff (eds) *The Divine Consort: Radha and the Goddesses of India*, Boston: Beacon Press.
—— (1989) 'Is there an Indian Way of Thinking? An Informal Essay', *Contributions to Indian Sociology* (n.s.), 23 (1): 41–58.
Ray, Rajat (1979) *Industrialization in India: Growth and Conflict in the Private Corporate Sector 1914–47*, Delhi and Oxford: Oxford University Press.
Robertson, Roland (1995) 'Glocalization: Time–Space and Homogeneity–Heterogeneity' in Mike Featherstone, Scott Lash and Roland Robertson (eds) *Global Modernities*, London, Thousand Oaks, CA and Delhi: Sage.
Robison, Richard and David S.G. Goodman (1996) 'The New Rich in Asia: Economic Development, Social Status and Political Consciousness' in R. Robison and D. S. G. Goodman (eds) *The New Rich in Asia: Mobile Phones, McDonald's and Middle-Class Revolution*, London and New York: Routledge.
Rosaldo, Renato (1993) *Culture and Truth: the Remaking of Social Analysis*, Boston: Beacon Press.

Sanderson, A. (1985) 'Purity and Power Among the Brahmans of Kashmir', in M. Carrithers, S. Collins and S. Lukes (eds) *The Category of the Person: Anthropology, Philosophy, History*, Cambridge: Cambridge University Press.

Sarkar, Sumit (1992) '"Kaliyuga", "Chakri" and "Bhakti": Ramakrishna and His Times', *Economic and Political Weekly*, July 18: 1543–66.

—— (1993) 'The Fascism of the Sangh Parivar', *Economic and Political Weekly*, January 30: 163–67.

Sen, A.P. (2000) *Swami Vivekananda*, Delhi: Oxford University Press.

Shah, Ghanshyam (1991) 'Tenth Lok Sabha Elections: BJP's Victory in Gujarat', *Economic and Political Weekly*, December 21: 2921–4.

Sharma, Ursula M. (1973) 'Theodicy and the Doctrine of Karma', *Man* (n.s.), 8: 347–64.

Shweder, R.A and Levine, R.A. (eds) (1984) *Culture Theory: Essays on Mind, Self and Emotion*, Cambridge: Cambridge University Press.

Sinclair-Brull, Wendy (1997) *Female Ascetics: Hierarchy and Purity in Indian Religious Movements*, Richmond, Surrey: Curzon Press.

Singer, Milton (1968) 'The Radha-Krishna Bhajanas of Madras City' in Milton Singer (ed.) *Krishna: Myths, Rites and Attitudes*, Chicago: University of Chicago Press.

—— (1972) *When a Great Tradition Modernises*, New York: Praeger.

Sil, N.P. (1997) *Swami Vivekananda: A Reassessment*, Selinsgrove: Susaquehanna University Press and London: Associated University Press.

Slocum, Carolyn (1988) 'Shakti: Women's Inner Strength' in Eleanor Zelliott and Maxine Burntsen (eds) *The Experience of Hinduism: Essays on Religion Among the Coorgs of South India*, Bombay: Asia.

Smith, Brian K. (1998) 'Questioning Authority: Constructions and Deconstructions of Hinduism', *International Journal of Hindu Studies*, 2 (3): 313–39.

Stein, Burton. (ed.) (1978) *South Indian Temples: An Analytical Reconsideration*, New Delhi: Vikas.

Swallow, Deborah A. (1982) 'Ashes and Power: Myth, Rite and Miracle in an Indian God-Man's Cult', *Modern Asian Studies*, 16: 123–58.

Tambiah, Stanley J. (1990) *Magic, Science, Religion and the Scope of Rationality*, Cambridge: Cambridge University Press.

—— (2000) 'Transnational Movements, Diaspora, and Multiple Modernities', *Daedalus*, 129 (1): 163–94.

Taylor, Charles (1985) 'The Person' in Michael Carrithers, Steven Collins and Steven Lukes (eds) *The Category of the Person: Anthropology, Philosophy, History*, Cambridge: Cambridge University Press.

—— (1989) *Sources of the Self: The Making of the Modern Identity*, Cambridge: Cambridge University Press.

Taylor, Donald (1987) 'Charismatic Authority in the Sathya Sai Baba Movement' in Richard Burghart (ed.) *Hinduism in Great Britain: The Perpetuation of Religion in an Alien Cultural Milieu*, London and New York: Tavistock.

179

Thapa, Vijay Jung (2000) 'A God Accused', *India Today*, XXV, 49.

Thapar, Romila (1989) 'Imagined Religious Communities? Ancient History and the Modern Search for a Hindu identity', *Modern Asian Studies*, 23: 209–31.

Tonnesson, S. and Antlov, H. (eds) (1996) *Asian Forms of the Nation*, Richmond, Surrey: Curzon.

Toomey, Paul M. (1990) 'Krishna's Consuming Passions: Food as Metaphor and Metonym for Emotion at Mount Govardhan' in Owen M. Lynch (ed.) *Divine Passions: The Social Construction of Emotion in India*, Berkeley: University of California Press.

Turner, Victor (1969) *The Ritual Process: Structure and Anti-Structure*, London: Routledge and Kegan Paul.

—— (1982) *From Ritual to Theatre: The Human Seriousness of Play*, New York: Performing Arts Journal Publications.

Upadhyaya, Prakash Chandra (1992) 'The Politics of Indian Secularism', *Modern Asian Studies*, 26 (4): 815–53.

Urban, Hugh B. (2003) 'Avatar for Our Age: Sathya Sai Baba and the Cultural Contradictions of Late Capitalism', *Religion*, 33: 73–93.

van der Veer, Peter (1987a) 'Taming the Ascetic: Devotionalism in a Hindu Monastic Order', *Man* (n.s.), 22: 680–95.

—— (1987b) 'God Must be Liberated: A Hindu Liberation Movement in Ayodhya', *Modern Asian Studies*, 21 (2): 284–301.

—— (1988) *Gods on Earth: The Management of Religious Experience and Identity in a North Indian Pilgrimage Centre*, London: Athlone.

—— (1994a) 'Hindu Nationalism and the Discourse of Modernity: The Vishwa Hindu Parishad', in M.E. Marty and R.S. Appleby (eds) *Accounting for Fundamentalisms*, Chicago and London: University of Chicago Press.

—— (1994b) *Religious Nationalism: Hindus and Muslims in India*, London and Berkeley: University of California Press.

—— (1996) 'Gender and Nation in Hindu Nationalism' in S. Tonnesson and H. Antlov (eds) *Asian Forms of the Nation*, Richmond, Surrey: Curzon.

—— (2001) *Imperial Encounters: Religion and Modernity in India and Britain*, Princeton, NJ: Princeton University Press

van der Veer, Peter and Lehmann, Harmut (eds) (1999) *Nation and Religion: Perspectives on Europe and Asia*, Princeton, NJ: Princeton University Press.

Vanaik, Achin (1997) *The Furies of Indian Communalism: Religion, Modernity and Secularization*, London and New York: Verso.

Varma, Pavan K. (1998) *The Great Indian Middle Class*, Delhi: Penguin.

Vaudeville, Charlotte (1996) *Myths, Saints and Legends in Medieval India*, Bombay and New York: Oxford University Press.

Wadley, Susan S. (1975) *Shakti: Power in the Conceptual Structure of Karimpur Religion*, Chicago: University of Chicago Press.

Wallis, Roy and Bruce, Steve (1992) 'Secularization: The Orthodox Model' in Steve Bruce (ed.) *Religion and Modernization*, Oxford: Clarendon Press.

Warrier, Maya (2003a) 'Processes of Secularisation in Contemporary India:

Guru Faith in the Mata Amritanandamayi Mission', *Modern Asian Studies*, 37 (1): 213–53.

Warrier, Maya (2003b) 'The *Seva* Ethic and the Spirit of Institution Building in the Mata Amritanandamayi Mission' in Antony Copley (ed.) *Hinduism in Public and Private*, Delhi: Oxford University Press.

Weber, Max (1958a) *From Max Weber: Essays in Sociology*, trans. and eds. H. H Gerth and C. Wright Mills, London: Routledge and Kegan Paul.

—— (1958b) *The Religion of India: The Sociology of Hinduism and Buddhism*, trans. and eds Hans H. Gerth and Don Martindale Glencoe, IL: Free Press.

White, Charles J (1972) 'The Sai Baba Movement: Approaches to the Study of Indian Saints', *The Journal of Asian Studies*, 31: 863–78.

Williams, G. M. (1991) 'The Ramakrishna Movement: A Study in Religious Change' in Robert Baird (ed.) *Religion in Modern India*, Delhi: Manohar.

Williams, R.B. (2001) *An Introduction to Swaminarayan Hinduism*, Cambridge: Cambridge University Press.

Wilson, Bryan R. (ed.) (1970) *Rationality*, Oxford: Blackwell.

Wittrock, Bjorn (2000) 'Modernity: One, None, or Many? European Origins and Modernity as a Global Condition', *Daedalus*, 129 (1): 31–60.

Zavos, John (2000) *The Emergence of Hindu Nationalism in India*, Delhi: Oxford University Press.

INDEX

aarati 37, 40, 54
Amrita apartments 128, 130
Amrita herbal products 26, 128
Amrita Institute of Medical Sciences
 35, 85; *see also* hospital
Amrita Vidyalayam 5, 7, 95
Amritapuri 1,6,113; contested
 meanings at 120, 136; disciples
 visiting 62; fieldwork in 20,
 21; multicultural interaction
 127–31
Appadurai, Arjun 62–3, 136
asceticism 4, 16, 70
ascetics 6, 59, 75; disciples 26, 35,
 53, 62, 83–6, 88, 128; *see also*
 brahmachari(ni); *sannyasi(ni)*
atman 44
atmic vigyan 111
aura 68
avatar-gurus 3,4, 36–7; accessibility
 42; authenticity 75, 78; perceived
 relations between 80, 81
avatars: contrast between 141–2; goal
 orientedness 53, 124; mission
 34, 7, 43, 46
Ayurveda clinic 128

Bhagavad Gita 36
bhajan 21, 121; at Amritapuri 84,
 129; during public programmes
 25–9, 37–8; as spiritual practice
 92, 98–9, 121
bhakti 5, 7, 38, 100
Bharatiya Janata Party 26
Bharatiya *samskara* 125

bhava darshan 34–5, 37–40, 74; *see
 also* Devi *bhava*; Krishna *bhava*
biography 32–4, 42, 69
blood donation camps 94
brahmachari(ni) 6, 7, 20, 94, 126; *see
 also* ascetics, disciples
brahmacharya diksha 6
brahman 44, 45, 56
Brahmasthanam 5, 7, 45, 51–4, 58,
 88; *mahotsavam* 54

cassettes, audio and video 21, 26, 65,
 98
caste 1, 4, 9; hierarchy 16; Mata's
 background 3, 32;
 networks/associations/groupings
 11, 12, 13, 15; priesthood based
 on 61; relevance of 76–7;
 transcendence of 37, 76
Catholics 126
chakra 45
charisma 1, 107–8
charitable activities 5, 21, 26, 35, 70,
 85, 94; beneficiaries 76
Chicago Tribune 121
Chinmayananda 73
Christ 55, 126–7
Christians 126
colonial rule/experience 8, 17, 141
communitas 104
community of sentiment 62
computer training institutes 5, 35, 61,
 86
congregational puja *see grahadosha
 shanti* puja

consecration 39, 40, 45
consumerism 10, 11, 96, 100, 134, 139
consumption patterns 9, 100
criminal activity of gurus 66

darshan 3; at Amritapuri 129, 130, 131; beneficial effects of 67–8; at initial encounter 27, 29, 30, 32, 41, 53, 65; long hours 69; in London 70; miracles during and after 75, 106, 112; *see also* Devi, *bhava*; Krishna, *bhava*
Devi 3, 33, 34, 45; *bhava* 3, 35, 37–40, 42, 73, 74, 84, 129
dharma 34, 36; *see also sanatana dharma*
disenchantment 117
Divine Life Society 71–2
divine stage manager 114
donations 10, 35, 60, 69, 95
Dumont, Louis 15,16

education 9, 14, 21, 22, 32, 120, 122; institutions 21, 35, 94; opportunities 11, 13; qualifications 41, 95, 100
egotism 48, 50–51, 57, 60, 90, 93, 139
electro-magnetic rays 68
embrace 3–4, 40–2, 58, 142; during Devi *bhava* 38; initial experience of 27–30, 100; intimacy of 67–70; life-transforming 50
emotions: during embrace 3, 28–30, 41, 100; feature of charismatic bonding 107–8; lack in modern world 47; revival 49, 50, 57–8, 142
engineering college 5, 35, 61, 85
experience 22, 49; construction through narrative 111–18; during embrace 29–30; of miracles 3, 30–1, 42, 52, 104–9, 112–14, 130

family shrine 88, 91, 93
fieldwork 20–1, 116
fisherfolk 3, 69, 128, 32, 122
flowers 25, 38, 54; garland 37
Friends of Amma 105

gadgetry language 111
Gandhi–King award 122
Ganesh/Ganapathi 25, 27
Ganges 57
global: contexts/processes 10, 11, 18, 19, 23, 24, 139, 140; Hinduism 37; orientation 119–37
globalization 1, 9, 20, 62–3
grahadosha shanti puja 51–4, 92
guru organizations 1, 3; popular middle class appeal 11–15; multicultural following 23; variety/diversity 65; boundaries between 79–81

hagiography 79
Hanuman 93; *chaalisa* 56
Hindu festivals 88
Hindu nationalism 9, 16–18, 125–7, 141–2
Hindu scriptures 117; *see also* Sanskrit, texts
horoscope 52, 93
hospice 5, 94
hospital 4, 37, 61, 35, 85
host–guest paradigm 131, 136–7

iconography 79
inclusivists and exclusivists 78–82
Indian Institute of Technology 86, 108
individuality 1, 116, 139
industrialization 8
insiders and outsiders 23, 55, 118
International Faith Congress 122
internet 11; *see also* websites

japa see mantra, *japa*
jiva 44
jnana 5

Kabir 127
karma 5, 44, 46, 60; karmic cycle 16, 84; *see also prarabdha; vasana*
Krishna 3, 27, 32, 36, 127; *bhava* 34–5, 74
kundalini shakti 45

Lalitha Sahasranama 53, 56, 58, 84, 92, 129

leper 76
liberal and conservative options 119–20
liberalization 8, 10, 13

Madonna 126; *see also* Virgin Mary
Malayalam 21, 26–8, 32, 71–2, 75, 78
management institute/college 5, 35, 61, 86
manasa puja 54
mantra 33, 54–6, 88, 93; *japa* 54, 55, 57, 92; *diksha* 55
masculinity 58, 141–2
materialism 46–7, 97, 124, 132–5
Matruvani 62, 95, 105, 121, 132
media 8, 11, 50, 61–3, 65
medical ventures 35, 41; *see also* Amrita Institute of Medical Sciences
meditation 6, 45, 54, 55, 57, 84, 92; techniques 10–11, 65, 88
middle classes 2, 4, 7–15, 21–2, 40, 118, 138, 142
Millennium World Peace Summit 122
miracles 3, 26, 34–5, 74–5, 81; *see also* experience
modern attitudes/lifestyles/world-views 2, 13, 17, 50, 64, 101
modernity 2, 11, 15–20, 41, 43, 60–4, 119, 136, 138–42; alternative and multiple 19–20; balanced 86, 101; imbalances of 50, 99, 132–4
moksha/salvation 46, 51, 84–5, 100, 120; seeking 5, 91; theodicies 16; attainment of 44
monkeys and kittens 114–16
Muhammad 127
multiple guru attachments 78–82, 118
Murugan 88

Nandy, Ashis 17–18, 141
narrative 67; levels of 2; of miraculous experiences 102–18, 130
new religious movements 15
New York Times 121
Nirmala Devi 12

old-age home 5
orphanage 5, 7, 94–5

parashakti 45
Parayakadavu 1, 32, 35
Parliament of World Religions 122
patriarchy 58
pension schemes 5
photographs 25, 79, 113
planetary influences 51–4, 92–3
postcolonial 139, 141
postmodernity 18–19
prarabdha 44, 51, 57, 68, 83, 85, 142
prasad 28, 29, 31
pratishtha 45
proxy control 103, 107–8, 114
psychiatrist 133
publicity 10, 21, 23–4, 54, 60, 121–2
puja 39, 40, 45, 51–4, 57, 91–3, 99
purna-avatar 34

Ram 27, 141
Ramakrishna 72, 126
Ramakrishna Math and Mission 6, 59, 72
Ramayana 93, 141
Rashtriya Swayamsevak Sangh 125
rationality 17, 18, 46–50, 58, 139
rebirth 44; *see also* karma
reflexivity 90, 115, 120, 140
renouncer 6, 16, 21, 36–7, 84; *see also sannyasi(ni)*
renunciation 45, 84, 123
renunciatory order 3, 4, 6

Sahaja Yoga 12
salvation *see moksha*/salvation
sampradaya 55
samsara 45, 56
San Fransisco Chronicle 121
sanatana dharma 4, 89, 126
Sangh Parivar 141
sankalpa 3, 41
sannyasa diksha 6, 35
sannyasi(ni) 6, 7, 84–5, 87, 113; interview with 125; 134–5; letter from 23; *see also* renouncer
San Ramon 5, 35, 135
Sanskrit 27; texts 73
Saraswati 27
Sathya Sai Baba 4, 12, 14, 36–7, 75, 78, 79–81, 100
Sathya Sai Mission 37

satsang 6, 45, 121, 130
science 48–9, 50, 109–11, 133, 139;
    see also rationality
selfhood 2, 14–15, 43, 63–4, 78, 99,
    114, 140–2; modern 2, 64, 95,
    99, 136; Hindu 15–18, 24, 101,
    119, 138, 140–2; Western 15,
    17, 119, 138; real and ideal
    114–16
self-realization 45
serpent 45
seva 7, 21, 22, 50, 59–60; rendered by
    ascetic disciples 84–6; at the local
    ashram branch 94–5; at
    Amritapuri 129–30
sex racket 66
Shaiva 5
Shakta 5
Shiva 45, 56, 129
spiritual drought 111
Srimad Bhagavatam 33
strategic essentialism 135
surrender 13, 29, 66, 78, 90, 93;
    attitude of 51, 54, 57, 85, 89
Swaminarayan 59

television 10, 21, 46, 53, 65, 98, 121
temples 39, 45, 88, 92, 93, 128;
    festival 45; *see also*
    Brahmasthanam

transnational: connections 10, 11,
    139; leader 1; organization 15, 23,
    36, 136; readership 23; *see also*
    global
tourist of gurus 78
tours: India 4, 35, 62, 70, 121
tribal welfare 5

UN Interfaith Celebration 122
unveiling 37–40

Vaishnava 5
Vaishno Devi 88
value-based education 86
vasana 44–6, 51, 57, 85, 142
Vedanta lectures 84
vibrations 66
video 63, 98; *see also* cassettes, audio
    and video
Virgin Mary 55; *see also* Madonna
Vishnu 36, 141; *sahasranama* 56
Vivekananda 59

The Washington Post 121
Weber, Max 16, 41
websites 21, 62, 65, 121
Western season 130
World Conference of Women
    Religious and Spiritual Leaders
    122